THE CAMBRIDGE COMPANION TO TED HUGHES

Ted Hughes is unquestionably one of the major twentieth-century English poets. Radical and challenging, each new title produced something of a shock to British literary culture. Only now is the breadth of his literary range and of his cultural influence being recognized. To the poetry and stories, writing for children and prose essays and reviews have been added, in recent years, the translations and letters. This *Companion* consolidates Hughes's life, writings and reputation. International experts from a variety of literary fields here confront the key questions posed by Hughes's work. New archival evidence is provided for fresh readings of his oeuvre with close attention to language, forms and the function of myth. Featuring a chronology and guide to further reading, this book is a valuable and insightful companion for those studying and reading Hughes in the context of his role in the development of modern poetry.

THE CAMBRIDGE
COMPANION TO
TED HUGHES

EDITED BY
TERRY GIFFORD

CAMBRIDGE
UNIVERSITY PRESS

CAMBRIDGE UNIVERSITY PRESS
Cambridge, New York, Melbourne, Madrid, Cape Town,
Singapore, São Paulo, Delhi, Tokyo, Mexico City

Cambridge University Press
The Edinburgh Building, Cambridge CB2 8RU, UK

Published in the United States of America by Cambridge University Press, New York

www.cambridge.org
Information on this title: www.cambridge.org/9780521145763

First published 2011

Printed in the United Kingdom at the University Press, Cambridge

A catalogue record for this publication is available from the British Library

Library of Congress Cataloguing in Publication data
The Cambridge Companion to Ted Hughes / edited by Terry Gifford.
p.   cm. – (Cambridge Companions to Literature)
Includes bibliographical references and index.
ISBN 978-0-521-19752-6 (hardback) – ISBN 978-0-521-14576-3 (paperback)   1. Hughes,
Ted (Ted James), 1930–1998 – Criticism and interpretation.   I. Gifford, Terry,
1946– II. Title. III. Series.
PR6058.U37Z63   2011
821'.914–dc22
2010051572

ISBN 978-0-521-19752-6 Hardback
ISBN 978-0-521-14576-3 Paperback

for Keith Sagar

CONTENTS

CONTENTS

ACKNOWLEDGEMENTS

First, I must thank the contributors for their patience with my questions and suggestions. The community of Ted Hughes scholars has always been generous with time and information. I thank them for decades of support and exchanges. For their particular contributions to this project thanks are due to Neil Roberts and Keith Sagar.

Any Chronology must acknowledge the work of Ann Skea, whose Timeline is available on her website, www.ann.skea.com/THHome. For comments on the Chronology thanks are also due to Olwyn Hughes, Carol Hughes, Keith Sagar, Steve Enniss, Helen Broderick, Ruth Crossley, Laura Webb and Lorraine Kerslake.

Chris and Bruce at the Watts Russell Arms, Hopedale, Staffordshire, England still provide the most convivial reading room in the world.

Seamus Heaney generously gave permission to quote from his poem 'On His Work in the English Tongue' in the Introduction.

The estate of Ted Hughes is thanked for permission to quote from unpublished material.

This book is dedicated to Keith Sagar, the pioneer of Ted Hughes studies, who became a friend and correspondent of the poet, eventually depositing his letters from Hughes in the British Library. Author of the first monographs on Hughes's work, Keith organized the first Ted Hughes conferences and edited the volumes of essays that resulted. His continuing scholarship on Hughes is widely referenced in this book. The generosity and support which Keith has extended to younger scholars exploring Hughes's works I first experienced over forty years ago. Now, all the contributors to this book are pleased to be able to acknowledge Keith's outstanding contribution to our knowledge and debates about the work of Ted Hughes.

Terry Gifford
Ednaston, Derbyshire

CONTRIBUTORS

JONATHAN BATE is Professor of Shakespeare and Renaissance Literature at the University of Warwick and author of *Shakespeare and the English Romantic Imagination* (1986), *The Genius of Shakespeare* (1997, 2008), *Romantic Ecology* (1991), *The Song of the Earth* (2000), *John Clare* (2003) and *Soul of the Age: The Life, Mind and World of William Shakespeare* (2008). He is also editor, with Eric Rasmussen, of *The RSC Shakespeare: Complete Works* (2007). Bate is currently writing for Faber and Faber *Ted Hughes: The Inner Life*.

PAUL BENTLEY is author of *The Poetry of Ted Hughes: Language, Illusion and Beyond* (1998) and *Scientist of the Strange: The Poetry of Peter Redgrove* (2002), and of various essays on contemporary poetry and Romantic poetry. He is Senior Lecturer in English at University College Plymouth St Mark and St John.

TRACY BRAIN is Senior Lecturer in English at Bath Spa University. Her book *The Other Sylvia Plath* was published in 2001. She is the author of 'Dangerous Confessions: The Problem of Reading Sylvia Plath Biographically' (2006), 'Sylvia Plath's Letters and Journals' (2006) and 'Unstable Manuscripts: The Indeterminacy of the Plath Canon' (2007). She is co-editor of *Representing Sylvia Plath* (2011), where her essay 'Fictionalising Sylvia Plath' will appear. Tracy Brain is currently working on a book about the representation of pregnancy and birth in the eighteenth- and nineteenth-century novel, and an essay about 'Sewing in *Jane Eyre*'.

RAND BRANDES is the Martin Luther Stevens Professor of English at Lenoir-Rhyne University in Hickory, North Carolina, USA. He has received two Fulbright Senior Research Fellowships to assist Seamus Heaney in Ireland. Brandes has published widely in the area of contemporary British and Irish poetry, including most recently 'Seamus Heaney's Working Titles' in *The Cambridge Companion to Seamus Heaney* (2009) and *Seamus Heaney: A Bibliography 1959–2003* (with Michael J. Durkan, 2008).

NEIL CORCORAN is Emeritus Professor of English Literature at the University of Liverpool where, until 2010, he was King Alfred Professor. He previously taught at the universities of Sheffield, Swansea and St Andrews. His books include *English Poetry since 1940* (1993), *The Poetry of Seamus Heaney: A Critical Study* (1998), *Elizabeth Bowen: The Enforced Return* (2004) and *Shakespeare and the Modern Poet* (2010).

ALEX DAVIS is a Professor of Modern English at University College Cork. He is the author of *A Broken Line: Denis Devlin and Irish Poetic Modernism* (2000), co-author of *Irish Studies: The Essential Glossary* (2003) and co-editor of three collections of essays on modern poetry, most recently (with Lee M. Jenkins) *The Cambridge Companion to Modernist Poetry* (2007).

TERRY GIFFORD is the author of *Ted Hughes* (2009), *Reconnecting With John Muir: Essays in Post-Pastoral Practice* (2006), *Pastoral* (1999) and *Green Voices: Understanding Contemporary Nature Poetry* (1995; 2nd edn 2011), together with six chapters in books on Ted Hughes. His seventh collection of poems (with Christopher North) is *Al Otro Lado del Aguilar* (2011). Chair of the UK's Mountain Heritage Trust, Terry Gifford is Visiting Professor at Bath Spa University and Senior Research Fellow and Profesor Honorifico at the University of Alicante, Spain.

JO GILL is Senior Lecturer in Twentieth-Century Literature at the University of Exeter, UK. She is the author of *Anne Sexton's Confessional Poetics* (2007), *Women's Poetry* (2007), and of *The Cambridge Introduction to Sylvia Plath* (2008). She is also the editor of *The Cambridge Companion to Sylvia Plath* (2007). During 2010, she held a British Library Eccles Centre Visiting Fellowship in North American Studies. She is currently writing a book entitled *The Poetics of the American Suburbs*.

CHEN HONG published in English her Ph.D. thesis on the role of animals in the poetry of Hughes and Lawrence as *Bestiality, Animality, and Humanity* (2005). A leading ecocritic in China, with several study periods at universities in Britain and America, Chen Hong recently organized a conference on literature and environment at Central China Normal University, Wuhan, where she teaches. She is currently writing a book on Hughes in Chinese.

JOANNY MOULIN, Professor of British Literature at Aix-Marseille University, France, is the author of *Ted Hughes: la langue remunérée* (1999), *Ted Hughes: New Selected Poems* (1999) and *Ted Hughes: la terre hantée. Biographie* (2007). He also edited *Lire Ted Hughes* (1999) and *Ted Hughes: Alternative Horizons* (2004).

NEIL ROBERTS is Emeritus Professor of English Literature at the University of Sheffield, where he taught for thirty-eight years, and Special Professor of D.H. Lawrence Studies at the University of Nottingham. He has published nine books including *Ted Hughes: A Critical Study* (with Terry Gifford, 1981), *Ted*

Hughes: A Literary Life (2006) and *Ted Hughes: New Selected Poems* (2007) and is the editor of the *Blackwell Companion to Twentieth-Century Poetry* (2001). He has recently completed *A Lucid Dreamer: The Life of Peter Redgrove* and an edition of Redgrove's *Collected Poems*, both Jonathan Cape, 2012.

VANDA ZAJKO is Senior Lecturer in Classics, University of Bristol. She has published many articles on the reception of classical literature, particularly in the twentieth century. She is co-editor of *Laughing with Medusa: Classical Myth and Feminist Thought* (2006) and of *Translation and the Classic: Identity as Change in the History of Culture* (2008). She is currently editing *The Blackwell Companion to the Reception of Classical Myth* and a volume on myth and psychoanalysis whilst working on a book for Cambridge University Press entitled *How to Read Classical Literature*.

NOTE ON REFERENCING AND ABBREVIATIONS

All references are to the British first editions unless otherwise indicated. So the abbreviation *SGCB* refers to the first 1992 edition of *Shakespeare and the Goddess of Complete Being*. Some references to *SGCB* in Chapters 7, 8 and 9 refer to the second 1993 edition, and the endnotes indicate this. If poems are published in *Collected Poems* they are referenced there. When referencing the two major Ted Hughes archives, 'Emory' refers to the Manuscript, Archives, and Rare Book Library (MARBL), University of Emory, Atlanta, Georgia, USA, and 'BL' refers to the Ted Hughes collections at the British Library, London, UK.

Abbreviations

BL	*Birthday Letters*
CP	*Collected Poems*
G	*Gaudete*
HW	*Howls & Whispers*
LTH	*Letters of Ted Hughes*
O	*The Oresteia*
SGCB	*Shakespeare and the Goddess of Complete Being*
SO	*Seneca's Oedipus*
SPCP	*Sylvia Plath Collected Poems*
ST	*Selected Translations*
TB	*Three Books*
TO	*Tales from Ovid*
W	*Wodwo*
WP	*Winter Pollen*

CHRONOLOGY

17 August 1930	Born 1 Aspinall St, Mytholmroyd, West Yorkshire, to William Henry and Edith (née Farrar) Hughes.
September 1938	Hughes, aged eight, moves with family to Mexborough, South Yorkshire, where they own a newspaper and tobacco shop.
1942	Mexborough Grammar School.
1945	First poems written.
1946	First poems published in School magazine, *Don and Dearne*.
1948	Wins Scholarship to Pembroke College, Cambridge University.
1949	National Service in the Royal Air Force.
1951	Enters Pembroke College, Cambridge to study English.
1952	Parents return to West Yorkshire to run a shop in Hebden Bridge, living first in Todmorden, then at The Beacon, Heptonstall.
1953	Fox dream: drops English to study Archaeology and Anthropology.
1954	Publishes poems in student magazines under pseudonyms Daniel Hearing and Peter Crew. Graduates from Cambridge.
1955–6	Living in 18 Rugby Street, London, and in Cambridge at weekends. Security guard, dishwasher at London Zoo, reader for J. Arthur Rank.

25 February 1956	At the launch of *Saint Botolph's Review* meets Sylvia Plath.
16 June 1956	Married to Sylvia Plath at St George the Martyr's Church, Bloomsbury, London.
July/August 1956	Honeymoon at 59 Tomas Ortunio, Benidorm, Spain.
November 1956	Living at 55 Eltisley Avenue, Cambridge. Teaching English and Drama at Coleridge Secondary Modern School.
April 1957	First poem, 'The Martyrdom of Bishop Farrar', read on BBC radio.
June 1957	To Plath's home in Wellesley, Massachusetts, USA, then on holiday at Eastham, Cape Cod.
August 1957	To 337 Elm Street, Northampton, Massachusetts, where Sylvia teaches at Smith College.
September 1957	*Hawk in the Rain* published.
Spring semester 1958	Hughes teaches at University of Massachusetts, Amherst, as instructor in English Literature and Creative Writing.
May 1958	Meets Leonard Baskin.
August 1958	Rents flat in 9 Willow Street, Beacon Hill, Boston.
Summer 1959	Crossing America by car.
September 1959	Yaddo Artists' Colony for eleven weeks. Meets Chou Wen-Chung and begins collaboration on *Bardo Thödol*.
December 1959	Return to parents' home in Heptonstall.
February 1960	Move to 3 Chalcot Square, Primrose Hill, London.
March 1960	*Lupercal* published.
1 April 1960	Daughter Frieda Rebecca Hughes born at home in London.
May 1960	First story, *The Rain Horse*, read on BBC radio.
April 1961	*Meet My Folks* published.

August 1961	Sell lease on London flat to David and Assia Wevill and move to Court Green, North Tawton, Devon.
November 1961	First radio play, *The House of Aries*, produced by BBC.
17 January 1962	Nicholas Farrar Hughes born at Court Green.
May 1962	*Selected Poems* with Thom Gunn published.
18 May 1962	David and Assia Wevill visit for the weekend.
10 July 1962	Plath insists on separation. Hughes leaves to live in London.
26 July 1962	Hughes and Plath travel to Wales together for three days for a joint poetry reading.
13 September 1962	Hughes and Plath visit Ireland to find her a house to rent near Richard Murphy.
11 February 1963	Sylvia Plath's suicide.
November 1963	*How the Whale Became.*
November 1963	*The Earth-Owl and Other Moon People.*
April 1964	*Nessie the Mannerless Monster.*
3 March 1965	Assia Wevill's daughter Alexandra Tatiana Eloise Wevill (Shura) born.
Autumn 1965	*Modern Poetry in Translation* (first editorial with Daniel Weissbort).
February 1966	Ted and Assia move to Connemara, Ireland, with the children, although return to Court Green later in the year.
May 1967	*Wodwo.*
July 1967	Hughes, with Patrick Garland, founds the first Poetry International, with Hughes speaking and writing broadsheet and programme notes.
October 1967	Assia and Shura move to London from Court Green.
December 1967	*Poetry in the Making* (five BBC radio broadcasts).
February 1968	*The Iron Man.*

1968	The Arvon Foundation established by John Fairfax and John Moat with Hughes's support.
23 March 1969	Deaths of Assia and Shura Wevill.
11 May 1969	Death of Hughes's mother, Edith Hughes.
Autumn 1969	Purchase of Lumb Bank.
December 1969	*Seneca's Oedipus* published, having opened in March 1968.
19 August 1970	Marriage to Carol Orchard.
October 1970	*Crow: From the Life and Songs of the Crow.*
April–September 1971	Works with Peter Brook in Paris before going to the Shiraz Festival, Persia to produce *Orghast*.
1971	Rainbow Press founded by Olwyn and Ted Hughes.
October 1972	*Selected Poems 1957–67.*
1972	Buys Moortown Farm land (95 acres) and runs it with Carol's father, Jack Orchard.
1974	Awarded Queen's Gold Medal for Poetry.
30 May 1975	*Cave Birds* and *Lumb's Remains* performed at the Ilkley Literature Festival.
October 1975	*Season Songs.*
February 1976	Death of Jack Orchard.
November 1976	*Moon Whales.*
May 1977	*Gaudete.*
1977	Awarded OBE.
February 1978	*Moon Bells.*
October 1978	*Cave Birds.*
May 1979	*Remains of Elmet.*
October 1979	*Moortown.*
1979	Fishing in Iceland with Nicholas.
1980	Fishing in Alaska with Nicholas.

February 1981	Death of father, William Hughes.
March 1981	*Under the North Star.*
February 1982	*Selected Poems 1957–81.*
October 1982	*The Rattle Bag*, edited with Seamus Heaney.
September 1983	*River.*
June 1984	*What Is the Truth?*
December 1984	Appointed Poet Laureate.
August 1986	*Ffangs the Vampire Bat and the Kiss of Truth.*
October 1986	*Flowers and Insects.*
June 1988	*Tales of the Early World.*
September 1989	*Moortown Diary.*
September 1989	*Wolfwatching.*
Spring 1990	*Capriccio* (fifty copies at $4,000 each).
April 1992	*Shakespeare and the Goddess of Complete Being.*
June 1992	*Rain Charm for the Duchy*
June 1993	*Three Books.*
September 1993	*The Iron Woman.*
March 1994	*Winter Pollen.*
October 1994	*Elmet.*
March 1995	*New Selected Poems 1957–1994.*
March 1995	*The Dream Fighter.*
August 1995	*Spring Awakening* performed at the Barbican Theatre, London.
October 1995	*Difficulties of a Bridegroom.*
October 1995	*Collected Animal Poems* (four volumes).
October 1996	*Blood Wedding* performed at the Young Vic Theatre, London.

March 1997	Archive of ninety-two linear feet in 186 boxes sold to Emory University, Atlanta, Georgia, USA.
Late spring 1997	Begins treatment for cancer.
1997	*The School Bag*, edited with Seamus Heaney.
1997	*Tales From Ovid.*
1998	*Phèdre* performed at the Malvern Literary Festival and the Almeida Theatre, London.
January 1998	*Birthday Letters.*
January 1998	*Tales from Ovid* wins the Whitbread Book of the Year prize.
March 1998	*Tales from Ovid* wins the W. H. Smith Literature Award.
Spring 1998	*Howls & Whispers* (100 copies at $4,000 each, plus ten deluxe copies).
October 1998	Forward Prize for Poetry awarded to *Birthday Letters.*
August 1998	Appointment announced: member of the Queen's Order of Merit.
28 October 1998	Ted Hughes dies.
January 1999	*Birthday Letters* wins T. S. Eliot Prize for Poetry.
January 1999	*Birthday Letters* wins the South Bank Award for Literature.
January 1999	*Birthday Letters* wins the Whitbread Book of the Year prize.
April 1999	*Tales from Ovid* performed by the Royal Shakespeare Company at the Swan Theatre, Stratford.
10 May 1999	Quentin Blake named first Children's Laureate, a post founded by Hughes and Michael Morpurgo.
13 May 1999	Memorial Service at Westminster Abbey.

August 1999	*The Iron Giant*, Brad Bird's animated film version of *The Iron Man*, is distributed by Warner Bros.
December 1999	*The Oresteia* performed at the National Theatre, London.
September 2000	*Alcestis* performed by Barry Rutter's Northern Broadsides Theatre Company at Dean Clough, Halifax, West Yorkshire.
2003	*Collected Poems*, edited by Paul Keegan, published.
2005	*Collected Poems for Children*, illustrated by Raymond Briggs, published.
March 2006	The Elmet Trust founded in Mytholmroyd to advance interest in Ted Hughes.
June 2007	First annual Ted Hughes Festival at Mytholmroyd organized by the Elmet Trust.
November 2007	*Letters of Ted Hughes*, selected and edited by Christopher Reid, published.
2008	British Library publishes *The Spoken Word: Ted Hughes*, two boxes of double CDs of BBC broadcasts by Hughes.
21 June 2008	Carol Hughes and Simon Armitage open 1 Aspinall St, Mytholmroyd for let by the Elmet Trust.
November 2008	*The Artist and the Poet: Leonard Baskin and Ted Hughes in Conversation 1983*, a documentary DVD by Noel Chanan published.
16 March 2009	Nicholas Hughes takes his own life in Fairbanks, Alaska, where he had worked as a fish biologist at the University of Alaska, Fairbanks.
April 2009	*The Story of Vasco* performed at the Orange Tree Theatre, London.
June 2009	*Phèdre* performed at the National Theatre, London.
September 2009	*Timmy the Tug* published.
March 2010	Dean of Westminster Abbey announces that Hughes is to be memorialized in Poets' Corner.

March 2010	Alice Oswald's *Weeds and Wildflowers* is the first winner of the Ted Hughes Award for New Work in Poetry, established in 2009 by the Poet Laureate, Carol Ann Duffy.
June 2010	British Library opens large addition to the Ted Hughes archive of 118 boxes.
October 2010	Draft poem 'Last Letter', from a *Birthday Letters* notebook in the British Library, published, with great media interest, in the *New Statesman* on 11 October.
January 2011	The Ted Hughes Society formed via the website www. thetedhughessociety.org.

TERRY GIFFORD

Introduction

When some of us who have contributed to this book were asked in 2009 to support the campaign to have a memorial to Ted Hughes (1930–1998) installed in Westminster Abbey, the question we were asked to answer by the Dean was whether Hughes would be a poet whose work would still be read by generations to come. In one sense, this is impossible to guess. In another sense we were being asked whether the work of Hughes was of the stature of the towering figures of twentieth-century poetry who were themselves the major influences upon his own work as a young poet – figures such as W. B. Yeats, D. H. Lawrence, Dylan Thomas and T. S. Eliot. At the end of the first decade of the twenty-first century it is probably true to say that Hughes's reputation as a poet has never been higher, both in the school and university curriculum and in British culture at large. There are also signs that, after largely ignoring his work during Hughes's lifetime, American critics and teachers are starting to catch up.[1] Hughes is often the only post-war English poet considered in books like Harvard professor Lawrence Buell's *Writing for an Endangered World* (2001) and Stanford professor John Felstiner's *Can Poetry Save the Earth?* (2009).[2] Any course in British Modern Poetry would be incomplete without the inclusion of work by Ted Hughes. In the four years prior to May 2010 six books on the work of Hughes were published – five monographs and a collection of essays[3] – plus two memoirs.[4] In the last months of his life the publication of *Birthday Letters* (1998), following a lifetime of apparent silence about the tragic death of his first wife Sylvia Plath, brought a new audience to his work. At the same time, his translation of *Tales from Ovid* (1998) won literary awards and was turned into a highly successful play by Tim Supple and Simon Reade (1999). Hughes's late flowering as a playwright translating classics of European theatre also added to the swell of praise that brought him a higher profile in his final years than individual volumes of poetry had done earlier in his life.

Important as this work has been to enhancing his reputation at the time of his death, Jo Gill and Vanda Zajko argue in this book that this late work also profoundly engages with a theme that has been a lifelong preoccupation: the responsibility in relationships for creating, against all other pressures, spaces for the negotiations between inner lives. Yet it is not for *Birthday Letters* and the late translations alone that Hughes deserves to be remembered and valued by future generations. The works of the five years between *Cave Birds* (1978) and *River* (1983) represent a breakthrough in the earlier quest to identify and critique the protections, limitations and restraints upon his vision and in the resolution of the tensions inherent in that vision. The image of the symbolic marriage in 'Bride and groom lie hidden for three days' at the crux of the *Cave Birds* sequence becomes a recurrent motif for releasing the potential for healing the splits between the different dichotomies with which Hughes engaged throughout his work: vitality/death; spirit/materiality; animality/ rationality; nature/culture; male/female; self/environment. But the potential for healing these tensions still had to be explored, fought for and rediscovered in each new work and in new forms. It is significant that, as Neil Corcoran has pointed out, the central figures of the mythic sequences are 'transgressive' in 'having their beings astride the boundaries between two worlds'.[5]

This is partly why narrative and dramatic tensions are such essential elements of Hughes's poetic works. As Tracy Brain argues below, each volume of poems needs to be read as an enquiring journey that is carefully constructed. It is often a mistake to attempt to find the complete Hughesian vision at the heart of a volume of poetry within any single poem. It is tempting to select the poem 'Egg-Head' (*CP* 33) from the first collection, for example, to illustrate the playful spirit of parody of the forms and consequences of human protections from fully feeling the forces of inner and outer nature in *The Hawk in the Rain* (1957). But that would risk ignoring the quiet, intimate grief of 'Six Young Men' (*CP* 45), although this poem's final line, and its implicit challenge to the reader to feel the body's vitality, is a remarkable echo of the challenge of 'Egg-Head' to feel 'the bolt of the earth'. Similarly, within the symbolic drama of the second collection of poems, *Lupercal* (1960), what appears to be a poem about a hawk roosting (*CP* 68) might actually be about the dominant human male attitude that explains the collection's final concern with female infertility in 'Lupercalia' (*CP* 87). At the same time, of course, the rejection and fear of femininity in the final poem offers insights into the hawk's closed death-obsessed nature. Voices and ironies qualify each other in the dramatic tensions of each collection of Hughes's poetry, even in those earlier volumes before the poet had discovered how he might develop a mythic narrative structure following his fourth collection, *Crow* (1970).

But the comprehensiveness and consistency of the whole work, in all its diverse forms, is remarkable and is the reason why, whilst we struggle to resolve dualities and debate their tensions, Hughes's work will continue to be essential reading for future generations. From the beginning of his career as a writer Hughes was exploring his central themes in plays and stories alongside the poetry. This was not always successful in the early stages. Stage plays, such as the lost play 'The Calm', were abandoned, and he eventually also abandoned writing short stories for adults as he found that they became weirdly prophetic. But their part in the Hughesian mode of enquiry is indicated by his inclusion of a play and five stories in his third collection *Wodwo* (1967) with a note to readers that they should be read as 'chapters of a single adventure'. Radio plays suited his interest in language and his lack of interest in staging. But two periods of writing for the theatre, for Peter Brook in the late 1960s/early 1970s and then in the final years of his life, are discussed by Vanda Zajko in Chapter 8. In Chapter 9 Neil Corcoran points out that Hughes's writing of stories for children has often been overlooked by critics of his poetry. Again, this is a form that he was exploring when he met Sylvia Plath and *How the Whale Became* (1963) was the focus of his writing during their honeymoon. His last collection of creation tales for children, *The Dreamfighter and Other Creation Tales* (1995), was published only three years before his death. Neil Corcoran also considers Hughes as an essayist, letter writer and literary critic. *Winter Pollen* (1994) collects early book reviews as well as brilliantly original long essays of criticism on poetics. In Chapter 10 Jonathan Bate evaluates Hughes's major critical work on Shakespeare, revealing not only Hughes's Shakespeare, but what he calls 'Shakespeare's Ted Hughes'.

More recently three further aspects of the diversity of Hughes's achievements as a writer have been revealed by new collections of his work. In his Introduction to *Ted Hughes: Selected Translations* (2006) Daniel Weissbort, with whom Hughes founded the journal *Modern Poetry in Translation* in 1965, claims that Hughes must be regarded as 'among the most important poetry translators in the English tradition'.[6] This is also a practice that was continuous throughout Hughes's career. Reviewers of *Letters of Ted Hughes* (2007) seemed to have been surprised by the depth and seriousness of what can now be seen to be a previously unknown significant body of work. Comparisons with the insights into the life of a poet in the letters of Keats were not uncommon in the reviews.[7] The editor Christopher Reid indicated that three more volumes just as big could have been compiled and would have provided something of interest on every page.[8] Thirdly, Hughes's career as a broadcaster for the BBC has been highlighted by the British Library's production of two boxes of double CDs, including previously unreleased recordings, giving a total of 284 minutes of richly voiced readings of poetry with introductions, stories and talks.[9]

The five talks published as *Poetry in the Making* (1967) remind us not just that Hughes was a huge supporter of educational radio broadcasting in its golden age, but that he was also a lifelong supporter of the burgeoning creative writing movement, especially for children. He judged children's writing competitions for decades, as Poet Laureate founded, with Michael Morpurgo, the appointment of a Children's Laureate, founded the Arvon International Poetry Competition and became a key supporter (though never a tutor) of the Arvon Foundation residential courses, offering his house at Lumb Bank, Heptonstall, West Yorkshire, as a second location for the scheme. Hughes also became increasingly active in putting his environmentalism into practice. Something of what Christopher Reid admits to omitting from his edition of the letters – Hughes's campaign of the 1980s on behalf of the rivers of south-west England – is indicated in Chapter 6 of this *Companion*, which provides detailed evidence of one aspect of Hughes's practical work on behalf of the environment that underpins his poetry. Here again, Hughes can be seen to be needing to attempt to heal the cultural dualisms of art and activism, science and poetry, politics and poetics, human health and the health of river life. Later, as Poet Laureate for the last fourteen years of his life, Hughes continued to lobby on behalf of the environment, believing that his books were an integral, if indirect, part of that activity. Chapter 6 reveals, for example, that, when it was first published, Hughes played with the idea of sending a copy of his children's story *The Iron Woman* (1993) to the prime minister and the members of his cabinet.

Behind this extraordinary range of literary and cultural activity there lay a coherent vision that was formed at an early stage of his life's work. Hughes's misunderstanding of the work of the nineteenth-century art critic and social theorist John Ruskin provides an opportunity to outline some of the key features of a vision that they actually shared, without Hughes realizing it. In doing so one might sense the trajectory of Hughes's imaginative achievement. In 1994, in an exchange of letters about the pollution of the River Don near my home in South Yorkshire, I enclosed in a letter to Hughes a copy of John Ruskin's famous tirade against the neglect of the environment in Victorian England, much abbreviated here:

> The first three principles [of political economy], I said, are Pure Air, Water, and Earth.
>
> Heaven gives you the main elements of these. You can destroy them at your pleasure, or increase, almost without limit, the available quantities of them.
>
> ... Your power over the rain and river-waters of the earth is infinite. You can bring rain where you will, by planting wisely and tending carefully; – drought where you will, by ravage of woods and neglect of the soil. You might have the rivers of England as pure as the crystal of the rock; – beautiful in falls, in lakes, in

living pools; – so full of fish that you might take them out with your hands instead of nets. Or you may do always as you have done now, turn every river of England into a common sewer, so that you cannot so much as baptize an English baby but with filth, unless you hold its face out in the rain; and even *that* falls dirty.[10]

Hughes wrote to me:

> My acquaintance with Ruskin is slight – more as a personality than as a body of works. My notion of his horror at the 'decay' of the Alps (he somewhere describes the changes seen by him during his lifetime) is also a notion of global paranoia – or was. I now see how much more there was to it. (He's always repelled me somehow – so I never read him.)[11]

Later, after a long period away, and unsure whether he had written in reply to me, he added in a postcard, 'The Ruskin on "Pure Air, Water and Earth" ought to be printed across the top of every page issueing [sic] from Dept. Of Env., NRA [National Rivers Authority, forerunner of the Environment Agency of England and Wales] and HMIP [Her Majesty's Inspectorate of Pollution].'[12]

Actually, Hughes was wrong about Ruskin, but for revealing reasons. Those who have not read Ruskin can find many legitimate reasons to be 'repelled' by his reputed 'personality'. His well-known sexual prurience, his reputation for bombastic moralism, his schematic mode of thinking and his divisive manner of making points by contrasts, are all aspects of Victorianism that would alienate any poet attempting, in his own words, to break out of the 'suffocating', 'cosy' conventions of the 1950s' Movement poetry, but especially one who was 'all for opening negotiations with whatever happened to be out there' that had led to the 'death camps and atomic bombs'.[13] If the Movement poets recoiled from the ideas of D. H. Lawrence, C. G. Jung and Robert Graves, whom Joanny Moulin argues in Chapter 1 were the influences on what he calls Hughes's 'ideology', Hughes recoiled from Ruskin's reputation and missed the opportunity to read *The Storm Cloud of the Nineteenth Century* (1884), the letter to the workingmen of England quoted above from *Fors Clavigera* (1871–84) and *Modern Painters* (1843–60), which might have had some ideas of interest to him. In the latter, which is driven by a defence of J. M. W. Turner's paintings and drawings, Ruskin praises Turner for seeing that 'decay having its use and nobleness . . . it ought no more to be omitted than, in the portrait of an aged man, the furrows on his hand or brow'.[14] The exaggeration of 'nobleness' here is parallel to Hughes's own later tendency towards the injection of religious nobleness in a line such as 'the tiger blesses with a fang' (CP 578). But the desire for respect for natural decay, disintegration and the death process Ruskin knew to be a radical one that would challenge the 'cosiness' of his own contemporary culture. Turner, Ruskin said, in discovering the true place of mountain decay in his vision of landscape, had to accept that he was 'not merely in *advance* of the men of his day, but in *contradiction* to them' (Ruskin's italics).[15]

Why was Ruskin's attitude to decay crucial to Hughes's view of him? Because from the beginning Hughes had wanted his poetry to enter negotiations with both the forces of life and the forces of death equally, indeed, to explore their reliance upon each other and the way they might be similar and different in the human animal and other animals, or in the long haul of the landscape and the short haul of the weather. The early shock of Hughes's poetry in *The Hawk in the Rain* and *Lupercal* was precisely because the processes of decay were introduced in deliberate contradiction to the dominant poetry of his day, and the protections against such shocks were exposed to satire, ridicule and horror by the poet. The radical, 'contradictory' impact of each volume of poetry throughout Hughes's career, and the challenging, revisionary tenor of his reviews, letters and essays, demonstrate how much Hughes was working against the dominant grain of his culture. Light and darkness are 'both essential to beauty', wrote Ruskin.[16] Once Hughes had had personal experience of the darkness of the deaths of Sylvia Plath and Assia Wevill, the latter quickly followed by his mother's death, he developed narrative sequences in which the protagonists' self-examination, disintegration, dismemberment were the necessary stages in negotiations that might make possible any wholeness of being, reconnection or 'redemption' as some critics like to characterize it.[17] Perhaps such a word requires caution for two reasons, both associated with a tendency to hubris in our species that Hughes constantly challenged.

Ruskin laid great emphasis on the essential humility required by the artist who sought to truly 'see' his subject. '*Pride is at the bottom of all great mistakes,*' wrote Ruskin, his heavy-handed italics ironically betraying his own difficulty in putting this notion into practice. In his early work Hughes often parodied a lack of humility, especially the arrogant assumption of being at the centre of the universe. In *Wodwo*, where the first explorations of the process of dismemberment of the ego are offered in the play 'The Wound', there are a number of poems in which the hubris of transcendence is exposed with irony as a self-deception. The most obvious is the Wodwo's humorous 'if I sit still how everything / stops to watch me I suppose I am the exact centre' (*CP* 183). Against this are the down-to-earth, materially anchored endings of poems typified by 'The Green Wolf': beautiful stars and flowers are sustained by decay and decomposition that is conducted 'In the scarves of dew, the wet hair of nightfall' (*CP* 160). What is so complete about the ending of the apparently uncompleted project of the *Crow* (1970) sequence of self-examination is the brilliant materiality of the forms of enlightenment in the last two poems, 'Two Eskimo Songs' and 'Littleblood'. What water learns in the former is that 'it lay at the bottom of all things // utterly worn out utterly clear' (CP 258). The wisdom gained by Littleblood through 'sucking death's mouldy tits' is already singing in the ear as it pulses through the body simply being itself (CP 258). 'Seeing' the profundity of material reality requires a humble acceptance of the special individuality of things in themselves. When the image of a marriage is earned by the diminishment of the ego in Cave Birds, the erotic mutual 'giving' that brings dualities to perfection in the modes of man and woman raises them, ironically, into 'two gods of mud' (CP 438). It is on the mud of the earth that human beings must learn to walk, make love, live with all their contradictory impulses and accommodate themselves ecologically. In the year following Cave Birds Hughes published Adam and the Sacred Nine (1979) in which Adam is encouraged to rise up into his humanity by the visits of nine sacred birds. But the transcendence of flying is not Adam's mode of being. He discovers, in the final poem titled 'The sole of a foot', that he must have his feet on the earth to be fully human. Possibly taking a line from the devotional writings of Gerard Manley Hopkins, Hughes concludes this sequence with the words 'I was made // for you' (CP 452).[18] If birds, animals and fish in Hughes's early poems were 'living the redeemed life of joy', as he put it in 1965, for humans it is not so simple.[19] Ecstasy and joy come with responsibilities for the mud and the relationship with it which we might now call the decentred 'human footprint' in it.

The sheer hard work of Moortown Diary (1979) and the detailed observation of River and Flowers and Insects (1986) could be argued to be the imaginative effort that earns, in these later collections, 'redemption' from the earlier engagements with decay and grief. Certainly the death process is a more integrated presence in these collections than in the sequences of disintegration. Certainly, too, Hughes invites the concept in his use of religious imagery, in River especially. The critical consensus is also strongly in favour of the view that Hughes's project is, at bottom, a 'religious' one (see, for example, Ann Skea,[20] Keith Sagar[21] and Neil Roberts[22]), 'if that word has not been too compromised,' adds Keith Sagar.[23] But the humility of Hughes's form of devotional stance and his depth of insight into natural mysteries do not lead to the transcendent moral position implied by 'redemption'. It is still a material world, as Skea, Sagar and Roberts each emphasize, in which these poems are anchored and in evocation of which they gain their insights. The feeling of being at one with the creative-destructive material world in Hughes's poetry may be like that of a god (as in 'like two gods of mud' at the climax of 'Bride and groom lie hidden for three days'), but the dualities of spirit and materiality, even at the moment of their reconciliation, do still need to be held in balance, against the temptation to privilege spiritual insight. Actually, the tiger does not, cannot, 'bless' with a fang, although in comparison to a machine gun which is the subject of 'Tiger-Psalm' it might be tempting to think that it does so.

The second reason to be cautious about 'redemption' is because, as the last lines of *Cave Birds* have it, 'at the end of the ritual / up comes a goblin' (*CP* 440). Again, Hughes might have agreed with Ruskin: 'There is a continual mystery caused throughout *all* spaces, caused by the absolute infinity of all things. WE NEVER SEE ANYTHING CLEARLY.'[24] In one sense this is the subject of *Gaudete* (1977), an unusually visual narrative which started out as a film script. Typical of Hughes's mixture of the storyteller's playfulness with his audience, humorous imagery and formal experimentation, with the most charged evocation of his deepest themes, *Gaudete* challenges the reader's perception of his purpose. In a narrative in which the characters are often shown to be voyeurs of each other, they cannot see that a 'wooden' priest of Christian love has replaced their previous one. The original priest, taken into the underworld, cannot see how to perform the healing vocation demanded of him. What he has seen there he records in the enigmatic poems of the Epilogue, which give glimpses of his having failed to fully engage, negotiate or find a fulfilling relationship with his female creator. As Jonathan Bate points out in Chapter 10, when Hughes elaborately charts Shakespeare's supposed search for the 'Goddess of Complete Being', Hughes is really betraying his own central preoccupation with such a figure in this huge prose work. For Hughes the poet she is elusive: her ultimate mystery is, he senses, embedded in the material world – in the mystery and materiality of a river, for example. Yet the 'creatures of light' Hughes is living among at the end of the *River* poem titled 'That Morning' are seen, not in religious transcendence, but with his feet in a river, standing, fishing, alive in his human mortality as the two golden bears also fishing there are alive in their own life cycles, fishing for the salmon that have brought them all there in their difference and their equivalence (*CP* 664). Nothing has been redeemed. There is no intrinsic guilt – no original sin – in human mortality, just as there is no stasis of permanent balance in living the recognition of contradictions and dualities. Perhaps a better model for Hughes's achievement is the continuous dynamic of juxtapositions in *Wolfwatching* (1989) and *Elmet* (1994) that is characterized in Chapter 6 as Hughes's 'social ecology'.

This kind of dynamic formulation has its origins in the early paradoxes of natural processes such as the single force at the heart of 'Crow Hill' that produces both erosion and vitality: 'what humbles these hills has raised / the arrogance of blood and bone' (*CP* 62). Despite the pain at a personal level of acknowledging and experiencing the 'humbling' and 'unmaking' of death and anguish, and the dangers of entering into poetic negotiations with those destructive forces in the process of symbolic dismemberment, the outcome is an ability to create, from *Cave Birds* onwards, successive volumes that can attempt to heal dualities by holding them in counterbalancing juxtapositions so that human life, in all its tensions and contradictions, can be understood to be part of those in the wider ecology in which we live. Of course, from that position a responsibility comes with being human. This cannot have the closure of 'redemption', but is a constant demand, to be continually remade and re-answered. So it is not just in the obvious farming responsibilities of *Moortown Diary* that the poet remakes his commitment, but in the counterbalancing of 'Salmon Eggs' with the 'epic poise' of death in 'October Salmon' in *River*. It is also in the placing of 'Anthem for Doomed Youth' next to the anthem for 'The Black Rhino' in *Wolfwatching*, the grief for the loss of human life alongside the grief for the anticipated loss of a species. The 'completeness of being' in creation helps the poet understand the mystery of his mother's tendency to sudden tears during his childhood, recalled in the poem 'Source'. The 'strange music' of crying is actually healing through a 'necessary' process of mourning that is characterized as 'repairing' (*CP* 757).

Awareness of such paradoxes, even as they are lived out, is what it is to be human, in Hughes's poetic vision. This is perhaps what the lizard meant when it said to Prometheus on his crag 'Even as the vulture buried its head – // "Lucky, you are so lucky to be human!"' (*CP* 294). As his punishment for stealing fire Prometheus has been condemned to live chained to his rock and each day the vulture feeds on his liver, which each night grows again. In the twentieth poem in this sequence Prometheus at last ponders the possible forms of 'the earth's enlightenment' that the vulture might be offering him. In the final poem he is reborn to freedom, a changed person who 'treads // On the dusty peacock film where the world floats' (*CP* 296). He treads with a new awareness and a responsibility for his footprint on the delicate, fragile, beautiful and dusty world. In 1849 Ruskin wrote,

> God has leant us the earth for our life; it is a great entail. It belongs as much to those who are to come after us, and whose names are already written in the book of creation, as to us; and we have no right, by anything that we do or neglect, to involve them in unnecessary penalties, or deprive them of benefits which it was in our power to bequeath.[25]

In 1993 Ted Hughes was considering the role of poetry in what had become, in his phrase, 'the Environmental Wars'. He knew that poetry's special role was not that of combative, ringing prose, such as Ruskin's for example, but closer to the puzzling whisper of the lizard in the ear of Prometheus:

Poetry has to be on all sides at once – or it has to take form at a level beneath that on which taking sides begins. In the Environmental Wars it is very easy to become righteously embattled against the individuals who seem responsible for the damage. The real problem, as I see it, is the difficulty of avoiding that easy but exhilarating battle with them, and of finding effective ways of making them painfully aware of the human folly in which we are all implicated.[26]

So Ted Hughes's great sense of responsibility as a poet is to offer us a complex vision that reconnects the dualities we struggle to reconcile in human culture with the contradictory tensions of the world in which we must make a sustainable home for future generations.

More than ten years after his death it has now become clear that in an always changing body of poetic work, and in a range of other literary modes, Hughes sought to raise questions for readers. This *Companion* introduces readers to the debates that have been developing over the last fifty years around the work of one of the most searching writers of the twentieth century. In the twenty-first century the questions Hughes's work raises have only become more urgent: What is it to be human within our universe? How might we understand our inner life in relation to the forces of nature around us? What is the moral scope for action within the paths already chosen? How can the contemporary imagination be a force for cultural change? What alternative forms of knowledge might we be ignoring? Is culture nature? What might be the healing role of literature in considering the problems we have created in our relationship with our environmental home?

The trajectory of Hughes's life and writing also raises some conundrums for readers and critics. The French biographer of Ted Hughes, Joanny Moulin, asks in Chapter 1 how the problems inherent in any biography are particularly focused by the challenge of narrating and understanding important episodes and recurring themes in the life of Ted Hughes. As Moulin narrates he also problematizes significant aspects of what he calls 'an unsolvable riddle'. In Chapter 2 Paul Bentley considers the underlying reasons for such vehement debate about Hughes's first volumes of poetry. Arguing that nature is actually also culture in Hughes's early work, Bentley traces the debates about 'violence' to historical and ultimately class origins in both the concerns of critics and the poet. The Chinese Hughes scholar Chen Hong also considers, in Chapter 3, the cultural implications of the early animal poems, demonstrating by close readings how animal totems function as critiques of human life. The question for her is how successful Hughes was in his poetic negotiations between the animal and the human realms. The creative negotiations between Hughes and Plath are the conundrum explored in Chapter 4 by the editor of *The Cambridge Companion to Sylvia Plath*, Jo Gill. What were the forms of the 'hidden supply lines', in Hughes's phrase, that fed into each other's work? How successful is Hughes, Gill asks, in the defence of those supply lines in the continued intertextuality represented by *Birthday Letters*? Hughes's mythic pursuit of the feminine in the form of the Goddess creator is the subject of Rand Brandes's chapter on the three epic works of Hughes's middle period: *Crow*, *Gaudete* and *Cave Birds*. This is followed by a chapter on the third period's major works: *Remains of Elmet*, *Elmet*, *Wolfwatching* and *River*. These collections offer me the opportunity in Chapter 6 to consider the exact nature of Hughes's mode of ecology, which seeks to embed humans in their environment. New evidence is revealed about the range of Hughes's work, combining art and activism, in the practice of what might be called his 'social ecology'. In Chapter 7 Tracy Brain takes the approach of a 'sympathetic feminist' in considering why feminist readers of the works have had difficulties with Hughes's representations of female figures. Brain pioneers a new approach to the complex relationship between masculine and feminine principles in Hughes's poetry. In Chapter 8 the recently excavated question of the role of the classics in Hughes's work, especially in the late body of translated plays, is approached by Vanda Zajko with an authoritative knowledge of both the original works and recent studies. Zajko reveals how what begins as an exploration of the archaic collective imagination expresses through its range of idioms material that ultimately 'opened inwardly for Hughes towards a first-hand experience both optimistic and transformative'. Hughes's late work also included much prose writing. Believing, at the end, that he had spent too much time writing prose, why did Hughes persist? Neil Corcoran makes the case, in Chapter 9, for Hughes's lifelong obsession with all forms of prose – stories, reviews, essays, letters, books – acting as both 'poison and cure' for Hughes's writing life. Of course, Hughes's major prose work, *Shakespeare and the Goddess of Complete Being* (1992), was both the main source of his anxiety about prose writing and the necessary outcome of another lifetime obsession. With new archival research, the Shakespeare scholar Jonathan Bate considers not only what Hughes reveals of Shakespeare, but what this work reveals about Hughes. In a parallel risk to his creative health and reputation, why did Hughes not only accept the role of Poet Laureate, but continue the tradition of writing for royal occasions? In Chapter 11 Neil Roberts traces a fascinating line of enquiry that leads to issues of class and the importance of the two world wars to Hughes's work in order to answer this question. Finally, in Chapter 12 Alex Davis provides a selective overview of the responses critics have made to the challenges of Hughes's work and some of the issues addressed by this *Companion*. Davis points out that the reception of Hughes' work 'has reached global proportions' as critics in China and India join those in Britain and America in the increasing international dialogue about the meaning and relevance of Hughes's imaginative challenges to the way we think we live.

'Every new child is nature's chance to correct culture's error,' wrote Hughes (*WP* 149). His belief in the imagination as a tool for healing the errors of culture can be extended to every new reader. Poetry, Hughes wrote, belongs to the reader rather than to the writer, suggesting that the imagination of the reader occupies the rooms of the house of the poem that is, once published, no longer owned by the builder.[27] This *Companion* is intended to open the doors of some of the rooms in the houses Hughes built and discuss alternative views from the windows. Of course, some of those views might be characterized as postmodern, or postfeminist, or post-pastoral in my own case, as I argued in 1994.[28] But Hughes's friend Seamus Heaney puts all such theoretical approaches to such powerful poetry into perspective in the first part of his poem 'On His Work in the English Tongue':

> Post-this, post-that, post-the-other, yet in the end
> Not past a thing. Not understanding or telling
> Or forgiveness.
> But often past oneself,
> Pounded like a shore by the roller griefs
> In language that can still knock language sideways.[29]

NOTES

1. The two notable exceptions are Leonard M. Scigaj's three books on Hughes (see Further Reading, below) and Diane Middlebrook's *Her Husband: Hughes and Plath – A Marriage* (London: Little, Brown, 1994).
2. Lawrence Buell's *Writing for an Endangered World: Literature, Culture, and Environment in the U.S. and Beyond* (London: Harvard University Press, 2001), pp. 250–1; John Felstiner's *Can Poetry Save the Earth? A Field Guide to Nature Poems* (London: Yale University Press, 2009), pp. 327–34.
3. Neil Roberts, *Ted Hughes: A Literary Life* (Basingstoke: Palgrave Macmillan, 2006); Susan Bassnett, *Ted Hughes* (London: Northcote House, 2008); R. D. Rees (ed.), *Ted Hughes and the Classics* (Oxford: Oxford University Press, 2009); Terry Gifford, *Ted Hughes* (London: Routledge, 2009); Keith Sagar, *Ted Hughes and Nature: 'Terror and Exultation'* (www.keithsagar.co.uk, 2009); Edward Hadley, *The Elegies of Ted Hughes* (Basingstoke: Palgrave Macmillan, 2010).
4. Ehor Boyanowsky, *Savage Gods: In the Wild with Ted Hughes* (Vancouver: Douglas and McIntyre, 2009); Daniel Huws, *Memories of Ted Hughes 1952–1963* (Nottingham: Five Leaves Publications, 2010).
5. Neil Corcoran, *English Poetry since 1940* (London: Longman, 1993), p. 118.
6. Daniel Weissbort, *Ted Hughes: Selected Translations* (London: Faber and Faber, 2006), p. xii.
7. As observed by American reviewer Carol Bere in her own review for *Contemporary Poetry Review*, www.cprw.com/Bere/hughes.htm, accessed 16 March 2009.

8. Christopher Reid (ed.), *Letters of Ted Hughes* (London: Faber and Faber, 2007), p. ix.

9. *The Spoken Word: Ted Hughes, Poems and Short Stories*, NSACD 54–55, British Library, 2008; *The Spoken Word: Ted Hughes, Poetry in the Making*, NSACD 56–57, British Library, 2008. See also 'Two of a Kind – Sylvia Plath and Ted Hughes in conversation' on *The Spoken Word: Sylvia Plath*, NSACD 71, British Library, 2010.

10. John Ruskin, *Fors Clavigera*, Letter v, 1 May 1871. E. T. Cook and Alexander Wedderburn (eds.), *The Works of John Ruskin*, 39 vols. (London: Allen, 1902–12), vol. XXVII, pp. 91–2.

11. Letter to T. G., 24 June 1994.

12. Postcard to T. G., 14 September 1994.

13. Interview with Ekbert Faas, Appendix II, Ekbert Faas, *Ted Hughes: The Unaccommodated Universe* (Santa Barbara: Black Sparrow Press, 1980), p. 201.

14. Ruskin, *Works*, vol. VI, p. 377.

15. *Ibid.*, p. 360.

16. *Ibid.*, p. 321.

17. *River* (1983) is taken to be the apotheosis of this achievement by Craig Robinson, Leonard M. Scigaj, Ann Skea and Keith Sagar. See Further Reading.

18. 'I was made for this'. Christopher Devlin (ed.), *The Sermons and Devotional Writings of Gerard Manley Hopkins* (London: Oxford University Press, 1959), p. 239.

19. John Horder, 'Desk Poet', *The Guardian* (23 March 1965), p. 9.

20. Ann Skea, *Ted Hughes: The Poetic Quest* (Armidale: University of New England Press, 1994), p. 226.

21. Sagar, *Ted Hughes and Nature*, p. 266.

22. Roberts, *Literary Life*, p. 188.

23. Sagar, *Ted Hughes and Nature*, p. 266.

24. Ruskin, *Works*, vol. VI, p. 75.

25. *Ibid.*, vol. VIII, p. 233.

26. Letter to T. G., 17 December 1993.

27. TH to Keith Sagar, 17 March 1975, Add. 78756, f. 20, BL.

28. Terry Gifford, 'Gods of Mud: Ted Hughes and the Post-Pastoral', in Keith Sagar (ed.), *The Challenge of Ted Hughes* (Manchester: Manchester University Press, 1974), pp. 129–41.

29. Seamus Heaney, *Electric Light* (London: Faber and Faber, 2001), p. 61.

I

JOANNY MOULIN

The problem of biography

All biographies are impossible, but Ted Hughes's is more impossible than others. One of the reasons for this is that he was made a character in the life-story of Sylvia Plath. Witness the title of one of the two Ted Hughes biographies to date: *Her Husband: Hughes and Plath – A Marriage*.[1] Of course, Diane Middlebrook came to Hughes from an interest in Ann Sexton and Sylvia Plath. Her approach testified to the construction of a personage called 'Ted Hughes' that took place early on in his own lifetime, originating in Sylvia Plath's poems and her extremely detailed journals and letters, which are one of the main documentary sources for any Hughes biographer. The earlier biography, Elaine Feinstein's *Ted Hughes; The Life of a Poet*,[2] while still relying heavily on Plath's writings, had already attempted to broaden the scope of what was then known by using first-hand correspondence and conversations with people who had been personally acquainted with the poet. Of course, huge new sources of information were discovered with the opening in the year 2000 of the Ted Hughes Archives in the Manuscript, Archives, and Rare Book Library of Emory University in Atlanta. This consists of a major part of Hughes's letters, drafts, notebooks and drawings, and it provides ample material for a literary biography of Ted Hughes that could not but lead to a genuine reappraisal of the figure of both the man and the poet. The full achievement of this remains impossible, however, because part of the archive remains sealed off, withdrawn from public inspection until the year 2023.

Poets' biographies are ultimately as impossible as poetry translations; like them, they require to be periodically redone. Whilst this is true for any work of a historical nature, in the case of the biography of Ted Hughes, one has to face the supplementary foreclosure of what he called his 'inner life', of which perhaps his own literary work is the only legitimate record. Here lies one of the central paradoxes of Hughes's career, which is that his whole work is an exploration of the inner life, in an age which was, at best, sceptical of this concept. For the biographer of Hughes the usual difficulty of establishing the 'facts' of a life, and distinguishing their statement from interpretation, is further complicated by the subject's ideology, which challenges this very process by privileging and protecting an elusively subjective inner life.

One of the major sources of discord between Plath and Hughes was directly linked to what has been called her 'confessional' poetic attitude. Plath insisted on offering for publication two poems about details of their private life, 'The Rabbit Catcher' and 'Event', which were personal fantasies about her husband. In addition to the example of Robert Lowell, Plath admired Theodore Roethke, from the days when Plath and Hughes worked as guests in the Yaddo community of artists in Saratoga Springs, just before they returned to the UK, and strove to emulate him by writing what she called 'mad poems' of her own. This was almost a recognition of the partly delirious nature of her fantasies in poems such as 'The Rabbit Catcher', and later 'Man in Black' and 'Daddy'. On the other hand, Hughes had, at that time, always insisted that one should not publish poems involving recognizable characters.

One remarkable point is the superimposition of the figures of Ted Hughes and of Sylvia's father, Otto Plath, especially in her poem 'Daddy'. In some accounts that Plath made of her psychoanalytical treatment with Dr Ruth Beuscher, she explains how she came to realize that she had constructed some mental overlap of the image of her husband and that of her dead father. Her hatred and resentment against her father, whom she felt had abandoned her and his family when he died, was somehow projected onto Ted, despite the fact that the two men were very different characters. The 'Ted Hughes' character that Plath writes about in poems like 'The Rabbit Catcher' has apparently got nothing in common with Otto, but he is very similar to a nocturnal character who haunts the poems of Ted Hughes's juvenilia in his *Collected Poems*, a poacher who stalks the moors and woods by night and absorbs the exotic stories and poetry of Rudyard Kipling by day.

Otto Plath was a scientist and an academic, a hard-working German-American, very strongly of a rational mode of thinking. There was also a serious-minded work ethic in the Methodist strain in Hughes's education, which he received from his mother, Edith Farrar Hughes. As a child Ted went with his mother to a Methodist chapel, and he would later satirize this particular religious mentality in poems like 'Mount Zion'. But at the same time, Ted inherited from Edith an altogether different style of spirituality, for Edith Hughes was psychic – she was a seer and had premonitory visions of tragic events; she also had a regular relationship with the ghost of her sister, who had died at the age of eighteen. Ted Hughes was convinced that he had inherited her gift and that he was a seer too.

In the series of BBC Radio talks called *Poetry in the Making* Hughes explained that finding a poem was very much like catching an animal. The comparison derived from his relationship with his elder brother Gerald, with whom, at an early age, he had got into the habit of leaving the house by night to go on hunting expeditions in the neighbouring countryside. Ted explained that Gerald's practical teaching developed in him a sixth sense, very much like their mother's psychic ability.

When the family left Mytholmroyd, Ted's birthplace in West Yorkshire, for the town of Mexborough in South Yorkshire, Gerald joined the RAF and then took up a position as a gamekeeper on an estate in Devon before emigrating to Australia for the rest of his life. This separation from Gerald was felt as a heart-rending and long-standing deprivation by Ted, who would long afterwards write a letter to his brother, saying 'Think how you deprived me – orphaned me, really'.[3] From time to time Ted would wish to be with his brother again, either by thinking of joining him in Australia, or by devising endlessly renewed money-making schemes to try and induce Gerald to return and live with him in England. One immediate consequence of Gerald's departure was that Ted had the terrible feeling that he was faced with the impossible task of making up for this loss to his mother. The shadow character of his juvenilia seems very clearly to develop from this situation; there is always the feeling, in these poems of his youth, which he published in the Mexborough Grammar School magazine *Don & Dearne* (named after the local rivers where the young Ted attempted to go fishing), that Ted the wanderer is constantly accompanied by a double, a ghostly doppelgänger, haunting his every step.

What are the implications of this for the biographer's understanding of the actual relationships with women by a poet whose whole work can be read as a search for a relationship with a female figure whom he comes to characterize (for Shakespeare's work) as the Goddess of Complete Being? One of Hughes's lovers, aware that there were others, said to Elaine Feinstein that 'Ted was a man who needed several women ... other men do, don't they? He isn't unique.'[4] Could it be that Hughes needed 'several women' because he was the spiritual heir of Robert Graves, whose *White Goddess* includes a theory of the necessity for a poet to keep falling in love with a muse to go on writing genuine poetry? Robert Graves famously explained that 'The White Goddess is anti-domestic; she is the perpetual "other woman", and her part is difficult for a woman of sensibility to play for more than a few years, because the temptation to commit suicide in simple domesticity lurks in every maenad's and muse's heart.'[5] Among the writers who spoke out against the sexual prurience of their times whom Hughes admired one should also add C. G. Jung and D. H. Lawrence. Ted Hughes once said that when he was reading D. H. Lawrence, he felt as if he was reading his own autobiography. In a letter defending fishing, Hughes referred to Jung's notion that if primitive impulses were not found an outlet – such as in fishing, Hughes suggested – one outcome might be, in Hughes's words, a 'hectic bout of adultery' (*LTH* 658).

The now well-known cases of Jill Barber[6] and Emma Tennant[7] offer two examples of women who temporarily played the part of the White Goddess for Hughes in the 1970s. But what were their own agendas? Barber sought an introduction to London literary life after following Hughes from a reading in Australia. Tennant quite readily admits that she had wanted to become Hughes's lover in the hope of gathering confidential information about what had really happened between him and Sylvia Plath. According to them, it seems that he offered both the same discourse about a spiritual marriage. In the case of Sylvia Plath, Hughes was accused by some American feminists of being an adulterous husband who was the chief cause of her suicide. How can a biographer ever know the full story of a separation and a suicide? Should the suicide of his wife make Ted Hughes's poetry unworthy of study, as has been the common attitude in American academia? If Plath's poetry has come to be, however misleadingly, read through her suicide, it is now clear that Plath's death haunted Hughes's work in the harrowing trials and dismemberments of his mythic sequences published well before *Birthday Letters*.

When he was a student in Cambridge, Ted Hughes and his friends used to meet to sing and recite poems at a pub called The Anchor, where the received opinion was that Sylvia Plath was not the right kind of girl for him, or perhaps even that marriage was not such a good idea in his particular case. Years after the tragedy of Plath's suicide, Al Alvarez said to the literary journalist Janet Malcolm that 'Ted kind of went through swaths of women, like a guy harvesting corn; Sylvia must have known that.'[8] There is no evidence from other contemporaries to corroborate this statement. On the other hand, Plath wrote in her journal, the day after meeting Hughes for the first time, that she had been told by her boyfriend, Hamish, that 'he is the biggest seducer in Cambridge', adding, 'I could never sleep with him anyway, with all his friends here and his close relation to them, laughing, talking, I should be the world's whore, as well as Roget's strumpet.'[9] In fact, one of Hughes's Cambridge friends, Daniel Huws, believes that 'Sylvia was far more sexually experienced than Ted.'[10] Which of these three views is the biographer to believe, and would it help to understand Hughes's problematic relationships with his Muses? What is the role of the biographer in unravelling 'the difficulties of a bridegroom', in Hughes's enigmatic and totemic phrase?[11]

Hughes the astrologer was convinced that he and Plath were, in fact, destined for one another, and would express it in his own vocabulary, saying 'the solar system married us' (*CP* 1051). In her turn, Plath wrote to her mother: 'It is ridiculous for us to separate our forces when it is such a magnificently "aspected" year.'[12] And marriage seemed to Sylvia the one obvious thing to do in such a situation. Ted followed suit. 'I didn't even ask her to marry me,' he said. 'She suggested it as a good deal and I said OK, why not?'[13] They were married in London on 16 June 1956 at the parish church of Saint George the Martyr in Holborn. Sylvia believed, wrongly, that her Fulbright scholarship would be compromised unless they had kept their wedding secret. However, there would soon be the first symptoms that the two poets were involved in something that looked like a reciprocal Pygmalion complex. Each of them soon proved to be dreaming up further idiosyncratic images of the other.

They went on honeymoon to Spain, with the fantasy that they would eventually become globe-trotting poets, very much like Frieda and D. H. Lawrence, spending every year in a different country. What for Sylvia was merely a holiday before she returned to Cambridge to complete her BA was for Ted a trial of his desire for a happy-go-lucky year in Spain teaching English as a foreign language to survive and write poetry. But return to Cambridge they must, so Ted Hughes found himself transformed into a school teacher in Cambridge against his heart's desire, while Sylvia Plath planned what she called her 'campaign to make Ted fall in love with America'. It should not be too difficult, she thought, since her 'big, unruly Huckleberry Finn'[14] of a husband loved fishing and the outdoor life, and so he was already very much like an American. Her vision of their future in those days was 'the American dream of a secure sinecure writing on campus'.[15]

The transition to America was facilitated by Hughes's collection *The Hawk in the Rain* winning Harper's first publication contest in New York. However, his discontent increased when they lived the lives of junior academics in Northampton, Massachusetts. That was partly because Hughes had the feeling of being trapped in a society that was cutting him off from the roots of his artistic creativity. In a letter to Lucas Myers, he said that for him, in America, the world was 'sterilised under cellophane' (*LTH* 105). He felt, as Coleridge had done, that the poet was dying in him.

So he had undertaken to begin his education in American literature over again, by rereading everything in chronological order. The American modernist poets repelled him. William Carlos Williams sounded to him like the 'most brainless American romanticism'; e. e. cummings he considered as 'prevailingly a fool, and essentially a huckster' (*LTH* 145). He was only interested in a very few contemporary artists and poets whom he met – especially John Crowe Ransom – and also Leonard Baskin, Robert Lowell and W. S. Merwin with whom he became friends. The only really important literary discovery that he made in those days were more folk-tales of the American Indians, which would be a seminal influence for his future masterpiece, *Crow: From the Life and Songs of the Crow*, published more than a decade later, in 1970.

Sylvia's pregnancy seems to have been what triggered their decision to return to the Old World, and it would soon be Sylvia's turn to suffer from a depression of which the causes were deeper than mere homesickness. In London, then in Court Green in Devon, each of them was attempting to persuade the other to his or her own idea of life. Just as Plath had failed in her tentative accommodation of Hughes to America, he would hardly have any more success in his efforts to win her to his own theory of literary creation. True, they practised various techniques of spiritualism, especially the Ouija board, which produced a spirit they called PAN that they conjured up all too easily and who apparently spoke through Sylvia's voice. (Daniel Huws has recently owned up to being PAN on the occasion recounted in the poem 'Ouija' in *Birthday Letters*.)[16] Ted also did peculiar exercises of concentration and complicated physical postures that sometimes left him with muscular cramp, and he went through a general discipline of work that proved productive for him. But Sylvia found these exercises much less effective for her, and they did little to vanquish her writer's block. In fact, Sylvia resisted the methods that Ted was trying to teach her. Perhaps one may presume that a plausible reason for this was that these methods were in conflict with the psychoanalytical work with Dr Ruth Beuscher that Sylvia had secretly resumed when they arrived in Boston.

Actually, it seems that Sylvia was not very receptive to Jungian psychology and proved a baffling pupil for Ted's sorcerer's apprentice tuition. Far from being won over to his developing cult of the Goddess, Sylvia soon felt the imperative need to go to church again. Because she thought it was 'the best way to grow into the community here'[17] she went to see the Anglican rector, who welcomed her, in spite of her 'heretical' Unitarian beliefs, and started attending church regularly and looking forward to sending their daughter Frieda to Sunday school. Very soon, however, she disagreed with the preaching and stopped her ears during the sermons. At home, she shed tears of joy over the beautiful sermons of the Unitarian minister in Wellesley, Massachusetts, which she asked her friend Marcia Plumer to send over to her. When their second child, Nicholas, was born, they decided to have both the children baptized. However, Ted Hughes was hardly a Christian any more, at least from his late teens onwards, and his anti-Christian opinions would keep asserting themselves as he grew older. In those days, Plath defined herself as a 'pagan-Unitarian at best!'[18] Whatever that means, one cannot help reading it as an expression of the dramatic tension inherent in their relationship.

Meanwhile, friends often came to visit the Hugheses on weekends. Ted Hughes was then an increasingly famous figure of the London literary world, whose voice was heard occasionally on BBC radio broadcasts. Among this crowd of old friends and new acquaintances, Assia Gutman, the wife of the Canadian poet David Wevill, half-jokingly made a bet with a friend that she was going to seduce Ted Hughes on their visit to Devon. Nevertheless, the love affair between Ted and Assia that developed from this visit was perhaps rather the consequence than the cause of the tensions in Sylvia's and Ted's marriage. In fact, only one meeting between Assia and Ted in London (for tea, Assia told William Trevor when she returned to the office)[19] can be documented before the fateful day when Assia asked a male colleague to make a phone call to Devon which Sylvia guessed was on Assia's behalf when she picked up the phone.[20] The blunder gave rise to a melodramatic scene resulting in Sylvia and Aurelia Plath driving Ted and his suitcase in their car to the railway station for the train to London. When Sylvia returned home she lit a bonfire of his papers. Might Hughes have been 'more sinned against than sinning' in the events that led to this separation? Can a biographer narrate this story without implying a view on this?

Perhaps the Hughes biographer might try to assess the importance of the Protestant ideology and especially a peculiar Nonconformist mentality inherent in Hughes's Methodist upbringing. One of the masterpieces of British literature on this subject is James Hogg's *Confessions of a Justified Sinner*, which identifies a schizophrenic tendency in the Scottish Presbyterian religion: the 'justified sinner'. Ted Hughes was aware of this kind of notion at least as early as 1961, when he and Sylvia Plath moved from London to their house in Devon. Evidence of this can be found in Ted's letters to his sister Olwyn in the Emory archives. Ted and Olwyn were always very close. In 1961, one year before his separation from Sylvia Plath, Ted Hughes was writing a letter to his sister in which he was trying to analyse his shortcomings and to understand what was going wrong in his own life. He said that there was something infantile about him, which amounted to a kind of incapacity to exert mental control and deliberate mental play in everyday life.

He put that down to his discovery of the writings of Carl Gustav Jung, already referred to above, at the age of eighteen. That year, 1948, was also the year when Robert Graves's *The White Goddess* was first published, and his English teacher at Mexborough Grammar School, John Fisher, had presented Hughes with a copy when he won his Open Exhibition to Cambridge. Hughes read Graves and Jung for the first time when he was doing his military service in the RAF before going up to Pembroke College. Jungian psychology made such a strong impression on him that he quite deliberately made the decision to impose upon himself some rules of behaviour that were meant to inhibit his conscious mind and rational thinking. In this way, he thought, his unconscious would compensate with an increased activity. This means that he hoped to foster the productivity and the growth of his creative mind, which he liked to call his 'factory', or his 'mental cabbage'.[21]

It was also in those years of his life that he very consciously took the decision to become a poet and nothing else. Hughes's poem 'Song', which came to him on a rainy night in 1948, can be read as a declaration of love to what Jung called 'the *anima*', the creative principle of male psychology, which is very close to what Graves called 'the White Goddess'. With Hughes, this had the seriousness of a religious vow. From then on, he told his sister, he adopted a self-imposed discipline to follow a list of 'seven laws' (unspecified). Thirteen years later, however, when he found himself up to his neck in 'the difficulties of a bridegroom', he looked back and realized that these eccentric rules of conduct, which suppressed his conscious life in order for his imagination to access the unconscious, had also rendered him rather ill-equipped to lead the life of a normal husband.

Furthermore, in 1961, when he was explaining all this in his letter to his sister, he went on to say that he was once again toying with the idea that he had already had in his Cambridge years, of emulating Fernando Pessoa by writing under several aliases, or at least in various poetic voices. He said, 'I'm now creating other poets.' But he now came to the realization that he had really succeeded in developing only *two* such distinct voices. One of these two poets in him pursued the exacting ideal of formal verse, putting the stress on detailed objective observation and the thorough development of ideas. The other poet turned his back on this 'rigid formalist' outlook, which he called 'puritanical'. This poet went for free verse and indulged in taking as many liberties as possible, in a resolutely 'experimental and lyrical' attitude. All this did not result in a Jekyll and Hyde division, for these two poets got on fairly well together: they were just as fluently outspoken as each other, and Hughes had the feeling that his own poems 'barged midway' between these two extremes.[22]

Of course, there are some obvious resemblances with Jung's well-known *animus/anima* dualism. However, the issue of the two-sidedness of Ted Hughes's personality, which played such an important role in the misunderstanding with Plath, and ultimately in the antagonism between the two poets, is a domestic aspect of an ideological debate which is still a matter of dispute.

The whole purpose and justification of Ted Hughes's poetic undertaking is to try and find a literary means of coming to terms with unconscious forces which, from his point of view, will play havoc in the Western world as long as they are suppressed. From Hughes's point of view the major suppressive forces in history remain essentially reformed Christianity and the rationalism it has led to. In this respect, he perpetuates Romantic ideology, and his dualistic take is very much derived from William Blake's and Percy Bysshe Shelley's discourses. In his *Defence of Poetry*, Shelley argues that 'the cultivation of those sciences which have enlarged the limits of the empire of man over the external world, has, for want of the poetical faculty, proportionally circumscribed those of the internal world; and man, having enslaved the elements, remains himself a slave'.[23]

Already in the Cambridge of the early 1950s, Ted Hughes encountered a dominant academic ideology characterized by a strong resistance to Jungian psychoanalysis, and he arrived on a literary scene that was under the influence of modernist discourse that defined itself in radical opposition to Romanticism. In what was still the prolonged aftermath of the Second World War, no-nonsense rationalism could easily appear to be the last resort bulwark against fascism, although perhaps not quite so when it came to the latest totalitarian threat. Such an opinion is still widespread today, in an intellectual tradition largely based on Thomas Mann's 1945 address to the Library of Congress 'Germany and the German', where he declared that, 'reduced to a miserable mass level, the level of a Hitler, German Romanticism broke out into hysterical barbarism'.[24]

More recently, one variant of this ideological discourse is the resistance to Jungian psychoanalysis, as most strongly expressed, perhaps, in the books of Harvard professor Richard Noll, *The Jung Cult*[25] and *The Aryan Christ*.[26] In the late twentieth century, anything Jungian encountered the ostracism of a large part of the academic world. However, Hughes might challenge Jung for cultural designation as 'black beast', because his neo-Nietzschean, anti-Christian ideas also alienate him from the opposite Christian conservative camp. Hughes's alleged responsibility for the suicide of Sylvia Plath has tended to be implicitly perceived as the unsurprising confirmation of deeper ideological beliefs.

The Hughes-baiting that followed the quickly rising posthumous fame of Sylvia Plath reached a noteworthy climax in a poem entitled 'Arraignment' by Robin Morgan in her 1972 collection *Monster*. She reproached Hughes with domestic violence and Nazi tendencies: "How can / I accuse / Ted Hughes / of what the entire British and American / literary and critical establishment / has been at great lengths to deny / without ever saying it in so many words, of course, / the murder of Sylvia Plath?' Morgan went on with an invitation to 'disarm him of that weapon with which he tortured us, / stuff it into his mouth, sew up his poetasting lips around it, and blow out his brains'.[27] Morgan is, incidentally, clearly harping on a Jungian archetype, although perhaps this Maenad was mistaking Dionysus for Bluebeard. In the 1970s, it became a badge of honour for Plath supporters to cry 'Murderer!' on the rare occasions that Hughes appeared at a public reading. He privately called them the 'Red Guards' and scornfully refused to retaliate or even reply. All this did very little to alleviate his occasional depression, and it certainly harmed his literary career in America in particular.

As has already been suggested, the intricate 'whodunit' of the circumstances that led to the suicide of Sylvia Plath in London in February 1963 is impossible to unravel. However, the personal and cultural after-effects were to be long-lasting. Actually, the news of his wife's death came to Ted Hughes as a surprise as well as a shock, for he had good reasons to believe that they would soon be reconciled. They had been seeing one another quite frequently in London, and on these occasions Sylvia had appeared to have mixed feelings about him. But, according to Hughes, at their last meetings they had talked of living together again soon. Hughes was appalled to realize that the people Plath had been corresponding with during the last months of her life, her mother, Aurelia Plath, her psychiatrist, Ruth Beuscher, and perhaps also her patron, Olive Prouty, had been urging her to consult a solicitor in London to initiate a divorce.[28]

Ted Hughes's life with Sylvia Plath had lasted seven years, and six years after her death, the tragedy repeated itself one step further up the ladder of horror, when Assia Wevill committed suicide in the manner of Plath, by using a gas oven, but also took the life of her little daughter Shura.[29] Faced with the blunt facts, perhaps Hughes could no longer avoid attributing to himself what he had called, in a letter to his brother, 'Sylvia's particular death-ray quality'.[30] What killed Assia, however, was the guilt-ridden depression in which she had irremediably sunk, haunted, as she had been, by the continuing posthumous presence of Sylvia in Ted's life. There had been a time when his house had become a cauldron of tension, when his parents had come to live with him and simply could not bear the presence of Assia. Ted had taken refuge in a wooden writing cabin built by his father in the garden.

The situation seems at some point to have been even more complicated in a way which an anecdote from Hughes's notebook reveals. In August 1968, the children were going on holiday to visit their American grandmother. While waiting for the plane, Hughes heard them talking together, and they were saying that he 'ought to marry Carol and Brenda', for then they would have one mother each. Hughes found the incident striking enough to jot it down in his pocket notebook.[31] And indeed, it would mean that, at this time of his life, he was seeing at least two women in addition to Assia, in a way that was conspicuous enough for his children to have been aware of it. Again, the biographer can only seek some kind of explanation in the gaps between the poet's life, his thoughts and his art, or rather his multiple lives.

Assia Gutman's German Jewish multilingual background was part of her attraction for Hughes, and he came to bring her linguistic resources into his developing fascination with translation. On New Year's Eve 1963, Ted Hughes had launched the idea of *Poetry in Translation* with Daniel Weissbort. The idea was to publish English translations of Eastern European poets such as Tadeusz Roszievich, Zbigniew Herbert, Miroslav Holub and Vasko Popa. He was interested in these poets because they had used poetry as a form of resistance against mental and spiritual oppression. He saw himself as an artist faced with the necessity to survive ideological oppression, in a modern Western world dominated, he thought, by forces that were aiming at ultimately closing up the unconscious and eradicating what he called the 'inner world' of spirits and poetic inspiration as so much superstitious mumbo-jumbo, or, in Philip Larkin's immortal words, a mere 'myth kitty'.

In Ted Hughes's own *Weltanschauung* the radical rationalism of the Western world was the disease of civilization. This for him was simply the continuation of the Christian religion as collective neurosis, as Freud had it in his book *Civilisation and Its Discontents*. One of the key issues was the Christian repression of sexuality, and more precisely the suppression of female sexuality – and the Goddess in all her forms – by reformed Christianity. For biographical reasons, the epitome of this nefariously narrow vision of the world was represented for Hughes in the ideology underpinning the American way of life, especially in its New England variant. Although Hughes never said so explicitly, he obviously had the feeling that this ideology was responsible for Sylvia Plath's long-lasting difficulties in accessing the unconscious. In his *Birthday Letters* poem 'You Hated Spain', Hughes describes Plath as a 'bobby-sox American' whose 'education had somehow neglected Spain' (CP 1068) – the Spain of Goya, bullfights and the *duende*. So her 'inner world' was like a desert from which all life had been napalmed out by the lightning of the ECT (Electroconvulsive Therapy) that she had undergone in Boston Hospital. From his point of view, this was the infernal world of Jehovah-Jupiter-Urizen-Krogon, and the whole castrating paraphernalia of the totalitarian scientific spirit of the West.

For the biographer writing about Ted Hughes it is difficult to avoid taking sides either for or against him, for merely to accept his preoccupations means placing oneself already outside the dominant Western ideology that he has challenged. Hughes was so aware of the problem, that he regarded biographers as among his worst 'black beasts'. 'These biographers,' he would write to Graham Ackroyd, are 'common burglars who creep into your life, defile everything, steal what they can lift, sell it with lies.'[32] He thought of founding a 'solidarity group', a kind of union of the victims of biographers with a 'vigilante commando' that could form a 'superego for the literary world',[33] exerting pressure on the publishers of libellous biographies.

In fact, a biographer who wants to eschew hagiography and arraignment equally will have to write in such a way as to present the subject as an open question. Since a biographical subject must always be misrepresented, it had better be so overtly and with a purpose. In other words, a worthy biographer has to admit failure from the start. A good biography, if there can be such a thing, has to be written as an unsolvable riddle.

NOTES

1. Diane Middlebrook, *Her Husband: Hughes and Plath – A Marriage* (New York: Viking, 2003).
2. Elaine Feinstein, *Ted Hughes: The Life of a Poet* (New York: Norton, 2001).
3. TH to Gerald Hughes, 21 December 1979, Mss 854, Box 1, ff. 28, Emory.
4. Feinstein, *Ted Hughes*, p. 165.
5. Robert Graves, *The White Goddess: A Historical Grammar of Poetic Myth* (New York: Farrar, Straus and Giroux, 1966), p. 449.
6. Gill Barber, 'Ted Hughes, My Secret Lover', *Mail on Sunday* (13 and 20 May 2001).
7. Emma Tennant, *Burnt Diaries* (Edinburgh: Canongate, 1999).
8. Janet Malcolm, *The Silent Woman: Sylvia Plath and Ted Hughes* (Basingstoke: Macmillan, 1994), p. 121.
9. Sylvia Plath, *The Journals of Sylvia Plath*, ed. Karen Kukil (London: Faber and Faber, 2000), pp. 213, 212.
10. Daniel Huws, *Memories of Ted Hughes 1952–1963* (London: Five Leaves Press, 2010), p. 37.
11. Hughes began using this title for various works in progress before it became the title of a radio play broadcast in 1963 and later of his collected short stories (London: Faber and Faber, 1995).
12. Sylvia Plath, *Letters Home: Correspondence 1950–1963*, ed. Aurelia Plath (London: Faber and Faber, 1976), 23 October 1956, p. 280.
13. Feinstein, *Ted Hughes*, p. 60.
14. Plath, *Letters Home*, 4 May 1956, p. 250.
15. *Ibid.*, 19 January 1957, p. 290.
16. Huws, *Memories of Ted Hughes*, pp. 43–4.
17. Plath, *Letters Home*, 13 October 61, p. 431.
18. *Ibid.*, 22 October 1961, p. 433.
19. Yehuda Koren and Eilat Negev, *A Lover of Unreason: The Life and Tragic Death of Assia Wevill* (London: Robson Books, 2006), p. 96.
20. Olwyn Hughes: 'Assia got a male colleague to call Ted – just in case Sylvia answered. I've corrected this several times but everyone wants to believe Sylvia's poem. As people do.' Letter to Terry Gifford, 5 August 2010.
21. TH to Gerald Hughes, 24 August 1961, Mss 854, Box 1, ff. 10, Emory.
22. TH to Olwyn Hughes, 1961, Mss 980, Box 1, ff. 9, Emory.
23. Percy Bysshe Shelley, *Shelley's Poetry and Prose* (New York: Norton, 1977), pp. 502–3.

24. *Deutschland und die Deutschen in 'Die Neue Rundschau'* (Stockholm: Heft, 1 October 1945). *Germany and the German*, trans. by Helen T. Lowe-Porter (Washington: Library of Congress, 1963), p. 64. Thomas Mann delivered this address at the Library of Congress, 29 May 1945.

25. Richard Noll, *The Jung Cult: Origins of a Charismatic Movement* (New York: Princeton University Press, 1994).

26. Richard Noll, *The Aryan Christ: The Secret Life of Carl Jung* (New York: Prentice Hall, 1997).

27. Robin Morgan, *Monster* (New York: Vintage, 1972), p. 76.

28. Plath, *Letters Home*, 26 September 1962, p. 463.

29. Here is the biographer's conundrum: Hughes was named as Shura's father on her birth certificate, but neither Frieda nor Olwyn Hughes regarded Shura as his child. Frieda: 'My brother and I knew Shura only as Assia's daughter; there was no indication from Assia that she was related to us.' 'The poison that drove Sylvia and Ted apart', *The Sunday Times*, 28 March 2010, p. 7. Olwyn Hughes: 'Assia said she didn't know. Ted told me when I asked, "I'm taking her on anyway."' Letter to Terry Gifford, 5 August 2010. Ted Hughes: 'I have two nice children . . . I had a third, a little marvel, but she died with her mother', *LTH* 293. *The Iron Man* was dedicated 'to Frieda, Nicholas and Shura'.

30. TH to Gerald Hughes, November 1962, Mss 854, Box 1, ff. 11, Emory.

31. Koren and Negev, *A Lover of Unreason*, p. 184.

32. TH to Graham Ackroyd, 22 October 1982, Mss 644, Box 185, ff. 1, Emory.

33. TH to 'Natasha and Stephen' [Spender], 17 December 1992, Mss 644, Box 53, ff. 5, Emory.

2

PAUL BENTLEY

The debates about Hughes

'Mindless violence' or metaphor?

'Everybody knows that Ted Hughes's subject is violence.'[1] By the time the opening words of this 'reappraisal' of Hughes were written in 1965 the association of Hughes's poetry with violence was so firmly established that such a remark could seem a statement of the obvious. What was far from obvious and settled, though, was what the nature and meaning of this violence was: the essay in which the above remark appears is one of a series of critical articles and exchanges at this time concerning this question. The early debates about Hughes's poetry register something of the shock of Hughes's first two books, *The Hawk in the Rain* (1957) and *Lupercal* (1960). In particular, the contentious nature of these debates about representations of 'natural' violence in Hughes, the sense of something radically new being grappled with, suggests that it is not simply 'nature' that is at stake here: 'nature' in these books, it will turn out, has a social and even political meaning.

In an early review of *The Hawk in the Rain* Edwin Muir used the phrase 'admirable violence' in relation to the imagery of this 'remarkable' new poet, a poet 'quite outside the currents of his time'.[2] The adjective 'admirable' anticipates, if not provokes, the debates that soon follow regarding the moral – or amoral – qualities of Hughesian violence (many critics would be quick to find the violence less than admirable). Muir also senses that the hawk, jaguar, macaw and wind of that volume have a 'symbolic meaning . . . whether it was intended to be there or not'.[3] Again following Muir, early reviewers and critics were much taken up with – and divided over – the question of whether Hughes's violent bestiary carried any symbolic or social significance. Questions of authorial intention and of Hughes's relation to the literary currents of the time would also prove difficult to settle. For example, while another critic follows Muir in identifying in Hughes 'a resilience to the pressures of the time because of the way his imagination responds to the fierce power of nature', for another, Hughes is very much of his time, his poetry belonging to 'the cult of the depressive attitude' in recent writing (as typified for this critic by the plays of John Osborne, Harold Pinter, Shelagh Delaney and Samuel Beckett, and the fiction of Kingsley Amis). For the latter, the 'vitalism' of Hughes's poetry 'is really a kind of naive admiration for animal life – a kind of raw nature cult, which assumes that human consciousness brings only limitation' (note how 'naive admiration' here corrects, whether intentionally or not, Muir's 'admirable violence'). Alternatively, Hughes exposes, 'with grim humour, the limitations of animal consciousness'.[4] Either way the violence in Hughes is felt to be brutally reductive.

What is perhaps most surprising about the early critical responses to Hughes is the resistance many critics register to the idea tentatively proposed by Muir that Hughes's animals have any symbolic meaning – that they might be read, as another reviewer puts it, as 'spokesmen for the hidden and violent beings that we partly are'.[5] One of the key players in these early debates about violence in Hughes, John Hainsworth, finds 'neither sophistication nor "intellectuality"' in poems like 'The Hawk in the Rain', 'Wind' or 'The Jaguar': Hughes's verse lacks 'inwardness', and while the poet 'probably meant to be allegorical', his hawk and jaguar 'so absorbed him that they distracted him'.[6] The same point is made again and again in early reviews and essays on Hughes: Hughes's subject is 'the bruising darkness of instincts and sensations, where the mind runs itself hard against the brute physical facts of blood and action, landscape and weather'; his gift is 'descriptive', 'a gift for rendering any physical appearance, movement, and sensation'; the poems are marked by an 'amoral, unmoralized factuality' – 'they do not read like compulsive surfacings of dark psychic undergrowths, still less as allegories of states of mind', but rather are 'turned outwards to the factual solidity of things seen'. This same critic goes on to insist in a second article that the poem 'Hawk Roosting' is 'a fiction' and 'not an allegory', and that 'the hawk remains a hawk'.[7] That Hughes's vision is 'elemental' in 'character', then, was soon taken to be 'self-evident'.[8] To attest that a point is self-evident is to short-circuit interpretation. More than that, the view of Hughes at this time as a poet of 'elemental' or 'universal' violence – whose subject is 'the power and violence of the universe', in whose work violence is 'the essential and universal condition of life'[9] – renders the poems virtually meaningless. Hughes emerges from these early debates as a poet of 'blind, instinctual thrust'; 'Because for him all life is a meaningless chaos, Hughes has no moral lessons to preach'; 'all is black, all is futile, all significance gone'; what the poems finally add up to is a 'heroic celebration of the mindless'.[10] Or else, though following the same line, a certain stoical quality might be admired in Hughes – the hawk in 'The Hawk in the Rain' is 'both metaphor and beacon of hard endurance' (the interchangeability of 'beacon' and 'metaphor' here again betrays an uncertainty over the figurative or non-figurative status of the hawk); 'The most man can do is to endure with dignity and courage' is the lesson we are to take from Hughes, although in terming the violence 'existential', this critic at least lends it a degree of philosophical dignity.[11] Stoical or depressive, futile or heroic, these are essentially the same readings, only differently inflected. In each case the violence the poems body forth is essentially regarded as meaningless.

The above assertion that Hughes's poems do not read like surfacings of dark psychic undergrowths – that, in other words, the animals are just animals, their violence, life itself, without meaning – is a response to A. Alvarez's championing of Hughes in his anthology *The New Poetry* (1962). In his Introduction Alvarez places Hughes at the vanguard of a 'new depth poetry', a poetry that challenges what Alvarez calls 'the Gentility Principle' of Movement writers such as Philip Larkin and Kingsley Amis, writers for whom, according to Alvarez, 'life is always more or less orderly, people always more or less polite, their emotions and habits more or less decent and more or less controllable'.[12] Alvarez places Hughes in the context of an age of psychoanalysis, an age coming to terms with new revelations about the Holocaust (Adolf Eichmann, the Nazi war criminal, was tried and executed in Israel in 1962) – revelations to which Sylvia Plath's poems explicitly respond. But when Alvarez comes to discuss Hughes's poem 'A Dream of Horses' in this context he is unable to bring the poem into any clear focus: the poem 'is unquestionably *about* something' – it re-creates, 'in the strongest imaginative terms possible, a powerful complex of emotions and sensations'.[13] Alvarez's is the most important attempt at this time to place Hughes's poetry in a cultural context and to detect in it a social or cultural relevance, though Alvarez, too, is uncertain when it comes to the figurative or factual status of Hughes's horses: 'Their brute world is part physical, part state of mind', their presence, finally, simply 'violent, impending'.[14]

Hughes on Violence

These early debates, which centre around the question of violence in Hughes (symbolic or factual? natural or cultural? physical or psychological? of its time or outside its time?), reveal that Hughes's subject is not so 'self-evident' after all. When asked about the critical controversy over his 'poetry of violence' in an interview in 1970, Hughes replied that the question was not a simple one:

> The poem of mine usually cited for violence is the one about the Hawk Roosting, this drowsy hawk sitting in a wood and talking to itself. That bird

is accused of being a fascist ... the symbol of some horrible totalitarian geno-
cidal dictator. Actually what I had in mind was that in this hawk Nature is
thinking. Simply Nature. It's not so simple maybe because Nature is no longer so
simple. I intended some Creator like the Jehovah in Job but more feminine.
When Christianity kicked the devil out of Job what they actually kicked out was
Nature ... and Nature became the devil. He doesn't sound like Isis, mother of
the gods, which he is. He sounds like Hitler's familiar spirit. There is a line in the
poem almost verbatim from Job.[15]

Why nature is no longer so simple has to do with its mediated status: refracted
through religion, myth and ideology, nature, in effect, becomes culture, and
powerfully so – Hitler's fascism was an ideology that was, of course, pre-
dicated on the belief that the Aryan race was *naturally* superior. If you are
naturally superior, no arguments need assert your right, as Hughes's hawk
knows (that the earth's face is upward for its inspection foregrounds the bird's
likeness to a fascist dictator). The violent effect of a poem like 'Hawk
Roosting' is not explicable with reference to how hawks behave, but is an
effect of the way the poem breaks up what is 'self-evident' (the hawk is a
hawk) by intimating and exploring the religious, mythical and historical
meanings already invested in nature (Isis, the devil, the hawk as a military/
ideological symbol in Nazism). We can now begin to see why early critics and
reviewers experienced such difficulty in placing, or accounting for, this type of
violence – a violence in effect performed on the very concept of 'nature' which
such readings are based upon – a difficulty compounded by the assumption
that this concept is self-evident: a hawk in Hughes is simply a hawk.

Hughes gives a fuller response to the early critical appraisals of his 'poetry
of violence' in his collection of non-fictional writing *Winter Pollen* (1992).
Referring to Muir's use of the phrase 'admirable violence' in his review of *The
Hawk in the Rain*, Hughes states that the question of violence is 'a social
question', one which depends 'wholly on context': 'And when the word is
used virtually without context, as in that phrase "poetry of violence", it is not
actually meaningless but it is a word still waiting to be defined' (*WP* 251,
253). Hughes distinguishes in this later response between two types of violence. The first type is 'negative' and entails the idea of violation or sacrilege. It
is this type of violence that Hughes suggests we associate with Hitler. The
second, 'positive' type of violence involves a reaction to the first: Hughes
describes this type of violence as 'a life-bringing assertion of sacred law which
demolishes, in some abrupt way, a force that oppressed and *violated* it' (*WP*
254, italics in the original). Taking his poem 'Thrushes' as an example,
Hughes proposes that his animals are 'innocent': 'their energy reaffirms the
divine law that created them as they are' (*WP* 259). This might seem on the

face of it to simply return the birds to nature: thrushes simply do what thrushes are self-evidently created to do, which is to kill and eat worms. But central to Hughes's argument here is the idea that 'positive' violence, such as the thrushes embody for Hughes, involves a corrective reaction to an oppressive and violating force. In the case of this poem and others the violating force in question, Hughes argues, is the culture that shapes the response of those readers who objected to what they saw as the poems' violence. It is in this sense that Hughes reads the poem as a '"critique" of a certain attitude' – of the kind of attitude that 'recoils from the poem in what I've called a stereotype, sentimental fashion'. This is the same attitude that for Hughes 'recoils from animals killing animals on the screen – with a disapproval that masks the speaker's implication in the process which among other things constructs the unspoken abattoir between the bullock in the field and the steak on his plate', an attitude that 'effectively denies its own guilt and openly condemns what it unconsciously colludes with and profits from' (WP 259). Hughes points out that the values that support that attitude '(whether we call them humanitarian or not) must be questionable' (WP 259).

Hughes returns here and at other points in the essay to the wording of the question put to him in 1970 regarding his 'poetry of violence': 'How does such poetry relate to our customary social and humanitarian values and to what degree can it be considered a criticism of those values?' (WP 251). On Hughes's reading, the 'positive' violence of his animals is a counterpoint to the invisible 'negative' violence inherent in 'customary social and humanitarian values': it implies a 'critique' of these values, of the very reaction the poems provoked. The meat industry is an example, for Hughes, of one such invisible form of violence that 'humanitarian' culture is implicated in, 'among other things'. What other things? Hughes then discusses Blake's 'The Tyger' as a symbol of 'the vast upsurge of psychic energy that accompanied, all over Europe, the French Revolution' (WP 263), while Yeats's 'rough beast' in his poem 'The Second Coming' is similarly linked with the idea of violent resistance to 'the "customary social and humanitarian values" of England's stranglehold policy on Ireland' (WP 265). For Hughes, Blake's Tyger and Yeats's 'rough beast' are political symbols – symbols of, following Hughes's argument, violent reactions to oppressive and violating social and cultural forces. It is important to note here that Hughes does not read Blake's or Yeats's poems – and by extension his own – as being political in a propagandist sense. 'The Second Coming', for Hughes, 'is an image of events, not propaganda' – such poems 'simply bear witness' (WP 265, 266). However, Hughes ends the essay hoping his poems might be 'floating on the banner' of the environmentalist movement, a cause for which Hughes became increasingly active in later life (WP 266).

Social contours

Hughes's argument about the forms of violence (political or industrial) concealed by 'our customary social and humanitarian values' has points of contact with post-Marxist thinking on this same subject.[16] Hughes suggests that 'our customary social and humanitarian values' mask our implication in forms of violence and, like other cultural critics, cites the meat industry as a graphic illustration of this point.[17] Hughes makes a crucial distinction between 'positive' and 'negative' violence, which clearly requires a social contextualization for such a distinction to be made. As Hughes writes, violence is 'a social question'. It follows then that to understand violence we need, as the cultural theorist Slavoj Žižek points out, 'to step back ... to perceive the contours of the background which generates such outbursts'.[18]

The presiding assumption behind the early debates about Hughes is that his subject is 'natural', or 'elemental' or 'universal' violence. Nevertheless, a social contour or background to the violence occasionally comes into view. Hughes's vision, it is occasionally noticed by some critics, is 'hard, northern and metallic', his voice registering a 'stubborn Yorkshire resistance' – 'Like Lawrence, he admires the natural warmth of working men, and is suspicious of the educated man's urbanity ... He rejects the "sophistries" and "indolent procrastinations" of Cambridge social life, and chooses as subject-matter for his verse the world of violent killing he observed as a boy among animals and birds in the Yorkshire countryside.'[19] When Hughes was a boy the Hughes family moved from Mytholmroyd in the West Yorkshire Pennines to Mexborough, which is situated between Barnsley, Doncaster and Rotherham, in the heart of the South Yorkshire coalfield. A little further off is Sheffield, the 'steel city' this coalfield supplied at that time. This is a landscape that everywhere bears the marks of the heavy industries of coal and steel. At primary school Hughes's friends were the sons of colliers and railwaymen. In contrast, the Cambridge to which Hughes would later win a scholarship was 'predominantly public school and upper middle-class'.[20] What Hughes refers to in a letter as the 'social rancour' (*LTH* 423) he experienced at Cambridge made him, in the words of one of his contemporaries there, 'very well aware of class'.[21] If Elaine Feinstein is right, at Cambridge Hughes 'held on all the more obstinately to the Yorkshire accent that would have been used to place him instantly'.[22] In an interview Hughes speaks of how, 'Whatever other speech you grow into', your dialect 'stays alive in a sort of inner freedom', and of the importance of dialect to his poetry.[23] Writing to a Cambridge friend in 1959, Hughes elaborates on T.S. Eliot's notion of a 'dissociation of sensibility' in English poetry by relating Eliot's term to the 'the inter-conflict of upper & lower classes in

England' and to a 'tabu on dialect as a language proper for literate men' (for Hughes in this letter the only poets using dialect since 1688 are Wordsworth, Keats, Blake and Burns) (*LTH* 146).[24]

Although Hughes does not use dialect in the way that, for example, Tony Harrison – a poet of Hughes's generation also from a Yorkshire working-class background – uses dialect in poems like *V.* or 'Them & [uz]', Hughes's early poems in particular are characterized by a bluntness and directness born out of Yorkshire speech patterns: 'The pig lay on a barrow dead . . . Its trotters stuck straight out' ('View of a Pig', *CP* 75); 'My manners are tearing off heads' ('Hawk Roosting', *CP* 69); 'And rain hacks my head to the bone' ('The Hawk in the Rain', *CP* 19). In Harrison's poetry the use of dialect is often aggressively foregrounded – figured as a form of linguistic and class violence done to English poetry: '4 words only of *mi 'art aches* and . . . "Mine's broken, / you barbarian, T. W.!" *He* was nicely spoken' ('Them & [uz]').[25] In contrast to Harrison, underpinning Hughes's ideas about dialect and poetry is the assumption that dialect is 'a language proper for literate men'; as English poetry's natural element, dialect in Hughes is not foregrounded as a sign of barbarism or illiteracy. This might make Hughes seem like a very different poet from Harrison. In Harrison's verse dialect is presented *as* dialect, as with the italicized *'mi 'art aches'* – its presence in the body of the poem is awkward, spiky, 'violent', and carries an obvious political force. In Hughes, on the other hand, dialect speech patterns are assumed *as* poetic language (though the effect of this can feel just as violent). In the Harrison poem quoted from above, Harrison reminds himself and his nicely spoken former English teacher that Keats was a Cockney, and that 'Wordsworth's *matter/water* are full rhymes' – much as Hughes names Wordsworth, Keats, Blake and Burns as poets who wrote out of their dialect. In different ways, then, both Hughes and Harrison seek to extend what is for them an old tradition of using dialect in poetry, and with both poets the redeployment of dialect is related to the 'inter-conflict of upper & lower classes in England': 'So right, yer buggers, then! We'll occupy / your lousy leasehold Poetry' ('Them and [uz]').

Although it was not conceived of in these terms, the violent effect of Hughes's early verse on literary sensibility at this time is clearly attested by the early reviews and articles. There is some evidence, though, that Hughes conceived of himself in these terms during his time at Cambridge, where he mixed with 'a sort of socialist group' of friends and sang Irish rebel songs.[26] Is this why Hughes was purportedly 'delighted to play Heathcliff'?[27] Whether this is true or not, the image followed Hughes.[28] For Feinstein the Heathcliff image attached to Hughes is 'misleading': 'None of his close Cambridge friends saw him as dangerous, despite his size, or discerned any malice in him.'[29] But Hughes's conduct or physical appearance would hardly account, in any case, for the potency of this image. By the time Hughes was reputedly 'playing' Heathcliff the social contours of Brontë's story of violent elemental passion, acted out on the Yorkshire moors, had been brought into clear focus. Heathcliff was now being read as a working-class rebel, his violence the rebellion of the oppressed and degraded labourer, his weapons the very weapons of his oppressors – property, wealth, class.[30] Terry Eagleton has further elaborated on this Marxist take on *Wuthering Heights* in a way that is of ready application to the debates about Hughes and 'natural' violence. For Eagleton, the raising of Catherine and Heathcliff's love to 'cosmic status' by Brontë constitutes 'a revolutionary refusal of the given language of social roles and values'. Their relationship thus appears 'as "natural" rather than social, since Nature is the "outside" of society'.[31] As with Hughes's animals, which turn out to be in a dialectical relation to 'customary social and humanitarian values', so nature in *Wuthering Heights* – in the form of Catherine and Heathcliff's symbolic association with the moor – is in a complex dialectical relation to culture, a projection of unresolvable social pressures onto a transcendent imaginary space where such pressures can be resolved (unable to be together in life because of class, Catherine and Heathcliff are together in spirit on the moor). Put another way, culture shapes the projection of nature in both Brontë and Hughes: in both, representations of violent 'natural' or 'elemental' or 'cosmic' forces imply a refusal and/or critique of 'normal' social values and of forms of violence hidden in such values. Beyond Hughes's 'craggily handsome'[32] looks and his reputed persona at Cambridge, what the Heathcliff image suggests is that the key to understanding 'natural' violence in early Hughes, as in Brontë, is class.

'In what furnace was thy brain?'

This is not to settle the question of Hughes's relation to the literary currents of his time by characterizing him as an Angry Young Man. Nor is it to resolve questions of whether nature in early Hughes is symbolic or factual, physical or psychological, by simply reading natural violence as symbolizing social violence, in the way that, say, Blake's 'The Tyger' can be read as symbolizing the French revolutionary Terror. Taken together, the early appraisals of Hughes clearly indicate that the poems resist being read in such terms. Neil Roberts provides a more productive way of thinking around the problem in his recent study of Hughes's 'literary life'. Discussing 'Mayday on Holderness', from *Lupercal*, Roberts points to 'a collapse between the categories of nature and history' in the poem: '"A loaded single vein" might suggest Nature's plenty, but it also combines potentially painful bodily connotations with mineral and implicitly industrial ones. The phrase "The effort of the inert North" can hardly be understood except in industrial and historical terms – condensing into one phrase the energy of the industrial past and post-industrial depression – an understanding that is reinforced by the name of one of northern England's most famous industrial cities [Sheffield].'[33] For Roberts 'Mayday on Holderness' looks forward to later work by Hughes such as *Remains of Elmet* (1979), which deals explicitly with post-industrial decline in Yorkshire, but the poem differs from other poems in *Lupercal* 'in its apparent determination to dissolve boundaries'.[34] In fact, Roberts's insight here into the way the poem collapses nature and history can be applied generally to Hughes's early poetry. Nature in early Hughes is virtually the product of heavy industry and industrial labour: a caged macaw 'stares at his furnace' in 'Macaw and Little Miss'(*CP* 20); in 'November' the cold is 'welding', the land 'Treed with iron' (*CP* 81); in 'October Dawn' ice is 'plate' and 'rivet', 'tons of chain and massive lock' (*CP* 37); a snowdrop's head in 'Snowdrop' is 'heavy as metal'(*CP* 86); a pig's squeal in 'View of a Pig' 'the rending of metal' (*CP* 76); the thrushes of 'Thrushes' 'More coiled steel than living' (*CP* 82). In the poem 'Ghost Crabs', from Hughes's third book, *Wodwo* (1967), 'the labouring of the tide / Falls back from its productions' (*CP* 149). It is precisely this trope – nature as industrial production – that is everywhere elaborated in early Hughes. This 'natural' landscape of coal, furnaces, machines and heavy metal is unmistakably South Yorkshire in character.

Not that this type of imagery went unnoticed by early reviewers and critics of Hughes. One reviewer anticipates Roberts's insight into the collapse of the categories of nature and history (or of factual and symbolic) in 'Mayday on Holderness' when he describes how Hughes 'hammers out his lines between the foundries of Sheffield and the "bog pools, dregs of toadstools" past which scurry the weasel, stoat and fox, red in tooth and claw'.[35] Here though, despite Sheffield coming into view, Hughes's animals are ascribed, as elsewhere, to a crude version of Darwinian nature, one which confirms Hughes's brutally reductive view of life: 'instinct, after all, is a form of life', another critic protests, 'not pure mechanism'.[36] Keeping the social contours of the poems in focus allows us to move beyond these reductive and misleading readings of the early poems as nature poems. It also enables us to see how the early debates themselves betray, through their reluctance or inability to conceptualize Hughesian violence in social terms – despite the repeated intuition or denial that this is somehow what its nature is – an essentially ideological operation, one bound up with the 'customary social and humanitarian values' Hughes refers to when he responds a second time to these debates. The same critic who misses the point when he objects that life is 'not pure mechanism' is right to identify the characteristic effect on the speaker/observer of Hughes's poems as being a 'sense of something not to be met with on his own terms and comfortably assimilated'.[37] This effect, as the early debates illustrate, extends also to readers at the time. Seamus Heaney intuits correctly for us the fundamental nature of the violence of early Hughes:

> Hughes's voice, I think, is in rebellion against a certain kind of demeaned, mannerly voice. It's a voice that has no truck with irony because his dialect is not like that ... I mean, the voice of a generation – the Larkin voice, the Movement voice, even the Eliot voice, the Auden voice – the manners of that speech, the original voices behind that poetic voice, are those of literate English middle-class culture, and I think Hughes's great cry and call and bawl is that English language and English poetry is longer and deeper and rougher than that. That's of a piece with his interest in Middle English, the dialect, his insisting upon foxes and bulls and violence. It's a form of calling out for more, that life is more. And of course he gets back from that middle-class school the enmity he implicitly offers.[38]

A political unconscious

Heaney's remark – and this chapter so far – suggest a degree of conscious solidarity on Hughes's part with his class, a dogged attachment to his dialect, his social background. But in the final analysis Hughes's relation to his class background is not so straightforward. Images of Hughes 'playing Heathcliff' at Cambridge, or, later, in America, practising his 'little private filthinesses' against the background of 'the general opulence' – 'I spit, pea [sic] on shrubbery, etc, and have a strong desire to sleep on the floor – just to keep in contact with a world that isn't quite so glazed as this one' (*LTH* 103) – certainly read like defiant and self-conscious assertions of Hughes's class background. Most of the *Lupercal* poems were written while Hughes was in America with Plath, and, if their themes are 'nostalgic' (*LTH* 153), it is a fierce and defiant nostalgia for Yorkshire they embody, for a world not quite so 'glazed'. But as a Cambridge-educated writer, now committed to a life on the move with a sophisticated American poet, Hughes can no longer fully identify with what he refers to in a letter of 1958 to a Cambridge friend as 'the mass, the proletariat ... a great senile toothless hairless white ape, blind, tied etcetera' (*LTH* 116). This image is used again in a letter of 1986, when Hughes objects to being portrayed by Anne Stevenson in a draft of her Plath biography 'as some crass chauvinistic working-class ape lounging with my beer' while Plath 'slaves at the sink' (*LTH* 523). Hughes's attitude to the working-class is complex and ambivalent, by turns prone to feelings of nostalgia (as in a poem like 'Dick Straightup') and abjection (the working class as 'a great senile toothless hairless white ape'). While is it his class background that enables Hughes to steel himself at Cambridge and resist a 'glazed' America, and to steel his early poems in an English literary scene dominated by literate English middle-class culture, it is this same background Hughes must detach himself from (and so experience as abject) to live the literary life.

It is for this reason that the question of authorial intention, which arises in the early debates, has to remain difficult to resolve with any precision. If not consciously written with feelings of class antagonism in mind, the early poems certainly bear the mark of a political unconscious[39] – of a kind of second-nature intimacy with a world traditionally represented (as Emily Brontë was well aware) as illiterate, unmannerly, brutish, muscular, violent. These mixed feelings about class would be brought to a head when Hughes accepted the Laureateship late in 1984 – at a time when once again the working class were routinely portrayed in the British media as violent, brutish and irrational. Hughes's appointment as Laureate occurs deep into the year-long miners' strike of 1984–5 – the most significant industrial confrontation of recent times, the violent crushing of which, as was clear at the time, was an act of class revenge on the part of Margaret Thatcher's Tory government (the miners' strike of 1974 having brought down the then Tory government).[40] In what might seem like an act of shamanistic divination by Hughes, the 'violent' industrialized South Yorkshire landscape of the early poems proved to be the front-line in the conflict. The scenes of mass picketing there and the (famously doctored) scenes of the massive and violent police response shown on TV must no doubt have still been fresh on Hughes's mind when he wrote that there was 'Nowt to be sorry at' in accepting the government-approved appointment to the Queen – that 'The Summit's/ Summat'[41] – thus confirming through negation the feelings of betrayal and sorrow he felt in relation to his besieged class.

NOTES

1. C. J. Rawson, 'Ted Hughes: A Reappraisal', *Essays in Criticism* 15 (1965), p. 77.
2. Edwin Muir, 'Kinds of Poetry', *New Statesman* 54 (28 September 1957), p. 392.
3. *Ibid.*, p. 392.
4. J. D. Hainsworth, 'Poets and Brutes', *Essays in Criticism* 12 (1962), pp. 101–2; David Holbrook, 'The Cult of Hughes and Gunn', *Poetry Review* 54 (Summer 1963), pp. 174, 175; J. D. Hainsworth, 'Extremes in Poetry: R. S. Thomas and Ted Hughes', *English* 14 (Autumn 1963), p. 227.
5. Norman MacCaig, 'Noise and Solemnity', *Spectator* (22 April 1960), p. 583.
6. Hainsworth, 'Poets and Brutes', pp. 100, 101.
7. A. Alvarez, 'An Outstanding Young Poet', *Observer* (27 March 1960), p. 22; J. M. Newton, 'Mr. Hughes's Poetry', *Delta* 25 (1961), pp. 8, 7; Rawson, 'Ted Hughes: A Reappraisal', pp. 81, 82; C. J. Rawson, 'Ted Hughes and Violence', *Essays in Criticism* 16 (1966), p. 127.

8. Brian John, 'Ted Hughes: Poet at the Master-Fulcrum of Violence', *The Arizona Quarterly* 23 (1967), p. 5.
9. Newton, 'Mr. Hughes's Poetry', p. 9; Rawson, 'Ted Hughes: A Reappraisal', p. 77.
10. 'The Renewing Voice' (unsigned review of *Lupercal*), *Times Literary Supplement* (15 April 1960), p. 238; C.B. Cox, 'The Violence of Ted Hughes', *John O'London's* (13 July 1961), p. 68; Holbrook, 'Cult of Hughes and Gunn', p. 169; Rawson, 'Ted Hughes: A Reappraisal', p. 91.
11. Rawson, 'Ted Hughes: A Reappraisal', p. 80; John, 'Poet at the Master-Fulcrum of Violence', pp. 8, 14.
12. A. Alvarez, ed., *The New Poetry*, revised edn (Harmondsworth: Penguin, 1966), pp. 35, 25.
13. *Ibid.*, p. 31.
14. *Ibid.*, p. 31. In his earlier review of *Lupercal* Alvarez had placed Hughes 'somewhere between' the 'factual little essays' of Marianne Moore's verse and D.H. Lawrence's 'dramatic colloquies'. 'An Outstanding Young Poet', p. 22.
15. Ekbert Faas interview with Ted Hughes, 'Ted Hughes and *Crow*', *London Magazine* 10:10 (1971), p. 8.
16. See, for example, Slavoj Žižek, *Violence* (London: Profile, 2008), p. 174.
17. See *ibid.*, p. 45.
18. *Ibid.*, p. 1.
19. G. Ingli James, 'The Animal Poems of Ted Hughes: A Devaluation', *Southern Review* 2 (1967), p. 202; John, 'Poet at the Master-Fulcrum of Violence', p. 6; Cox, 'The Violence of Ted Hughes', p. 68.
20. Elaine Feinstein, *Ted Hughes: The Life of a Poet* (London: Weidenfeld and Nicolson, 2001), pp. 13, 22.
21. David Ross, cited in *ibid.*, p. 31.
22. *Ibid.*, p. 23.
23. Faas, 'Ted Hughes and *Crow*', p. 11; see Chapter 11, p. 154.
24. See Chapter 11, p. 153.
25. Tony Harrison, *Selected Poems* (Harmondsworth: Penguin, 1984), p. 122.
26. David Ross, cited in Feinstein, *Life of a Poet*, p. 31.
27. D.D. Bradley, cited in *ibid.*, p. 26.
28. *Ibid.*, p. 26.
29. *Ibid.*, p. 26.
30. Arnold Kettle, *An Introduction to the English Novel 1*, 2nd edn (London: Hutchinson, 1967), pp. 130–45.
31. Terry Eagleton, *Myths of Power: A Marxist Study of the Brontës* (London: Macmillan, 1975), p. 108.
32. Brian Cox, cited in Feinstein, *Life of a Poet*, p. 26.
33. Neil Roberts, *Ted Hughes: A Literary Life* (Basingstoke: Palgrave Macmillan, 2006), p. 52.
34. *Ibid.*, p. 53.
35. Kenneth Young, 'Poet from the Pennines', *Daily Telegraph* (14 April 1960), p. 17.
36. James, 'Animal Poems', p. 199.
37. *Ibid.*, p. 193.
38. John Haffenden, interview with Seamus Heaney, *Viewpoints: Poets in Conversation with John Haffenden* (London: Faber and Faber, 1981), pp. 73–4.

39. I adapt the term from Fredric Jameson's *The Political Unconscious: Narrative as a Socially Symbolic Act* (London: Methuen, 1981). Jameson's term implies 'the recognition that there is nothing that is not social and historical', his book proposing that the task of the Marxist critic is 'the unmasking of cultural artefacts as socially symbolic acts', p. 20.

40. See for example Seamus Milne, *The Enemy Within: The Secret War Against the Miners* (London: Verso, 2004).

41. Roberts, *Literary Life*, p. 14.

3

CHEN HONG

Hughes and animals

Hughes's poetry from his first book to the last can be regarded as expressing one poet's personal myth of his quest for what Keith Sagar has called 'healing truths' that both he himself and his society needed.[1] For Hughes the poet, one way of achieving such insights is by taking a shamanistic approach to thinking and writing about animals. In one of his letters to Moelwyn Merchant in 1990, Hughes explains his long-standing interest in shamanism and the role of animals in it. He said that it was actually shamanism that had helped him see the connection between 'everything that concerned [him]', such as his 'preoccupation with animal life', his mythologies and a series of his recurring dreams (*LTH* 579). And underneath them all, what he found was a deeper connection between animal life and the divine world, a world that animals have always been living in and that humans are separated from, a world that is sometimes termed 'the animal/spiritual consciousness'. In Hughes's view, what he called 'the divine being' is the state of a shaman whose cultural ego has collapsed and who has then plunged back into an animal/spiritual consciousness that is not only his own, but that of his whole group.[2]

From the very first Hughes undertook the discipline of partly leaving the usual human domain to look for the healing truths in the animal world that had fascinated him since childhood. For this reason, he has been said to be practising, in Alan Bleakley's words, 'a modern animal-centred shamanism'.[3] Bleakley's definition of the shaman as someone whose worldview 'offers continuity between what we would separate out as literary and psychological animals' represents the poetic task that Hughes set himself from his first collection onwards.[4] In trying to articulate human existence 'through the medium of animal life, as a sur-reality', Hughes shows his imaginative capacity, or 'animalizing imagination' in Bleakley's terms, absorbed by the poet from the traditional realm of totemism 'where biological, psychological and conceptual animals come to overlap, to fuse'.[5]

This chapter undertakes a reading of the first three collections of Ted Hughes by looking at the animals which abound in his early works and which, for their multiple appearances in different realms or orders of experience, are clearly being used as animal totems. While the totemic meanings of the animals are explored, Hughes's purpose of invoking animal totems to invite a serious critique of the human condition will also be discussed, often in the light of the poet's persistent, mythic quest, which he continued in different forms and modes throughout his writing career.

The Hawk in the Rain

If one poem is to be selected as the most typical example of Hughes's animalizing imagination, it must be 'The Thought-Fox'. Being one of his earliest poems, it is also often regarded as one of his best animal poems since it seems to be magically holding three animals in one: the biological, the symbolic and the textual. When the imaginative eyes of the working poet look through the window into the midnight forest, when a sense of movement outside in the darkness penetrates the lonely heart, and when the actual fox merges with the one in the poet's memory at the point where the eye appears as 'A widening deepening greenness', and when these fuse to jump onto the pages by the way of 'the dark hole of the head', the usual boundaries between different worlds collapse, and the triple transformation is made. Imitation of the fox's alertness is evident in the hesitant rhythm of the lines: 'Two eyes serve a movement, and now / And again now, and now, and now' (*CP* 21). In this way, the fox – for it is also being the thought-fox as well as the text-fox – is a totem or shamanic animal with the power to move freely out of its own physical existence into the spiritual/mythic realm whilst communicated as a textual force from beyond, yet obviously expressed within, human culture.

But the move between the different realms might not be as effortless or spontaneous as it appears. Richard Webster detected a 'conflict of sensibility' in the poem, a tension between 'the extraordinary sensuous delicacy' of the fox image and 'the predatory impulse' which he sees in the poet's attempt to capture the animal in the process of poetic creation by having the feminine sensuality of the poem 'purified by, or subordinated to, a tough, rational, artistic will'.[6] Webster's observation about Hughes's 'conflict of sensibility' has brought out a split that I see existing within the poet in the early period of his career. It is a split caused by what Sagar described as the poet's preoccupation with 'a fiercely dualistic attitude to life' that made the poet see human and nature as against each other in both the real and the symbolic sense, though this attitude is expressed much less overtly in 'The Thought-Fox' than in most of his other early poems.[7] Influenced by Jung, Hughes felt deeply about 'the separation of the two psychic halves' and regarded it as a basic human condition in which every human being, including himself, was implicated.[8] Whether inspired or not by Jung's emphasis on the importance of symbols as the third ground for the meeting of the two polarized halves, Hughes tried to use animal totems to join the two, though his attempt did not seem to be very successful at this stage.

The reason that shamanism, through the mode of totemism, has been widely practised by ancient and diverse cultures is that there seems to be, as people of those cultures believe, a kind of natural continuity between energy possessed by different beings in their lived experience, including human beings. Hughes was fascinated by this view, and the first two poems in *The Hawk in the Rain* could be seen as his evocation of the mysterious workings of life-sustaining energy stored in the bodies of powerful animals. In the title poem, descriptions of the hawk, which is as 'Steady as a hallucination in the streaming air' and is like 'The diamond point of will that polestars / The sea drowner's endurance', suggest that the animal power is internalized into what might resemble the will-power of human beings or even mythologized into a kind of universal energy when the hawk becomes 'the master- / Fulcrum of violence' (CP 19).

Like the hawk, the jaguar is a creature full of energy powerful enough to mesmerize the watching crowd at a zoo. Facing the jaguar as if it were 'a dream', the crowd seems to be penetrated by 'the drills of his eyes', just as the 'prison darkness' is drilled through. The dreamy moment thus becomes the moment when the closed door to the inner world of the crowd, which we may understand as the collective unconscious of human beings, opens temporarily up to forces of the outer world. But the jaguar does not need any impetus from the outside to break out of the bondage. The cage no longer exists for him as he strides in 'wildernesses of freedom'. When comparing the *Hawk in the Rain* version of the ending of this poem with the earlier published version in *Poetry (Chicago)*, we may notice an obvious shift of emphasis to the internal world of the animal in the later version through the poet's attempt to visualize what the jaguar might be seeing: 'Over the cage floor the horizons come' (CP 19–20).[9] The novelist J. M. Coetzee appears to have been deeply impressed by the way Hughes attempted to push his powers of understanding beyond their limit, so much so that his fictional character Elizabeth Costello gives a lengthy lecture about 'The Jaguar' and what she sees as its 'primitivism'. According to Costello, Hughes has a rare gift of 'feeling his way toward a different kind of being-in-the-world', which she also describes as the power of 'inhabiting another body' that was once possessed by our ancestors and is now lost to us.[10] As far as the poem is concerned, Hughes's acceptance of primitivism has indeed presented itself in the honour and respect he pays to the jaguar as the totem animal, which is basically a primitive attitude, as well as in his criticism of humans – childlike consumers of caged displays – who are much inferior to the jaguar in terms of energy and completeness of being.

Different from Costello, whose remark about the poem seems to suggest an unreserved acceptance of the jaguar on the poet's part, Terry Gifford read this poem and many others, including 'The Hawk in the Rain' and 'The Horses', as ironic and ambivalent in stance. Admitting the poet's admiration for the sheer vitality of the animals, he argued that 'The will of the hawk and the intensity of the jaguar were each presented as to some extent self-delusions'.[11] But Hughes's reservation about the power of the hawk and the jaguar must also indicate some defence inside him against an unobstructed flow of such energy between the human and the animal, for when the jaguar works as a totem of unbounded energy, isn't there the danger of the poet's being blinded, just as the animal is, by the intensity of that energy?

Despite the resistance, which could be unknown to the poet himself, other poems in the first collection, such as 'Macaw and Little Miss' and 'The Horses', also envision the flow of energy across times and spaces. As in 'The Jaguar', the dream in 'Macaw' is the point where the unconscious of the girl arises to link up the real and the mythological in a potential, desired, sexual force, whereas the dream in 'The Horses' leads to the enforced penetration of the human mind by the harsh elements and the horses' patient endurance of them. In both poems, we see an obvious lack of preparation by humans to engage with the shock of the otherness of the natural forces both outside and inside ourselves. Knowing already the poet's own reservations about the dangers of full engagement with animal power, we may understand his attack on humans in these poems as a self-criticism as well.

In fact, the note of self-criticism sounds rather strong in poems such as 'The Horses' and 'The Meeting'. The latter poem can be read both as an affirmation of the ultimate power of nature symbolized by the goat and as a psychological drama of self-discovery. A more complex lesson is taught in 'Egg-Head'. Being what Gifford calls a 'manifesto poem', 'Egg-Head' could well be a concluding piece for Hughes's first collection for pointing out explicitly the necessity of dropping defences and breaking down the boundaries between human intellect and the elemental energies of nature in both the inner and outer worlds.[12] In spite of his involuntary resistance, the poet is well aware that the removal of boundaries is the foundation of all shamanic experiences and is therefore vital for his writing to be able to explore the possibility of making various connections.

One crucial connection Hughes always takes care to make is the one between energies he sees in inner and outer nature and that in the language of his poetry. Many critics have commented on Hughes's meticulous use of language in his first collection and its taut, tense style, and those who discern a purpose behind this would accept the word 'mimetic' as a general description of that style. When it comes to the animals in his poems, Hughes's mimetic act is clearly a result of his conscious attempt to return to matter, which, to use Hugh Underhill's expression, is an attempt to re-establish 'the sacred materiality of the universe' that has been ignored ever since the elevation of the intellect above material and emotional experience.[13] Realizing Hughes's interest in so-called 'primitivism' and its deep effect on his life and work, it may even be said that this early mimetic style was dictated by the poet's initial trust in the physical reality of the animal world, from which he came to develop a faith in the material essence of all the energies in the universe. Yet, there might exist another reason for the reader's much-justified impression of a forced and deliberate style in Hughes's first book, which, in my opinion, lies in the gap between Hughes's intellectual conviction in the crucial importance of the raw energies of the material world to the healthy development of the human psyche and his actual failure to reconcile the two. That such a gap could hinder the poet from fully experiencing his shamanic explorations in the way he might have wished is evident in the first book as well as those published in the following dozen years.

Lupercal

Hughes's second collection is generally accepted as a development on *The Hawk in the Rain*. But, except that the use of language becomes more fluent and direct, there is not much dramatic 'development' in the sense of improved realization on Hughes's part in the way he regards his familiar subjects. As far as his animal poems are concerned, they are mostly a continuation of his earlier concerns about the expression of irrational energy in the physical and psychological worlds, though very often the focus seems to be more on the inner world of the human psyche. Together with this inward move, one other change to be found in some of the poems is an increasing, ambiguous fear of the instinctive energy in both humans and animals.

Poems such as 'The Bull Moses', 'February', 'A Dream of Horses' and 'Esther's Tomcat' bear traces of the first book to a different extent, though on the whole they dwell obviously more often in the realm of dreams than those earlier poems. The wolf, a powerfully totemic figure, is a predominant presence in 'February' and reappears in the background of the title poem of the book. Its feet, which are still wandering, not only disturb dreams, the only realm where it now lives in Britain, but also 'pursue, siege all thought' in the waking mind. So the realization of the indestructibility of the wolf or wolfishness has risen from the unconscious level to the conscious. Knowing the impossibility of human attempts to try to keep the wolf within whatever bond, whether physical or mental, the 'him' in the poem is afraid that the wolf's wandering feet might 'choose his head' to enter. Ironically, masks of totem animals, normally used to provide channels for the flow of energy between the animal and human worlds, are now constructed by the man as an ultimately unsuccessful protection against the animal soul. In the end, the wolf has its control of the human psyche, or of all people in the world despite the man's defence, as the mouths of the wolf-masks 'clamped well onto the world' (CP 61).

Compared with the self-conscious man in this poem who is left making his wolf masks, the grooms in 'A Dream of Horses' are more passive, or perhaps more intuitive in accepting the wild power potent in dreams. The masks made of the 'little orange flare' of the grooms' lanterns around their 'each sleep-dazed face' became an invitation to the 'horses / That whinnied and bit and cannoned the world from its place'. The attack of these wild horses on the human psyche seemed to be full of violence, but the grooms were submissive to their power as they 'longed for a death trampled by such horses', or when they kept 'listening' to 'the thunder of the horses' in their dream 'like drunkards'. Besides the grooms' involuntary capture by the thunderous disturbance of the horses, which we see in their act of 'listening', in their clear-mindedness they are also brave enough to wish that 'doomsday's flames be great horses' (CP 66). Such a continuity or consistency of the human attitude to the wild power represented by the horses, in both the grooms' conscious and unconscious states, is not seen in any of the previously discussed poems. The horse as a shamanic totem is thus extremely effective in making the men drop their consciousness to enter and stay in the divine world of animals. But how much the poet identifies himself with the poor grooms remains an unanswered question.

In fact, what happens in 'A Dream of Horses' makes up the central theme of Hughes's early poetry, which, as Neil Roberts rightly observes, is 'the usurpation or invasion of the world that the rational intellect has constructed, by a power that is represented as greater and ultimately more real'.[14] Roberts's use of the words 'usurpation' and 'invasion' for the natural force seems to reveal Hughes's view of nature at that time as something powerfully fascinating and inescapable, yet also threatening. In some of his *Lupercal* poems, Hughes expresses a fear of the dark forces of nature that exist outside as well as inside, a fear that, though still ambiguous, is now presented, as it has never been before, as a predominant mood and often in fearful images. Intended by Hughes to represent the innocent violence of nature, the hawk in 'Hawk Roosting', however, is often associated by the reader with egomaniac humans or even some arbitrary force of divinities. For those such as Gifford who observe a sense of irony in the earlier hawk poem, it is interesting to see how the self-deceptive confidence of the earlier stoic figure fully develops into a kind of blind and bloody faith held by this self-appointed lord of the world who holds 'Creation' in his foot. Though both poems admire the power of the hawk to a certain extent, they also show the mindless limitations of animal instinct that the poet seemed to see in the hawk.[15] Roberts must have observed the contradiction when he recognized 'Hawk Roosting' as 'a hybrid creation, in which the concept of a splendid, innocent natural creature is shadowed by something more human and sinister'.[16]

Roberts's remark has actually recognized an emerging tension in much of *Lupercal*, a tension between the poet's admiration for the animal power and his fear of it. Alongside, there is also the tension between the poet's desire and struggle for humanity and his consciousness of its handicaps: the danger of being out of touch with one's inner intuitive life. A full play of these tensions is to be seen in 'Thrushes' and 'Pike'.

In 'Pike' the speaker at the end of the poem is obviously experiencing a dilemma as he 'silently cast and fished / With the hair frozen on [his] head' in that pond full of 'Pike too immense to stir'. That fishing is both a physical sport and a psychological activity has been repeatedly emphasized by Hughes himself. In a letter to Gifford, he explicitly defined fishing as a means of 'putting the individual back in contact with the primitive being' (*LTH* 600). But as we see in the above quotation from the poem, the pike as the symbol of one's primitive impulse is both desired and feared by the speaker. Once the predatory nature of the pike goes deep into the unconscious world of dreams, it becomes a horror to the powerless human, who can only listen in the darkness, though being aware all the time of the 'watching' eyes of the dream that 'Darkness beneath night's darkness had freed' (*CP* 85–6). Here I would agree with Roberts, who found the speaker 'threatened rather than fulfilled by the imaginary predatory creature'. But Roberts did not forget to remind us that, like the fox, the pike is 'a manifestation of creative power' and is 'the inner resource that the poet is desperate to preserve'.[17] Hughes's apparently ambivalent view of the dark power he found in such animals as the pike and the thrush is a distinction made by the poet between his attitude towards the kinds of powers at work in predatory animals and that towards the same powers working in the inner world of humans.[18] This is a distinction that emerges first in *Lupercal* and is to be emphasized again and again in Hughes's later work.

Such poise is reflected in the language of *Lupercal*, where the poet appears more relaxed and less concerned about being self-consciously artful. The stressful and deliberate voice we hear in the earlier book has modulated into a voice that is more relaxed and less loud, except when in character, such as in

'Hawk Roosting'. Nevertheless, tensions to be confronted and reflected upon are everywhere within the freer form of the poems. The reason for that could be, as Hughes admitted himself in a letter to Lucas Myers, that there was a 'lack of the natural flow of spirit and feelings' during the time of the book's composition (*LTH* 178). The flow should also be there, of course, between the inner and outer animals, those of dream and reality, and the ultimate block of the flow in all the animal poems in *Lupercal*, with the only exception of 'A Dream of Horses', is proof of the inconclusive, ambivalent workings of Hughes's animal totems, or at least a reserved acceptance of them by the human mind.

Wodwo

Knowing Hughes's view of the troubled relation between the outer material world and the inner world of humans, we may be able to understand the increasing dependence of the poet on myth since his third collection, *Wodwo*. Though there is always a mythic element in many of Hughes's earlier poems, it never stands out so prominently as in *Wodwo*, where the creation myth alone appears several times, for example. In Hughes's important essay 'Myth and Education' he explains, in the second version included in the second edition of *Winter Pollen*, that myth provides a vehicle for 'negotiations between the powers of the inner world and the stubborn conditions of the outer world' (*WP* 151). Here again we see the influence of Jung on Hughes, whose use of animal totems for human critique could have been a result of his acceptance of Jung's idea about how myths or archetypes may remind us of our 'deficiency in consciousness'.[19]

Unlike Hughes's first two books, *Wodwo* comprises three parts, with poems in the first and the third parts, and five stories and a radio play in the middle part. The animals in the first part appear to be much more symbolic in function than those in the previous books. The first half of 'Second Glance at a Jaguar' recalls the earlier jaguar, but this one is much more pitiable because of his unmistakable sense of confinement and debasement in the real world. When we hear him 'Muttering some mantrah, some drum-song of murder / To keep his rage brightening' and see him 'Rounding some revenge', we are witnessing the magical metamorphosis of a hurt animal into a revengeful spirit with his own conjuring 'mantrah', and in doing so, the jaguar himself becomes the shaman. Therefore in the end of the poem we see him no longer in confinement, but already free and 'Hurrying through the underworld, soundless'. Like the ghost crabs, the jaguar becomes a wandering spirit outside the sphere of human consciousness, where he keeps on 'looking for a target' of his revenge (*CP* 152). The confrontation between the conscious and the unconscious seems irresolvable in the jaguar's relentless hate.

47

Other symbolic animals include the serpent in 'Reveille' and the title animal in 'The Bear'. Whereas the serpent is clearly a vengeful spirit like the jaguar, the bear is a shamanic figure in trying to arouse the spirits for the purpose of human salvation. Moreover, being established by the poet as an absolute authority with the power to decide the fate of human beings, the bear is actually an example of what Frazer described as 'the evolution of a god from a totem animal'.[20]

The second part of *Wodwo* shows a similar concern about the consequence for humans of their wrong treatment of the animal and whatever it may represent, though expressed perhaps more explicitly or dramatically in the stories than in the poems, an example of which is found perhaps in the not-so-close relationship between the story 'The Rain Horse' and the poem 'The Horses' from the first book. That 'The Rain Horse' is a psychological drama is clear at the beginning of the story, where the young man takes the path towards the central event as if everything was pre-determined and he himself was expecting a special experience, though 'he didn't quite know what'. At the end of the story, when the young man finally gets away from the pursuit of the horse and is alone, when his 'ordeal with the horse had already sunk from the reality' (W 45), instead of feeling safe he feels 'as if some important part had been cut out of his brain' (W 55). The sense of loss we see here is similar to that of the speaker in 'The Horses', who, at the end of the poem, has only his memory about the horses to cling to against the 'din of the crowded streets' (CP 23). Hughes's explanation of shamanism in an interview with Ekbert Faas might lead us to believe that he had probably designed the whole story to act out the drama of a man's refusal of an invitation from the spirit of an animal, the consequence of which is the death of the selected man or, at least as it happens in the story, 'a heavy spiritual price' paid by the man.[21] When we set the story against 'A Dream of Horses', we may come to understand the reason for the human characters' different reaction towards the invitation and their different outcomes as lying in the contrast between the young man in his grey suit and the grooms with 'mice in [their] pockets and straw in [their] hair', one being obviously self-conscious and the other much less cultured or controlled by human con-sciousness (W 45; CP 66).

The animal poems in the third part of *Wodwo* are various in style, tone and animal imagery, showing, perhaps, the poet's uncertain view of nature. There are, on one hand, celebrations of the natural world in poems such as 'Skylarks' and 'Gnat-Psalms', and on the other animals with no sense of purpose or confidence in 'The Howling of Wolves' and 'Wodwo'. 'Skylarks' seems to have offered a corrected view of the predatory nature of the birds in 'Thrushes' by concluding the skylark's hunt as well as the poem with the remark 'Conscience perfect' (CP 176). A changed view of the animal is also offered in 'The Howling of Wolves', though the change goes in a totally different direction. Unlike the wolves in 'February', whose relentless pursuit goes on day and night, the wolves here know no purpose, being no more than 'steel traps' or the 'steel furred'. Machine-like, the small wolf in the second part of the poem is urged on by an impulse little known to the creature itself to 'feed its fur'. The human observer is less certain about the condition of the wolf: whether it howls 'out of agony or joy', and he shows little admiration for its innocence that 'crept into minerals' (CP 180–1). Looking into the wolf symbols in Hughes's poetry, Ann Skea recognized the 'ambivalent nature of Hughes's wolves and the mixed feeling of attraction and fear which they arouse'.[22] But of all the wolves appearing in the first three books, including the one in the story 'Sunday', plus others coming up in later books such as Wolfwatching, the small wolf in 'The Howling of Wolves' is exceptional in that it is deprived of all powers, whether natural or supernatural. The shamanic spirit stops working here where the animal becomes a pitied victim rather than a totem guide. Knowing that the poem was written after the suicide of Plath, we may take it as an outpouring of human grief through the voice of the wolf, which then becomes the poet himself with all his bewildered loneliness. In this case where the poet is transformed temporarily into a wolf, the beast is perhaps a totem after all, being where the soul of the man now resides.[23]

When we come to the end of the book, we have again a mythological creature whose name is 'Wodwo'. Having a magic power that enables it to be anywhere, the creature is, however, in no better condition than the howling wolves, for it knows nothing about itself, and the whole poem becomes a series of poignant questions. The extreme uncertainty of the creature is reflected in the halting lines running on throughout the increasingly unpunctuated poem. Comparing 'Wodwo' with 'Hawk Roosting', Roberts found in the creature's humble acknowledgement of its ignorance 'a developing consciousness' and 'emerging humanity', which are, however, accompanied by its having 'no intuitive sense of its own being' that may eventually lead to its becoming 'out of touch with its inner life'.[24] This view accepted, it may be said that by the end of 'Wodwo' the poet still cannot reconcile humanity with animality, and whether the two can be reconciled remains an open question. Sagar, however, differed from Roberts when he identified the wodwo as 'a creature of the unfallen world, before the human, animal and spirit worlds become separated in Western consciousness'.[25] Whether the poem is as negative as the majority of the book, or an upbeat ending in Sagar's view, the whole book, in being 'too subjective', exemplifies a split between the conscious and the unconscious which the poet could not bring together at that time (LTH 274).

49

When comparing *Wodwo* with Hughes's first two books in terms of language, the predominant use of free verse in the animal poems of the last book stands out immediately, distinguished further by the frequent use of irregular stanzas and irregular punctuation. The free form culminates, finally, in the title poem, where punctuation disappears totally in the second half of the poem and capitalization is dropped except, ironically, for the word 'I'. But rather than create a sense of effortless flow of ideas or emotions, the voice in the final poem sounds extremely hesitant and unconfident with its endless and unanswered questions. Such is perhaps the poet's state at this stage of his poetic quest to find modes of negotiation between inner and outer, human and animal, worlds.

What we see in Hughes's first three collections is the poetic exploration into the inner world of both himself as an individual and representatives of the human race, carried out as an adventure of engagements with animals and birds in their physical, totemic and mythic roles.

The fact that the ten years between the publication of his first book and that of his third did not convince Hughes of the possibility for humans to embrace the whole of nature is an indication of the deep dilemma faced by Hughes during this time. Underhill sees this as a dilemma for the Romantic imagination:

> Hughes's imagination, with its vitalist vision, belongs to that Romantic tradition which repudiates the mechanical, utilitarian and rational: that it should come to the contradictory point of perceiving nature as mechanism would seem to reflect an impasse of the Romantic imagination.[26]

The problem confronted by Hughes through his first three books has actually been the problem of the relation between objectivity and subjectivity, or that between the outer material world and the inner world of humans. In the second 'Myth and Education' essay published in *Winter Pollen*, Hughes talked about the relation between the two and explicitly recognized children as those who can best accept our inner world because they are 'the least conditioned by scientific objectivity to life', and that 'they are aware that this inner world we have rejected is not merely an inferno of depraved impulses and crazy explosions of embittered energy. Our real selves lie down there' (W 149).

The 'Myth and Education' essay, most explicitly in its earlier 1970 form, makes it clear that Hughes's writing for children is a search for 'healing truths'.[27] What he hopes he may finally achieve is a kind of mature divine innocence beyond this original state in children, in which the animal and the human can find a true relationship that is both symbolic and real. Hughes's first three books constitute the beginning stage in the poet's persistent quest for the voice that is finally able to declare 'The tiger blesses with a fang' (*CP* 578), or to picture golden bears 'swim[ming] like men / Beside us' (*CP* 664). In a remarkable letter to his son Nicholas, Hughes refers to 'a visionary dream' in which he saw a ship loaded with salmon on top of which jaguars slept. In his dream he failed to engage and 'wandered away, drunkenly, dazed ... So that boatload of truths, insights, wisdoms from the other side ... I simply abandoned. I wasn't up to it' (*LTH* 711). This was the kind of challenge that the poet undertook in his earliest poetic encounters with animals, attempting to discover what being 'up to it' might mean, risks that were to be redeemed in his final meetings with animals, birds and especially fish.

NOTES

1. K. Sagar, *The Laughter of Foxes: A Study of Ted Hughes*, 2nd edn (Liverpool: Liverpool University Press, 2006), p. 4.
2. In explaining his idea about shamanism in the letter mentioned, Hughes used expressions such as 'the divine self', 'a divine animal' and the 'lost "divine" consciousness'. To me it is obvious that Hughes understood shamanism as a divine state, something that might be called 'the divine being'. For his discussion on the issue, see *LTH* 581.
3. A. Bleakley, *The Animalizing Imagination: Totemism, Textuality and Ecocriticism* (London: Macmillan, 2000), p. 79.
4. *Ibid.*, p. xvi.
5. *Ibid.*, pp. xiii; xvii; xvi.
6. R. Webster, '"The Thought-Fox" and the Poetry of Ted Hughes' (www.richard-webster.net, 1984), p. 5.
7. K. Sagar, *Ted Hughes and Nature: 'Terror and Exultation'* (www.keithsagar.co.uk, 2009), p. 163.
8. C. G. Jung, *Collected Works*, 20 vols. (London: Routledge and Kegan Paul, 1957–79), vol. IX, part 2, p. 180.
9. For the first version of the poem, refer to *CP* 1242.
10. J. M. Coetzee, *The Lives of Animals*, ed. Amy Gutmann (Princeton: Princeton University Press, 1999), p. 51.
11. Terry Gifford, *Ted Hughes* (London: Routledge, 2009), p. 35.
12. *Ibid.*, p. 34.
13. H. Underhill, *The Problem of Consciousness in Modern Poetry* (Cambridge: Cambridge University Press, 1992), p. 272.
14. N. Roberts, *Ted Hughes: A Literary Life* (Basingstoke: Palgrave Macmillan, 2006), p. 28.
15. That Hughes might be showing some admiration for the power of the hawk in 'Hawk Roosting' may not be accepted by some scholars. Sagar, for example, is obviously denying any admiration in the poem when he accused Hughes of being 'dishonest' in Hughes's essay 'Poetry and Violence'. According to his argument, Hughes here 'foists onto "Thrushes" ... and "Hawk Roosting" untenably "posi-tive" interpretations deriving from his unwillingness to admit in retrospect the degree of hostility to nature which had actually informed his poems at that time'

(*Ted Hughes and Nature*, p. 68). In my view, there is at least some admiration in the poem for the instinctive power of the animal, especially in comparison with the human, since it has 'no falsifying dream' and 'no sophistry in [his] body', etc.

16. Roberts, *Literary Life*, p. 51.
17. *Ibid.*, pp. 46–7.
18. Sagar once made a comment about this distinction in *The Art of Ted Hughes*, 2nd edn (Cambridge: Cambridge University Press, 1978), p. 46. In his latest book on Hughes, however, Sagar came to a very different view of some of the poems in *Lupercal*, such as 'Thrushes' and 'Pike', saying that they are and were 'clearly intended' by the poet to be images of 'nature's insanity' (*Ted Hughes and Nature*, p. 68.). But I still prefer Sagar's earlier interpretation and believe what Hughes said in 'Poetry and Violence' about the distinction between animal violence and human violence to be true.
19. Jung, *Collected Works*, vol. x, pp. 218–20.
20. J. G. Frazer, *Totemism and Exogamy*, vol. II (London: Macmillan, 1935), p. 138.
21. For Hughes's talk about shamanism in the mentioned interview, see Ekbert Faas, *Ted Hughes: The Unaccommodated Universe* (Santa Barbara: Black Sparrow, 1980), p. 206. The quoted expression in the sentence is from Roberts, *Literary Life*, p. 60.
22. Ann Skea, 'Wolf-masks: From *Hawk* to *Wolfwatching*' (http://ann.skea.com, 2000), p. 7.
23. In interpreting the wolf as a totem of a different kind, I'm following Frazer, who explicitly recognized the widespread belief in the external souls of living people as an integral part of totemism. Frazer, *Totemism and Exogamy*, p. 598.
24. Roberts, *Literary Life*, pp. 62–4.
25. Sagar, *Ted Hughes and Nature*, p. 72.
26. Underhill, *Problem of Consciousness*, p. 282.
27. 'Myth and Education', *Children's Literature in Education* 1 (1970), pp. 55–70.

4

JO GILL

Ted Hughes and Sylvia Plath

When Ted Hughes and Sylvia Plath first met in 1956 both were already, in Hughes's words, 'curious' about the other.[1] Both had acquaintances in common and both were publishing poetry in the various literary magazines that proliferated in Cambridge at this time. Two early Plath poems, 'Epitaph in Three Parts' and '"Three Caryatids Without a Portico" by Hugh Robus. A Study in Sculptural Dimensions', the first that she published in England, appeared in the Winter 1956 issue of *Chequer*.[2] Two years earlier, Hughes had published some of his poems, 'The Jaguar' and 'Casualty', in the same magazine. Several of his friends were frequent contributors.[3] Plath's poems were mocked in a 'broadsheet of literary comment' which Hughes's 'poetic gang' (his words) produced. And although this particular review was penned by Hughes's friend Daniel Huws, it is clear from the former's subsequent recollection of events that this was to some degree a collaborative enterprise with Huws acting, at least implicitly, on behalf of 'our group'.[4]

When they finally met in person at the launch party for another periodical, the short-lived *St. Botolph's Review*, each knew, or knew of, the other's work. Plath's first move was to call out to Hughes the words of some of his poems.[5] He found himself having to explicate and exculpate his friend's (and by extension his group's and his own) response to Plath's poetry.[6] It is writing and reading, then – the thrilling potential of words and the devastating consequences of their misreading – which are fundamental to the Hughes and Plath relationship from the outset. But there are also, as the events surrounding their meeting and the subsequent narrative of their relationship indicate, wider literary and cultural contexts which have informed the emergence and reception of their work.

'Call and response'

Diane Middlebrook has called theirs a relationship of 'call and response', wherein each poet in turn initiates a poetic reply from the other. She cites

53

Hughes's 'Lines to A Newborn Baby' as one example of an opening call, to which Plath responded with 'Morning Song', a poem which then solicited a further response in his 'Full Moon and Little Frieda'.[7] She also points to echoes of Hughes's 'Jaguar' and 'Law in the Country of the Cats' in Plath's 'Pursuit' (written just days after the couple first met) – echoes which reverberate in 'Trophies' from *Birthday Letters*. We see the same influence on 'The Hidden Orestes' in *Howls & Whispers*, where 'Orestes / Is padding up the long trail / Like a black panther' (CP 1175). The panther is then likened to a 'black velvet bagful / Of family emeralds' – an image which attenuates the Plath connection while also establishing an association with Assia Wevill, whose 'gem-stones (rubies, emeralds)' are finally lost to her in the *Capriccio* poem 'Descent' (CP 787).

Other critics have concurred in arguing that the influence is mutual and two-way. Margaret Dickie Uroff was one of the first to evaluate the poets' close textual relationship, suggesting that, 'although their purposes were different and their home territories widely separate, Plath and Hughes share a view of poetry as a raid on the inner life ... their poems should be read together as raid and counter-raid, gathering intensity as they developed'.[8] Her militaristic metaphor, as we will see shortly, anticipates some of the rhetoric which Hughes uses in describing their creative relationship. For Tracy Brain, the poets are in 'conversation' with each other and with a wider literary context.[9] Brain, like others, including Middlebrook, Susan Van Dyne and Heather Clark, has used archival evidence to trace what she calls a literally 'back-to-back [on the page] relationship between Plath's work and Hughes's'.[10] Stephen C. Enniss and Karen V. Kukil's introduction to a New York exhibition of Hughes and Plath manuscripts from the Emory University and Smith College Archives, respectively, refers to 'the young couple's emphatic commitment to a shared writing life'.[11] Terry Gifford describes some of the practicalities of this 'collaboration': 'Hughes set lists of titles for Plath to explore while she set readings in American poetry for him, and they exchanged dreams, and played with tarot cards and the Ouija board to find ideas for poems'.[12] For Neil Roberts, 'their mutual influence is obvious, and it would even be true, if a partial truth, to say that they created a common text, in which many important motifs cannot be straightforwardly assigned to one or the other writer/protagonist'.[13]

Some commentators, though, see the relationship as more combative than affirmatory. Clark points to the 'contradictory messages about their "collaborative" relationship' which each sent in a 1961 BBC interview and suggests that both poets 'at turns embrace and reject each other's influence'.[14] Vivian Pollak's critique of Hughes's poem 'The Literary Life' notes the 'necessarily unstable' alliances between Hughes, Plath and other poets.[15] Gayle Wurst similarly highlights the difficult dynamics of such a bond: 'rather than providing an enabling myth which permitted her to see herself as poet-god and co-creator, Plath's deification of her husband played into, and quickly exacerbated, her life-long dread of her own poetic sterility'.[16] Plath herself disavows Hughes's influence in the BBC interview mentioned earlier: 'I've always thought that our subject matter in particular and also the forms in which we write, the forms, are really quite, quite different.' Hughes confirms the point, saying that even when they write on similar themes (for example, in his poem 'View of a Pig' and her 'Sow'), they 'treat' it 'differently'.[17]

As this indicates, the question of influence is complex and highly contested. In his *Paris Review* interview, Hughes credits Plath's role in introducing him to American literature, but he also speaks about the importance of resisting influence, of 'tuning out the influences, the static and interference'.[18] He similarly seeks to cover his traces in a 1971 interview with Ekbert Faas: 'It's a mystery how a writer's imagination is influenced and altered . . . this whole business of influence is mysterious.'[19]

'Supply lines'

In his *Paris Review* interview, Hughes refers to the 'hidden supply lines' which fuel his work. The metaphor of 'supply lines' is interesting for a number of reasons, not least because it draws on militaristic notions of survival in a war of attrition (a supply line is the means by which nourishment is provided to those under attack in the field). By deploying Hughes's image of 'hidden supply lines' in this study of influences on his work, we can escape binaristic and competitive debates about who exerted the greatest power over whom, and we can open out the enquiry in order to give full consideration to the multiplicity and fluidity of both poets' sources.

Raphaël Ingelbien has argued that 'the huge impact of *Birthday Letters*, to which Hughes's death has granted the status of last will and testament, means that much of his work will inevitably be read through the lens of its interconnectedness with Plath's'.[20] Before turning to Plath's incontrovertible presence in *Birthday Letters*, it is useful to pause and examine some of the ways in which her work influenced his earlier writing.

Paul Bentley makes an extended case for Plath's impact on Hughes, citing Hughes's comments on the admirable directness of her speech in his 1966 essay 'Notes on the Chronological Order of Sylvia Plath's Poems' and suggesting that her later poems provide 'the most important influence on the style of the *Wodwo* poems'.[21] Gifford and Roberts make a similar point: 'it seems to us likely that the greater rhythmical freedom, compression and elliptical language of Hughes's poetry from *Wodwo* onwards owe something to the example of Plath's later work'.[22]

Throughout his poetry Hughes has arguably inherited from Plath a way of talking about his own (and others') suffering and need of exoneration or cleansing. Such a quest is vividly and persistently realized in both poets' work through metaphors of burning as simultaneously punishment, purification and illumination. In his 1965 comments on Plath's *Ariel* (which he had recently edited for publication), Hughes notes that her poems are 'charged with terrific heat', that they are like 'explosions', 'burningly luminous' (*WP* 161). In 'Notes on the Chronological Order' he comments on the radiance of her language, concluding that 'every word is *Baraka*: the flame and the rose folded together'.[23] With the exception of, say, 'The Martyrdom of Bishop Farrar', such imagery is not characteristic of Hughes's own early work. From *Crow* (1970) onwards, though, we find similar images of 'conflagration', to quote 'Crow's Last Stand'. 'A Grin' closes with a face in an 'electric chair', while in 'Crow Tyrannosaurus' man's murderous mind is shown 'incinerating' the innocents' 'outcry'. In 'The Black Beast', Crow 'roasted the earth to a clinker' (*CP* 210, 213, 215, 224). A clinker is the solid, forged residue of burning in a furnace. Hughes returns to the same theme in *Cave Birds* (1978), where in 'The Accused' the subject offers up his body, skin, heart, desire and mind for testing and purification by fire. There, 'his atoms are annealed'. Annealing (which means to toughen by prolonged exposure to a heat source) transforms his 'mudded body' into something more permanent and more aesthetically and spiritually valuable – into 'rainbowed clinker and beatitude' (*CP* 425).[24] In 'Ophiuchos' (from *Moortown*'s 'Orts' sequence), 'fire inexhaustible' is charged with 'Fining the marital metal' (*CP* 574). 'Fining' is a process which connotes purification by fire of metal or glass.

Imagery such as this responds to Plath's poetry, for example, to her 'Poppies in July' (from *Ariel*), where the speaker finds herself frustratingly unable to offer herself up to the flames: 'I put my hand among the flames. Nothing burns.'[25] Her 1960 poem 'The Hanging Man' opens with an electrocution – as, of course, does her novel, *The Bell Jar* – while, famously, 'Fever 103°' references smoke, ash and heat and finally settles on the image of the 'pure acetylene virgin'. The 'red // Eye, the cauldron of morning' which closes 'Ariel' synthesizes many of these images and – in the metaphor of the cauldron – provides a place wherein Hughes's processes of annealing and fining might occur (*SPCP* 141, 231, 239). 'Earth-numb' in *Moortown* opens with an image of the dawn as a 'smouldering fume of dry frost. / Sky-edge of red hot iron' (again recalling the 'red // Eye, the cauldron') and subsequently refers to 'an electrocuting malice / like a trap' thereby recapitulating Plath's use of this motif (*CP* 541). Many of the poems of *Birthday Letters* are nourished by these supply lines. 'Astringency' is set among the 'cindery air / A waft of roasted iron' of Plath's native Boston while 'The God' alludes to smoke, fire and sacrificial flames, and 'Suttee' features immolation: subject and object in this poem are consumed by the 'Babe of dark flames and screams' (*CP* 1093, 1163, 1140). The title *Birthday Letters* itself gestures towards Plath's poem 'Burning the Letters' (*SPCP* 204) and connotes both the destruction and the potential renewal which this act of purgation by fire might bring about.

Another important supply line is Plath's representation of Devon voices and landscapes in a number of poetry and prose texts. In the prologue to *Gaudete* (1977), Hughes's characterizations of people and settings bring to mind Plath's sketches of 'Rose and Percy B.' and 'Charlie Pollard and the Beekeepers'.[26] *Gaudete*'s depiction of the blacksmith's wife recalls the suspicious atmosphere and mutual mistrust among the women of the Mothers' Union in Plath's story 'Mothers':

> Evans' wife is vivid and tiny,
> Startling like a viper.
> A magnet for local scandal fantasies, spoken and unspoken ...
> She is Secretary of the local W.I.
> What goes on at those W.I. meetings?   (*G* 66)

Hughes was looking through Plath's prose in preparation for its publication in 1977 at the same time as he was working on *Gaudete*. Just two years later, *Moortown*'s 'The Formal Auctioneer' offers a similarly jaundiced view of local figures and places – a perspective which, as we will see later, owes something to Plath's defamiliarizing, American eye (*CP* 534). Middlebrook traces the wider effects of this process of defamiliarization on Hughes's writing, suggesting that Plath's reactions to the unfamiliar new world of his family on their first visit north after their marriage subsequently influenced him: 'Her response to Yorkshire seems to have opened his own eyes to the possibility of bringing the Calder Valley into his work.'[27] From this point of view, the effect of Plath's presence is to turn Hughes back to his roots and to what critics have subsequently identified as his true theme and voice.

Birthday Letters

It is in *Birthday Letters* that Hughes's debt to Plath – or his continued haunting by her memory and words – is most clearly visible. The word 'haunting' is used cautiously and with qualification here to connote not a ghostly presence, but an absence, and not a personal influence, but one comprising textual traces.[28]

The 1998 publication of the book provided startling confirmation of the strength and persistence of the two poets' literary relationship. These poems had, it transpires, been written over some three decades (an unpublished postcard from Hughes to Keith Sagar dated 17 November 1997 indicates that they were written between 1972 and that year).[29] A handful had emerged, with little notice, in *New Selected Poems: 1957–1994*. Also in 1998, 110 copies of a fine-press edition of related poems, *Howls & Whispers*, appeared. A collection of poems, *Capriccio*, nominally addressed to Assia Wevill (the woman with whom Hughes was involved at the time of Plath's death) had been published in a limited fine-press edition of fifty copies some eight years earlier.[30] *Birthday Letters* caught the public by surprise. Here, it seemed, for the first time, Hughes was revealing the true story of his married life, 'breaking decades of diplomatic silence' and, finally, 'set[ting] the record straight'. The media interest in the appearance of a previously unpublished poem, 'Last Letter', which was found in the British Library's collection of Hughes papers and featured in the magazine the *New Statesman* on 11 October 2010, confirms the open-endedness of this particular narrative, and the persistence of the public's fascination with it.[31]

On the surface, *Birthday Letters* does indeed revisit Hughes's relationship with his former wife. It attempts to reopen the lines of communication (in Peter Davison's telegraphic terms 'Ted Hughes finally addresses Sylvia Plath').[32] But I think it a mistake – and a disservice to both poets' work – to read the collection as merely a diaristic account of events. The collection is more fruitfully read as a complex, profoundly textual and highly tentative exploration of what it means to read and to write about one's own experience and that of others. It is not Plath's influence *per se* that we might detect in *Birthday Letters*, but the influence of her words – and by extension other textual representations of their experience – as Hughes encounters them afresh on each and every rereading. 'Visit' and '18 Rugby St' are explicit about this creative process. In the former, 'Ten years after your death / I meet on the page of your journal, as never before, / The shock of your joy' and in the latter, 'Your journal told me the story of your torture' (*CP* 1047, 1055). In a letter to Keith Sagar recounting his original attempts to deal in poetry with the experience of Plath's loss, Hughes explains that he had originally thought of using the story of Orpheus but that he rejected the myth, realizing that the living Plath was permanently beyond reach: 'I saw my little note about it the other day. The shock twist was that Pluto answered: No, of course you can't have her back. She's dead, you idiot' (*LTH* 723). It is letters alone which remain; in the closing words of 'Visit': 'You are ten years dead. It is only a story. / Your story. My story.' This exchange of letters, or correspondence, at one and the same time unites the two parties and confirms their separation or what Middlebrook terms their 'complex dynamic of sameness and difference'.[33]

This notion of exchange is important in light of our overarching question about Ted Hughes and influence. Are the *Birthday Letters* the first in an exchange of letters to which Plath, as implied addressee, is invited to respond? Or are these Hughes's responses to messages which he has already received through the medium of Plath's extant writing? The collection, I would argue, leaves this question open as a sign of the fluidity, or indecipherability, of meaning and as confirmation of the backwards and forwards flow of ideas across and between the two poets' work.

Numerous poems in *Birthday Letters* can be seen to write back to, or correspond with, Plath's. This is most obvious in poems which share titles (such as 'Wuthering Heights', 'Brasilia', 'The Rabbit Catcher'), or explore similar areas (Hughes's 'The Bee God', for instance, which evokes Plath's bee poems, and his 'Night-Ride on Ariel' and 'Sam', which bring to mind 'Ariel'), or which re-enact roles prescribed in Plath's poetry ('A Picture of Otto' and 'Daddy').[34] But more subtle influences can also be traced. For example, images of performance and display in 'Fulbright Scholars', 'Caryatids (2)', 'Visit', '18 Ruby Street' and 'Chaucer' bring to mind similar interests in Plath's 'Lesbos' and 'Lady Lazarus'. The latter finds an explicit echo in Hughes's 'The Table', with its contemptuous reference to 'your peanut-crunchers', who are now free to pore over 'the ink-stains, the sigils' that are all that remain of her writing life. There is a preoccupation here with the writer's relics (the writing table that Hughes had made for Plath, supposedly to 'last a lifetime', as line two of 'The Table' puts it, is reduced in the closing stanza to 'a curio' (*CP* 1132)). 'The Shot' places the speaker in the position of privileged and voyeuristic member of Plath's 'peanut-crunching crowd' (*SPCP* 244): 'I managed / A wisp of your hair, your ring, your watch, your nightgown' (*CP* 1053). Similarly, in 'Trophies', mentioned above, the speaker faces a bruising encounter with a figure metaphorically represented by the panther who escapes with the 'trophies' (the spoils of war, perhaps, to return to the combative rhetoric noted earlier) of his addressee's 'hairband' and 'ring' (*CP* 1054).

In addition to their debt to Plath's poetry, several of the *Birthday Letters* enter into a dialogue with her prose work. 'The Table' and 'The Rag Rug' implicitly reference Plath's *Letters Home* and *Journals*. 'The 59th Bear' responds to Plath's story 'The Fifty-Ninth Bear',[35] which itself fictionalizes an experience shared by the couple and recorded in Plath's *Letters Home* (349–50) and in a letter from Hughes to his parents (*LTH* 150). 'You Hated Spain' similarly draws on shared experience and on sketches and stories in *Johnny Panic*, the *Journals* and *Letters Home*. The presence of these palimpsests confirms, once again, the textuality of these aptly named 'Letters' and the multiplicity of supply lines.

Capriccio

In *Birthday Letters*, its companion volume *Howls & Whispers*, and its precursor *Capriccio*, Hughes at last permits – or steels – himself (in a letter to Seamus Heaney he mentions the 'courage' it took (*LTH* 703)) to examine his own memories of his past relationships. It is here that he engages with the haunting textual traces of both addressees – Plath and the woman with whom he subsequently formed a relationship, Assia Wevill.

The evocation of Assia's presence and influence in *Capriccio* is unsettling in several regards. The poems were first published in a limited fine-press edition as though to give Hughes the necessary release that publication offered without too visibly broadcasting his sources (*LTH* 704). In the case of *Birthday Letters* and *Capriccio*, Hughes's correspondence makes clear that there was no conscious motive or plan behind their creation. Of the latter, he writes to Leonard Baskin (the artist whose illustrations accompany the text) that they were the result of 'no programme' (*LTH* 688). Of the former, in the letter to Heaney cited above, Hughes continues: '[I] wrote them en masse for some time – not knowing what I'd end up with or where I'd end. Till suddenly – between one day and the next – I realised that was it' (*LTH* 704). Hughes thus presents himself as being impelled by some larger force or influence outside himself and his immediate muses. This deterministic narrative in which the poet is mere witness to events and forces that he is powerless to prevent – fate, historical circumstances, the Freudian family romance – is apparent in the poems themselves as well as in Hughes's extratextual comments on them.[36] In 'The Hands' and 'A Picture of Otto' (*Birthday Letters*), the addressee is depicted as the already doomed victim of the underworld powers associated with the loss of the father. In 'Fanaticism' and 'The Error' (*Capriccio*), she is agent and victim of her own death wish.

In *Capriccio*, the relentless force of astrological and occult powers is hammered home in the opening poem with its relentless return at the beginning of three successive, central stanzas to the ominous date 'Friday the thirteenth'.[37] The date sounds like a knell throughout the text, situating speaker and addressee as passive victims of its influence. The intractability of this force is demonstrated by its re-emergence in a near-identical poem, now under the new title 'Superstitions', in *Howls & Whispers*. The second poem in *Capriccio*, 'The Locket', reads the subject's (Assia's) death as a '*fait accompli*' (*LTH* 784); we should note the aural rhyme of '*fait*' and 'fate'. In the third poem, 'The Mythographers', the subject is cast in the simultaneous roles of Lilith and

Nehama.[38] Denied agency, she can only play out the role for which, in this narrative's terms, she is destined. The move here is reminiscent both of Hughes's casting of Plath in the role of perpetually grieving victim of an Electra complex in *Birthday Letters* and, in turn, of Plath's own précis of 'Daddy', which he quotes in the notes to his 1981 edition of her *Collected Poems*: '"Here is a poem spoken by a girl with an Electra complex. Her father died while she thought he was God ... she *has to* [my emphasis] act out the awful little allegory once over before she is free of it"' (*SPCP* 293). It also foreshadows Hughes's unavoidable casting of himself as Orpheus throughout *Birthday Letters* – an effect which is all the more telling given his explicit reluctance to take on this role in the letter to Heaney quoted earlier.[39] In 'The Minotaur (2)' from *Howls & Whispers* the speaker is clear about the forces which direct his moves, leaving him powerless to deviate from some pre-ordained script: 'I saw the plot unfolding and me in it' (*CP* 1178). From this point of view, if Plath (or Wevill) do influence or otherwise haunt Hughes's writing, they do so not of their own volition, but as agents of some larger power.

In *Capriccio*, *Howls & Whispers* and *Birthday Letters*, the forces are not only esoteric. History exerts its own influence on players and events. In *Capriccio*, 'Descent' pictures the subject (Assia) as the victim of historical and political circumstances, compelled (hence the repeated phrases 'You had to' and 'You were forced to') to remake herself again and again until nothing remains but the story – 'the book' as the poem's final word puts it – of her passing (*CP* 787). Here, as in *Birthday Letters*, there is no direct relationship between speaker and addressee. Influence is mediated by language. And the speaker can only read and reread his 'other' in an increasingly fraught attempt to make sense of their shared past. In 'Folktale', both participants read – or misread – each other in terms of national and cultural stereotypes. Hughes orientalizes Assia, by which I mean that he projects onto her his own forbidden, disavowed fears and desires. What each party 'wanted' from the other is hammered home fourteen times as though to emphasize the egotistical neediness of both. *Cappricio*'s 'The Error' similarly portrays an outsider's misreading of the signs:

> You must have misheard a sentence.
> You were always mishearing
> Into Hebrew or German
> What was muttered in English.   (*CP* 795)

In *Birthday Letters*, 'Error' depicts an English speaker's misreading of an outsider's (an American's) needs. Both poems expose the process of defamiliarization; the American and German Jewish 'others' prompt the English speaker to look afresh at his own landscape, culture and identity.

Assia's cultural identity as a Jewish woman of Russian and German ancestry, forced into exile first in Canada and then in Israel, provides a fruitful supply line for Hughes. This background interested him for several reasons – political, spiritual and mythological – as evidenced in his responsiveness to the Jewish American artist Leonard Baskin's work in the essay 'The Hanged Man and the Dragonfly' (*WP* 84). Gifford and Roberts suggest that 'Hughes's most important affinity is with the post-war poets of Eastern Europe' – an affinity that Wevill was able to foster.[40] Hughes worked alongside Wevill in bringing to public attention a number of European writers and in translating the work of Israeli poet Yehuda Amichai.[41] According to Sean O'Brien, 'the vigilant and unadorned language of some poets from Eastern Europe can perhaps be heard to influence Hughes's work from around the period of *Wodwo* (1967)'.[42]

'America and American literature in person'

In his *Paris Review* interview, Hughes twice credits Plath with introducing him to America and its culture: 'To me, of course, she was not only herself: she was America and American literature in person'.[43] The point is dramatically realized in '18 Rugby Street', where the addressee is metonymized as 'Beautiful, beautiful America' (*CP* 1055). As he proceeds to explain, 'When I met Sylvia I also met her library, and the whole wave hit me. I began to devour everything American' (*Paris Review*, p. 85).[44] Even here, though, it would be a mistake to see the influence as one-directional. Speaking to Faas, Hughes notes that he was able to turn Plath back to hitherto overlooked aspects of her own cultural tradition: 'I was infatuated with John Crowe Ransom when I first met her, and I brought her into that infatuation as well. And that had an immediate impact on the style of her writing at the time'.[45] Another important influence that both poets shared was Emily Dickinson (*LTH* 169–70).

Elaine Feinstein contends that in his reading of the 'more ambitious' writing then emerging from the American poetry scene, Hughes was able to find his own voice. She also reminds us that it was in America that Hughes 'achieved his first recognition'.[46] In his well-known introduction-cum-manifesto to his anthology *The New Poetry*, Al Alvarez implicitly aligns Hughes's work with exciting new American voices. Sagar accounts for the development in his writing from *The Hawk in the Rain* (1957) to his next book, *Lupercal* (1960), by suggesting that Hughes 'may have learned from the American poets he came to know in his years in America'.[47] In all of these cases, Plath forms the entrée, but it is the wider tradition which fuels his creativity.

The same might be said of Hughes's introduction to the nascent environmental movement in the United States, spearheaded by the publication in the *New Yorker* (of which Plath was an avid reader, and in which both published poetry) of Rachel Carson's 'The Sea Around Us', 'Under the Sea Wind' and 'Silent Spring'. In a 1958 letter, Hughes indicates that they had read the first two while in the United States (*LTH* 127) and in later correspondence with Tracy Brain confirms that they had read the last on its 1962 publication.[48] As recent work on Hughes's environmental concerns by Gifford has shown, this was to prove a lasting influence. His eco-consciousness is evident throughout his poetry and prose and in children's books such as *The Iron Man* and *The Iron Woman*, the first of which is, in Gifford's and Roberts's words, a 'reaction to the failure of children's literature he had read in America to reflect "the collision with the American technological world"'.[49]

Beyond Plath and Wevill

As this indicates, there are plentiful other lines of influence beyond the nexus of Plath and Wevill. In one of his interviews with Faas, Hughes explains: 'in the way of influences I imagine everything goes into the stew'.[50] Hughes himself credits the importance of his immediate family (his mother, who introduced him to folklore and was sensitive to the esoteric; his brother, Gerald, who instilled in him a love of nature; and his father, from whose war-time experience he learned vital lessons about the power of silence).[51] Extended family, too, supply sustenance; Uncle Walt, who features in *Elmet*, provides a valuable connection to community, family and self. Hughes's childhood move from Mytholmroyd to Mexborough proved similarly influential. For Feinstein, it was 'crucial to his development as a poet'.[52] In the 1961 'Two of a Kind' interview for the BBC, Hughes describes the significance of this move and the attendant loss of a childhood shared with countryside and animals. On moving to the town of Mexborough, he says, 'all that then was sealed off'. He emphatically reiterates the point: 'it really sealed off my first seven years' and again, 'it was sealed off in that particular way'. His metaphor is echoed in Plath's memoir of her childhood, 'Ocean 1212-W', written the following year, which concludes: 'My father died, we moved inland. Whereon those nine first years of my life sealed themselves off like a ship in a bottle – beautiful, inaccessible, obsolete, a fine, white flying myth'.[53]

There are also other literary palimpsests beyond the work of Plath and stretching further back than contemporary East European and American writers. Hughes cites Chaucer, Shakespeare, Marlowe, Blake, the Romantic poets, Hopkins, Yeats, Eliot, Lawrence and Dylan Thomas as important supply lines.[54] *Birthday Letters* reveals traces of the work of numerous other writers. Walt Whitman's elegy for President Lincoln, 'When Lilacs Last in the Dooryard Bloom'd', is echoed in 'A Pink Wool Knitted Dress'. Wilfred Owen's 'Strange Meeting' informs 'A Picture of Otto'. Coleridge's 'Frost at Midnight' is an important presence in 'Visit', where in places, for example in line two, Hughes even borrows his metre. 'Daffodils' and 'Perfect Light' write back to Plath's poem 'Among the Narcissi' but also suggest other sources, including Wordsworth, Christina Rossetti and Thomas Hood. 'The Literary Life' summons the presence of Plath and Marianne Moore (as Pollak has shown, the poem reflects on their anxious literary relationship) but also draws on a number of other intertexts including Elizabeth Bishop's 'Invitation to Miss Marianne Moore' and Philip Larkin's 'The Less Deceived', Yeats's 'The Stare's Nest by My Window' and Shakespeare's *King Henry VIII*.[55] In this way the relationship with Plath is con-textualized – placed alongside and inflected by other writers, other voices.

This, finally, is what Hughes's poetry reveals about the nature of influence. It is mutable and multifaceted, elusive and unreliable. In many of the poems of *Birthday Letters* we are witnesses to the failure of influence; Hughes's defence of his precious supply lines is not always successful. In poem after poem we are shown the difficulty of making and maintaining a meaningful connection. In 'The Rabbit Catcher', for example, the speaker cries out in frustration: 'I could not find you, or really hear you, / Let alone understand you.' In the end, it is this plangent silence which continues to haunt the poetry.

NOTES

1. 'Ted Hughes: The Art of Poetry LXXI', interview with Drue Heinz, *Paris Review* 134 (1995), p. 76. Various first- and second-person accounts of their first meeting exist. As well as Hughes's 1995 essay, Plath writes about it in a letter to her mother and in her *Journals*. See Sylvia Plath, *Letters Home: Correspondence 1950–1963*, ed. Aurelia Plath (London: Faber and Faber, 1976), pp. 219–21, and Sylvia Plath, *The Journals of Sylvia Plath, 1950–1962*, ed. Karen V. Kukil (London: Faber and Faber, 2000), pp. 210–12. Numerous biographers have revisited the scene, including Anne Stevenson, *Bitter Fame: A Life of Sylvia Plath* (Harmondsworth: Penguin, 1990); Elaine Feinstein, *Ted Hughes: The Life of a Poet* (London: Weidenfeld and Nicolson, 2001); and Diane Middlebrook, *Her Husband: Hughes and Plath – A Marriage* (London: Viking, 2003). Daniel Huws recalls it in his *Memories of Ted Hughes 1952–1963* (Nottingham: Five Leaves Publications, 2010).
2. Stephen Tabor, *Sylvia Plath: An Analytical Bibliography* (London: Mansell, 1987), p. 110.
3. Feinstein, *Life of a Poet*, pp. 38, 39.
4. Hughes, 'Art of Poetry', p. 76.
5. Plath, *Journals*, p. 211. See Middlebrook, *Her Husband*, pp. 18–19 for a reading of Plath's textual response to meeting Hughes.

6. Gayle Wurst, 'Words to "Patch the Havoc": The Imagination of Ted Hughes in the Poetry of Sylvia Plath', in Joanny Moulin (ed.), *Ted Hughes: Alternative Horizons* (London: Routledge, 2004).

7. Diane Middlebrook, 'The Poetry of Sylvia Plath and Ted Hughes: Call and Response', in Jo Gill (ed.), *The Cambridge Companion to Sylvia Plath* (Cambridge: Cambridge University Press, 2006), pp. 161–3.

8. Margaret Dickie Uroff, *Sylvia Plath and Ted Hughes* (Urbana and Chicago: University of Illinois Press, 1979), p. 38.

9. Tracy Brain, *The Other Sylvia Plath* (Harlow: Longman, 2001), pp. 167–8.

10. *Ibid.*, p. 203. See Susan Van Dyne, *Revising Life: Sylvia Plath's Ariel Poems* (Chapel Hill: University of North Carolina Press, 1993); Heather Clark, 'Tracking the Thought-Fox: Sylvia Plath's Revision of Ted Hughes', *Journal of Modern Literature* 28:2 (2005). See also Heather Clark, *The Grief of Influence: Sylvia Plath and Ted Hughes* (Oxford: Oxford University Press, 2011).

11. Stephen C. Enniss and Karen V. Kukil, *No Other Appetite: Sylvia Plath, Ted Hughes and the Blood Jet of Poetry* (New York: The Grolier Club, 2005), p. viii.

12. Terry Gifford, *Ted Hughes* (London: Routledge, 2009), p. 13.

13. Neil Roberts, 'The Common Text of Sylvia Plath and Ted Hughes', *Symbiosis* 7:1 (2003), p. 157.

14. Clark, 'Tracking', pp. 100–1.

15. Vivian R. Pollak, 'Moore, Plath, Hughes and "The Literary Life"', *American Literary History* 17:1 (2005), p. 112, n. 2.

16. Wurst, 'Words', p. 19.

17. 'Two of a Kind: Poets in Partnership', Ted Hughes and Sylvia Plath interviewed by Owen Leeming, BBC, recorded 18 January 1961, British Library National Sound Archive, NP7400WR C1. Also available in *Sylvia Plath (Spoken Word)*, audio CD (London: British Library, 2010).

18. Hughes, 'Art of Poetry', pp. 85–6.

19. Ekbert Faas, *Ted Hughes: The Unaccommodated Universe* (Santa Barbara: Black Sparrow Press, 1980), p. 203.

20. Raphaël Ingelbien, *Misreading England: Poetry and Nationhood Since the Second World War* (Amsterdam and New York: Rodopi, 2002), p. 142.

21. Paul Bentley, *The Poetry of Ted Hughes: Language, Illusion and Beyond* (Harlow: Longman, 1998), p. 27; Ted Hughes, 'Notes on the Chronological Order of Sylvia Plath's Poems', *Tri-Quarterly* 7 (1966).

22. Terry Gifford and Neil Roberts, *Ted Hughes: A Critical Study* (London: Faber and Faber, 1981), p. 22.

23. Hughes, 'Notes on the Chronological Order', p. 88.

24. For an extended reading of these metaphors see Jo Gill, '"Your Story, My Story": Confessional Writing and the Case of *Birthday Letters*', in Jo Gill (ed.), *Modern Confessional Writing: New Critical Essays* (London: Routledge, 2006), pp. 67–83.

25. Sylvia Plath, *Collected Poems*, ed. Ted Hughes (London: Faber and Faber, 1981), p. 203. Future references to Plath's poetry quote this source and are identified by the abbreviation *SPCP* followed by the page number.

26. Sylvia Plath, *Johnny Panic and the Bible of Dreams* (London: Faber and Faber, 1979), pp. 226, 240, 106.

27. Middlebrook, *Her Husband*, p. 81.

28. See Jacqueline Rose, *The Haunting of Sylvia Plath* (London: Virago, 1991), for a discussion of these and related issues.

29. TH to Keith Sagar, 17 November 1997, Add. 78760 f. 199, British Library. For more on the background to *Birthday Letters* see, among others, *LTH* 703ff., and Erica Wagner, *Ariel's Gift: Ted Hughes, Sylvia Plath and the Story of Birthday Letters* (London: Faber and Faber, 2000), pp. 1–31.

30. For more on the background to *Capriccio* see Carol Bere, 'Complicated with Old Ghosts: The Assia Poems', in Moulin, *Alternative Horizons*, pp. 29–37. Poems from all three books are now included in *CP*.

31. Robert Potts, 'Well Versed', *Guardian* (27 November 1998), p. 44; Al Alvarez, 'Ted Hughes', in Nick Gammage (ed.), *The Epic Poise: A Celebration of Ted Hughes* (London: Faber and Faber, 1999), pp. 210–11; Ted Hughes, 'Last Letter', *New Statesman* (11 October 2010), pp. 42–4.

32. Peter Davison, 'Dear Sylvia', *Boston Globe* (8 February 1999), p. G1.

33. Middlebrook, 'Call and Response', p. 163.

34. See Wagner, *Ariel's Gift*, for a poem-by-poem commentary on *Birthday Letters*.

35. Plath, *Johnny Panic*, p. 94.

36. See Leonard M. Scigaj, 'The Deterministic Ghost in the Machine of *Birthday Letters*' in Moulin, *Alternative Horizons*, pp. 1–15.

37. For a reading of astrological and occult codes in *Birthday Letters* see Ann Skea, 'Poetry and Magic', in Moulin, *Alternative Horizons*, pp. 57–66, and Neil Spencer, 'Stargazer Laureate', in *Observer Life Magazine* (1 February 1998), p. 43.

38. See Bere, 'Complicated with Old Ghosts', pp. 33–4, for an explanation of these figures.

39. See Lynda K. Bundtzen, 'Mourning Eurydice: Ted Hughes as Orpheus in *Birthday Letters*', *Journal of Modern Literature* 23 (2000), pp. 455–69 for a reading of this motif.

40. Gifford and Roberts, *A Critical Study*, p. 25.

41. Yehuda Koren and Eilat Negev, *A Lover of Unreason: The Life and Tragic Death of Assia Wevill* (London: Robson Books, 2006), pp. 165 ff.; Gifford, *Ted Hughes*, p. 88.

42. Sean O'Brien, *The Deregulated Muse* (Newcastle upon Tyne: Bloodaxe, 1998), p. 36.

43. Hughes, 'Art of Poetry', p. 77.

44. *Ibid.*, p. 85.

45. Faas, *The Unaccommodated Universe*, pp. 210–11.

46. Feinstein, *Life of a Poet*, p. 76.

47. Keith Sagar, *The Art of Ted Hughes*, 2nd edn (Cambridge University Press, 1980), p. 37.

48. Brain, *The Other Sylvia Plath*, p. 86.

49. Gifford and Roberts, *A Critical Study*, pp. 44–5.

50. Faas, *The Unaccommodated Universe*, p. 202.

51. Hughes, 'Art of Poetry', p. 59.

52. Feinstein, *Life of a Poet*, p. 13.

53. Plath, *Johnny Panic*, p. 124.

54. Hughes, 'Art of Poetry', pp. 60, 73; Faas, *The Unaccommodated Universe*, p. 202.

55. Paul Muldoon, *The End of the Poem: Oxford Lectures on Poetry* (London: Faber and Faber, 2006), pp. 36–43.

5

RAND BRANDES

The anthropologist's uses of myth

There is only one poem in the 1972 Faber and Faber revised edition of *Crow: From the Life and Songs of the Crow*, the edition used for the *Collected Poems*, that has never been collected in a US edition: 'Crowcolour'. The 1972 Faber edition 'Publisher's Note' states: 'This new edition of *Crow* contains seven new poems which did not appear in the original edition. They are: ...'[1] Since all seven of the new poems had appeared in the 1971 first American edition, the note gives the impression that the only difference between the 1970 Faber first edition and the 1972 augmented Faber are the new poems. The note does not mention that one poem, 'Crowcolour', was deleted from the 1970 Faber first edition before the seven new poems were added to the American edition.

Crow poems were appearing regularly in American magazines in the late 1960s and early 1970s, and 'Crowcolour' was one of them, published on its own on 14 November 1970 in the *New Yorker*, its first and last US appearance. The poem is so understated, slipped between the monumental twins of 'Crow Improvises' and 'Crow's Battle Fury' in *Crow*, that one would not notice its disappearance. 'Crowcolour' also has the fewest words of any poem in the Faber first edition – thirty-three ('Glimpse' has thirty-four). So, simply in terms of length, impact and narrative importance, the decision to exorcise 'Crowcolour' makes sense. However, there are several possible non-literary reasons for 'Crowcolour's' disappearance, the most obvious of which are political, as suggested by the heart of the poem, which reads: 'He was as much blacker / Than any negro / As a negro's eye-pupil' (CP 243).

Even though the 'negro' of 'Crowcolour' was a quasi-acceptable term of the period in the US, here it stands in for 'African' or even 'aboriginal'. The analogy between Crow's blackness and the 'negro' was for Hughes a positive one, built upon the connection between Crow's primal powers and that of the uncivilized, and thus unfallen, negro. Readers, especially race-sensitive American ones, would have found the analogy reductive or even racist, especially when juxtaposed to 'coloured' resonating in 'colour'. Somewhere

67

during the editing process for the first American edition, Hughes must have seen, or been made aware of, his own blindness in the 'eye-pupil' of the poem. But this tiny example is indicative of the much larger challenges faced by Hughes and his work as a result of his belief in, and use of, myth and its magical and mystical precepts gleaned from anthropology.

Crow, while being a truly innovative poetic work, was riding on a new wave of world poetry. Songs, stories and sacred poems that had been part of ancient oral traditions were appearing everywhere transcribed and translated. Along with these songs came the myths and rituals that had been buried in the notes of anthropologists and ethnographers. The Otherness of the world was suddenly made manifest and offered a spiritual alternative to the chaos and confusion of the 1950s, 1960s and eventually 1970s. The non-Western mythic past, and the indigenous peoples that were still connected to it through their dances and trances, dreams and drugs, singers and shamans, were the new Adams and Eves in Paradise. By the time Hughes had published *Crow*, he had internalized this primitivist worldview, or 'batty syncreticism' as one reviewer called it, through his immersion in anthropological works and their mythic manifestations.[2] Hughes does not employ a premeditated 'mythic method'. In sharp contrast, what makes Hughes's myths so powerful is their intense spontaneity. Hughes does with anthropology, as Yeats argues the poet must do with philosophy: learn everything and then forget it when writing. 'Crowcolour' highlights the limitations and liabilities of the mythic – limitations Hughes encountered in the two other mythic works of his middle period, *Gaudete* and *Cave Birds*.

Ted Hughes knew from the very beginning that the vast array of myths, symbols and magical arts that he absorbed from anthropological sources from around the world would define his work and defy his audience. He enhanced these anthropological sources over time by adding a full range of materials from the occult sciences and esoteric philosophies he found in poets like W. B. Yeats and Robert Graves in addition to the depth psychology of Carl Jung and Mircea Eliade's work on comparative religion. The typically ancient and often non-Western sources that these writers mined shaped what he wrote, how he wrote and, most importantly, why he wrote. Hughes, as mythic poet, wrote to liberate and to heal – the soul, the body, the mind, the community and the world. It would be the shaman and his mythic quest that served as the primary paradigm and sacred script for the poet as healer and liberator.[3]

Myth is the language of crisis, and for Hughes myth expressed a spiritual condition not just a psychological state. In this way, mythic poetry serves the same function as religion, as Hughes asserts in a letter to Bishop Ross Hook: 'Poetry is forever trying to do the work of religion – as local "healers" are perpetually setting up as an alternative to orthodox Medicine. Some very great poets have come near formulating what was, pretty well, an alternative religion – a new religion. It's the shaman streak in the poetic temperament' (*LTH* 460–1) When fully realized, myth can operate in the public, political sphere as a liberation theology by first liberating the individual, and then society, through the power of the poems. When Hughes switched his course of study at Cambridge from English to Anthropology he did so because he had experienced what he believed was the shaman's call, the most dramatic manifestation of which appeared to him in a waking dream (*LTH* 422).[4] Supernatural forces had intervened, and Hughes was willing to sacrifice mass-appeal and easy access for the spiritual rewards and poetic powers he hoped to acquire from his sacred quest. Hughes fought self-doubt and constant criticism to fulfil his commitment to his art and life through the healing powers of myth in conjunction with the occult arts. Of all of his work, *Crow* (1970), *Gaudete* (1977) and *Cave Birds* (1978) most powerfully document these struggles as the poet explores the cosmos, community and self through myths, mysticism and magic in search of truths that will heal – if the reader and society are ready and willing to be healed through poetry.

Collected in various groupings and formats, and published sequentially in trade editions at the mid-point of his writing life, the poems of *Crow*, *Gaudete* and *Cave Birds* tell the same story. In fact, they are the same story – the story of crisis, death and resurrection. The story is told from book to book from three different perspectives in three slightly different voices with three different but connected endings in which the hero achieves the final goal of full Jungian individuation and self-actualization with varying degrees of success. Like a mandala comprised of three concentric circles, the field of action of each book becomes more focused as one moves from *Crow*'s cosmos and creation myths, to *Gaudete*'s cultural critique and country comedy, and on to *Cave Birds*' individual and wholly internalized psychic drama. It is a world of sacred performance designed to make things happen, to restore and free. However, for the healing to take place, the poet/healer must create a dynamic space outside of – that is, removed from – contemporary England as reflected in Crow's outsider's view, *Gaudete*'s Ireland or *Cave Birds*' Egypt.

As noted in relation to 'Crowcolour', the mythic, not to mention the mythomagical, is open to challenges from many (theoretical) quarters, especially when used by a white, middle-class male from England writing at the end of the twentieth century. This intensified as Hughes's life imploded and became fodder for gossip columns and tabloids. In contrast to the charges faced by Hughes, the mythic, when originating from postcolonial, indigenous, displaced or marginalized peoples, benefits from the permissions given to, or earned by, authentic expression often rooted in a bloody present or pure past. For instance, contrast Ted Hughes's use of 'negro' with Langston Hughes's use of the word in 'The Negro Speaks of Rivers'. Furthermore, the mythic shares many of the same modes of experience and expression as magic realism, the fantastic, the surreal and the visionary. Literary works that draw upon these modes, however, are not typically subject to the same rules of engagement applied to writers like Hughes, who, whether justified or not, represent the empire even when ironically trying to subvert it. One can quickly compile a list of responses critical of Hughes's poetry, and especially *Crow*, *Gaudete* and *Cave Birds*. These responses can be grouped under the headings of history, consciousness, culture and gender.

Some critics have argued that the mythic dimension of Hughes's work, especially when combined with primitivism, ignores reality and the efficacy of history.[5] Even though the myths come out of history and can stay rooted in history, as in anthropology, the mythic transcends history when considered by thinkers like Jung and Eliade. Jung and Eliade lived through modern history's bloodiest years, so it is not surprising that both developed epistemologies that not only denied history's ability to shape our lives and destinies, but also obliterated it. Jung's and Eliade's theories are fundamentally anti-historical. In addition, Hughes as nature poet and neo-Romantic believed that we must live like Nietzsche's beast of the fields, 'unhistorically', if we are to reconnect with nature and live wholly in the world.[6] Hughes stakes out his position on history in relation to the mythic when speaking of Yeats: 'His mythology is history, pretty well, and his history is as he said "the story of a soul".'[7]

Myth is the translation of ritual (dance and drama) into song and story that comes from and leads to a heightened awareness and an altered state of consciousness. The highly symbolic language of myth is similar to the language of dreams, and thus evokes a separate reality. In the mythic this is a spiritual reality with a logic and location of its own. For many, therefore, the mythic is delusional, self-indulgent and escapist. Furthermore, it can be argued that Hughes's appropriation of non-Western and primitive mythic materials, including the shaman and his quest, ignores the cultural conditions that produced them. His use of these sources is reductive at best, relying on essentializing stereotypes, and exploitative at worst by dealing in the often eroticized exotic, often colonial, past. Critics assert that the mythic, in addition to being trans-historical and trans-cultural, is inherently elitist – privileging the individual experience outside of the political realities of community, class and economic conditions. These critiques were not just being aimed at Hughes by literary critics, but also at the entire 'counter-cultural' movement of the 1960s by anthropologists like Marvin Harris, who wrote in 1974 in *Cows, Pigs, Wars, and Witches*:

In the lifestyle of the counter-culture, feelings, spontaneity, imagination are good; science, logic, objectivity are bad. Its members boast of fleeing 'objectivity' as if from a place inhabited by plagues . . . A central aspect of counter-culture is the belief that consciousness controls history. People are what goes on in their minds; to make them better, all you have to do is give them better ideas. Objective conditions count for little.[8]

Harris continues:

Counter-culture celebrates the supposedly natural life of primitive peoples. Its members wear beads, headbands, body paint, and colourful tattered clothing; they yearn to be a tribe. They seem to believe that tribal peoples are nonmaterialistic, spontaneous, and reverently in touch with occult sources of enchantment.

In the anthropology of counter-culture, primitive consciousness is epitomized by the shaman, a figure who has light and power but never pays electric bills. Shamans are admired because they are adept at 'cultivating exotic states of awareness' and at roving 'among the hidden powers of the universe'. The shaman possesses superconsciousness.[9]

Hughes did not accept blindly the principles of the counter-culture; he was a student of history and in touch with the objective realities of his time. Nonetheless, many of Harris's charges echo those of reviewers and critics distrusting Hughes's mythic vision.

In addition to being trans-historical and trans-cultural, the mythic is trans-gender, operating in the same way in men and women. This last transgression is at the heart of Hughes's mythic sensibility as a result of his preoccupation with the Goddess, which was heavily influenced by Graves and Jung among others. The Goddess is the total embodiment from Hughes's perspective of the (pro)creative, harmonizing and unifying feminine principle. Some critics argue that there is a serious dishonest, even destructive, disconnect between Hughes's worship of a mythic feminine principle and the realities of Hughes's life and the women in them.[10] Where Hughes sees female power, they see submission; where Hughes sees female beauty, they see objectification; where he sees female religious authority they see a patronizing patriarchy; where he sees the sacred female, they see diminution of the Other. Finally from a rough psychological reading of Hughes's work, they argue that what he sees as an absolutely necessary painful pursuit of the Goddess they see as projections of (sado)masochism and guilt. To these critics the ironies are obvious and the apparent hypocrisy disturbing. Hughes believed that mythic poetry served the same function as religion in the way that it gives passionate access to deeper truths and higher realities. The sacred feminine principle informing the most important of his mythic sources reaffirmed his commitment to the Goddess and her archetypes. So, in the end, given all of his options, Hughes put his faith in myth and the mythic quest. Thus *Crow*, *Gaudete* and *Cave Birds* stand at the nadir and nexus and nucleus of Hughes's poetic being.

That *Crow*, the words on the page, the pages between the covers, the covers between our hands, exists at all makes it the most hopeful and promising of all of Hughes's mythic works. For myths to heal they must, like modern mandalas, be spontaneous responses to personal crises. As Jung writes:

> The fact that images of this kind have under certain circumstances a considerable therapeutic effect on their authors is empirically proved and also readily understandable, in that they often represent very bold attempts to see and put together apparently irreconcilable opposites and bridge over apparently hopeless splits. Even the mere attempt in this direction usually has a healing effect, but only when done spontaneously. Nothing can be expected from an artificial repetition or a deliberate imitation of such images.[11]

There is a sense throughout *Crow* that everything is provisional, that everything may fail at any moment. Even after we read the last poem, 'Little Blood', there is a sense of disbelief that the poet has actually made it through, that the triage has worked. If the poet as shaman, and Crow as the shaman's spirit guide and avatar, can survive Crow's world, there is hope:

> She has come amorous it is all she has come for
> If there had been no hope she would not have come
> And there would have been no crying in the city
> (There would have been no city)   (*CP* 237)

If Hughes had stayed 'in hell' with Crow and not published *Crow* there would be no *Gaudete*, no *Cave Birds*, nor any of the books that followed.[12] What *Crow* truly conquers is silence and the inarticulation of being – the weapons of depression and despair.

Crisis is the catalyst for much of Hughes's work, and *Crow* is a response to both personal and public crisis. 'My whole writing career sometimes presents itself to me as a search for not one style in particular, but the style for this crisis or that' (*LTH* 629). The first personal crisis, Sylvia Plath's suicide, provoked Hughes's friend the American artist Leonard Baskin to involve the poet in a project based upon images of crows; the second, the deaths of Hughes's partner Assia Wevill and her daughter, Shura, ended the *Crow* project. The public crisis described above required a radical myth – a myth Hughes constructed out of historical, philosophical and religious fragments. *Crow* establishes all of the pre-existing conditions and preoccupations of Hughes as mythic poet. Crow destroys Platonic philosophy and eats logic for breakfast. Crow deconstructs Christianity and tears the Bible apart. God, Adam, Eve and the Snake are like puppets in a play. Lear lingers in the wings as the Reformation drives men crazy and Mary is tied to the maypole where she is burned alive. Hughes's Crow disdains the heartless pursuit of science and the carnival of consumerism and its detritus. Civilization and culture are okay if they are in touch with nature and the passionate lives of people. Myths and folklore from outside the empire and removed in time are particularly effective remedies to the daily news and TV. Among many others, African, Aboriginal, Asiatic, Indian, Native American and Celtic sacred stories, songs and symbols work their magic in *Crow*. Anything from anywhere and anytime, outside the forces and events that produced the modern Western world and consciousness, has the potential to heal. Hughes used every trick in the shaman's book to counter these crises through the mythic.

While there are many mini-crises throughout the book, the main ones are encapsulated in 'Crow's Account of the Battle', where 'Theorems wrenched men in two' and

> Reality was giving its lesson,
> Its mishmash of scripture and physics,
> With here, brains in hands, for example,
> And there, legs in a treetop.   (CP 222)

Theorems, scripture and physics lead the self away from the instincts that make us healthy and whole. They separate us from divine creation and our natural spiritual needs. Over time and in isolation they produce a desensitized and fragmented self and society capable of unimaginable atrocities. Hughes's position does not unquestioningly celebrate the irrational, and is not exclusively anti-Christian: 'I identified, you see, the sacrificed God, the divine self which has to die to come into life, with the whole animal & vegetable kingdom, which culture tortures and destroys' (*LTH* 580). He looks through history for confirmation of his diagnosis:

> This had happened too often before
> And was going to happen too often in future
> And happened too easily   (CP 223)

The healing truths in myth offered modern people a way out of the endgame where 'The demolition is total / Except for two strange items remaining in the flames – / Two survivors, moving in the flames blindly. // Mutations – at home in nuclear glare' (*CP* 212). In contrast to, and perhaps as a response to, the Armageddon blast of many of the *Crow* poems, the volume ends with a prayer, the last lines of which are whispered in an underbreath: 'Grown so wise grown so terrible / Sucking death's mouldy tits. // Sit on my finger, sing in my ear, O littleblood' (*CP* 258). The labyrinth of the outer mandala has reached its end as has the shaman's flight through Crow's otherworld guided by the 'spiritual consciousness' embedded in myths.[13]

As one finds hope in the hopelessness of *Crow*, one finds hopelessness in the hope of *Gaudete*. To make *Crow* work on the page Hughes had to suppress his linguistic energies. In *Gaudete* these energies fill the narrative with some of Hughes's most fertile tropes and dynamic images. Despite the poetic accomplishments of the book, *Gaudete* fails in the same way that Lumb fails as a saviour/messiah. *Gaudete*, especially when compared to *Crow* or *Cave Birds*, is by far one of Hughes's most under-realized works, and he knew it. Part of the problem is that the book began as a film script; this explains the highly visual aspects of the writing and the episodic but fast-paced plot. Anyone who believes that Hughes was blind to the practical limits of his mythic perspective and the shaman's quest just needs to read *Gaudete*. As Hughes says of the working subtitle of the book: 'The subtitle of the book has always been "An English Idyll" – but the irony of that seemed a bit precious' (*LTH* 377). Hughes was always aware of the ironies of the utopian impulse that informs his desire to heal and liberate, and he knew that transformative change at the social, public level takes time and resources.[14] Lumb's failed attempts to revitalize the community take on a farcical feel, with elements of the mock-heroic and Shakespearean parody. More than likely, the Prologue and main narrative will be relegated to the realm of minor works, as their absence from the *Collected Poems* implies; but the 'Epilogue' poems will join some of Hughes's finest works.

With Lumb's death the possibility of personal and social regeneration through ritual and a return to nature dies as well. England, and by extension the entire Western world, is beyond hope with one notable exception – Ireland. Hughes's obsession with folklore began at an early age with the myths and legends of Ireland.[15] After meeting Plath and while writing *Crow*, *Gaudete* and *Cave Birds*, Hughes spent a significant time in Ireland, which became his spiritual home since 'Ireland has an inner space – which England almost wholly lacks. To my feeling, Ireland is a bit like muslim countries' (*LTH* 615). As with the source myths in *Crow*, Hughes imagines a site outside the empire that is more in tune with and open to the 'nameless female deity' (*G* 9). The association of Ireland with Muslim countries (informed by Hughes's fascination with dervish dancers in Persia) explains why a whirling Irish dervish-like figure with the 'face of a tinker' guides Lumb to the opening ritual: 'A flapping shape – A wild figure gyrating toward him. / A flailing-armed chimpanzee creature' (*G* 13). The juxtaposition, and even conflation, of 'tinker' and 'chimpanzee' pops on the racist radar like 'negro' in 'Crowcolour'. Again, Hughes would see both references as positive and pointing to the wildness of the world outside the empire and modern civilization itself, as represented by the 'tenth century anchorite in the West of Ireland' that closes the book (*LTH* 385).

Hughes refers to the 'Epilogue' poems as 'vacanas', which come out of the Hindu oral tradition of mystical song and devotional poetry (*LTH* 634). The blending of Eastern and Western religious traditions is typical of Hughes's approach to myth, so the vacanas share the mystical language and surreal imagery of all sacred praise poetry, Indian and Irish. The shaman and the guru and the starry-eyed Irish saint whirl with the dervish down the *via negativa* towards the dark enlightenment and rebirth. Since the Irish anchorite is the one who transcribes the poems in the 'Epilogue', the poems may also be seen as 'glosses' in the margins of *Gaudete* and of the mind. Glosses grace the margins of many ancient Irish texts capturing the inner and outer spiritual journeys of the scribe. The 'Epilogue' poems trace Lumb's renegotiations with the Goddess he has failed. In the spirit of the mystical tradition, most vacanas begin with a question; consequently, the first 'Epilogue' poem begins: 'What will you make of half a man ... How will you correct / The veteran of negatives / And the survivor of cease?' (*CP* 357). As with most religious parables and mystical journeys the answer is hidden in the question. The poems look back to *Crow* in their compression and improvised fragmentation, and forward to *Cave Birds* in their piety and promise. The poems drift through space forming clusters, but never constellations. Everywhere in the poems is the cutting edge of leaf, the scraped-out skull, the destruction of creation, the defamation of the spirit and the longing to be healed and in harmony with the world.

This is the world of myth, the world of every time and everywhere with few specific historical cultural references. It is a 'Horrible world', and yet the poem continues 'Where I let in again – / As if for the first time – / The untouched joy' (*CP* 371). This is the joy of *Gaudete*'s 'rejoice': intoxicating, not ironic. The poetic lift is real as the pilgrim joins the ecstatic holy men drinking the divine wine, and the divine wine drinks them: 'Like a bunch of grapes. // Now I am being drunk / By a singing drunkard' (*CP* 370). Given the myriad of violent images of death and rebirth, this one flows from a more celebratory mystical tradition. The 'Epilogue's' closing poems point to a fuller recognition of the Goddess followed by redemption and rebirth. The drunkard begins to dance, a freedom Hughes has not allowed his suffering, searching shamans the freedom to do until now: 'And maybe he dances and sings // Because you kissed him' (*CP* 374).

The sacred oak that opens *Gaudete* as Lumb's soulmate reappears in the 'Epilogue's' final two poems. 'Your tree – your oak' blends the poems' prehistoric Celtic content with Christian imagery of the main narrative with its 'Agony in the garden. Annunciation.' The tree is 'A guard, a dancer / At the pure well of leaf' (*CP* 374). The dancing imagery continues: 'Waist-deep, the black oak is dancing' (*CP* 375). The surreal image of the dancing tree follows the symbolic trajectory of the mystical experience. This is the language of dreams and is consistent with Hughes's mythic vision. Like the shamans who ride their magical steeds of wood to the otherworld, 'The oak is flying / Astride the earth' (CP 375). The oak is the Goddess's tree, which helps make sense of the sexual suggestions of 'astride'. The merging of male and female principles suggests that Lumb's failures have been forgiven and that a balance has been temporarily restored. The 'half a man' of the 'Epilogue's' first poem is now healed and whole as a result of his mystical meditations, deaths and rebirths. One of these closes the book: 'So you have come and gone again / With my skin' (CP 375). The purged pelt is all that remains of the animal self and is all that is left after the encounter with the divine. The reader, too, closes the book of prayers, not sure what just happened, what these strange songs mean, but knowing that it was important to Lumb and Hughes and that 'what they meant' is not the right question, but 'what they did'. The purgatorial experience of *Gaudete* prepares the poet, shaman, healer, for the consummate death and rebirth in *Cave Birds*. However, *Cave Birds* has a mystic centre hidden at its core.

Like *Crow*, *Cave Birds* was inspired by a series of primitive-looking bird images by Leonard Baskin. *Cave Birds* first appeared as a limited folio edition of ten poems published in 1975; opening the over-sized edition was like unsealing a sarcophagus. Hughes added nineteen poems and the subtitle, *An Alchemical Cave Drama*, to the 1978 trade edition. Hughes's bibliographers argue of the trade edition that 'This edition is so expanded and revised from the limited edition as to constitute in effect a new work.'[16] The significant differences between the two editions are not just the number of poems and the instructive narrative suggested by the sub-title. There is also a major shift of emphasis from the purification process, the journey to the underworld and the death of ego that ends in a lightness of being in the folio poems, to the rebirth and resurrection of a powerful masculine self in the trade edition. The original impulse of the poems is more muliebral in the limited folio edition, which ends with 'The Good Angel', than the macho trade edition ending with 'The Risen'. The major differences can be seen by comparing 'Walking Bare' and 'The Risen'. 'Walking Bare' immediately precedes 'The Good Angel' in the folio *Cave Birds*. 'The Risen' immediately follows 'The Good Angel' in the trade edition.

Both *Cave Birds* editions draw upon the sacred and magical cave paintings of prehistoric people and the hieroglyphs of ancient Egypt in Baskin's images. Hughes's working sub-title for the book was 'The Death of Socrates and His Resurrection in Egypt'; however he cancelled it because it was too 'curious-good' (*LTH* 395). While there are suggestions of many archetypal journeys to the underworld from Virgil to Dante to Milton to D. H. Lawrence's poem

'Ship of Death', Hughes concentrates on the narrative and symbolic content of Egyptian mythology and the mystical operations of alchemy in addition to completing this phase of the shaman's quest at the mandala's centre. For Hughes, Socrates represents the *overly* logical, abstract, ethereal man that has lost contact, like most of the Western world, with his intuitive, emotional and natural self. Egypt, ancient Egypt, represents the Other, the sensual, magical, ceremonial and feminine life in touch with the rhythms of nature and forces of the otherworld.

From a postcolonial perspective, Hughes engages in the colonial process of feminizing colonial nations and cultures. He looks back to the mythological remains and not the historical realities of Egypt. The trade edition's central poem, 'Bride and groom lie hidden for three days' has a setting suggestive of Egypt, with Isis as the bride and the Socratic hero as groom. Hughes has offered an interpretation of the poem: 'So the marriage is (a) the ritual reassembly of the shattered fragments of his total being (b) his reunion with his lost "life" – with the divine renewing healing life of his natural being (his "bride"), and (c) the conception or begetting of his "rebirth"' (*LTH* 618–19). The inverted commas suggest that these terms are subjective and not exactly objective. So, the bride is not really his 'bride' but his 'natural being'. There is really only the female half of the male character's 'natural being'. At the most critical moment in the drama the female presence is absent. In fact one could argue that there are no female actors (even the healers) in the drama of *Cave Birds*, just projections of the male hero's 'natural life'. At the moment of the alchemical wedding's reconciliation of opposites and unification of tensions, when the suffering abstracted male ego and logos seek completion in the sacred sensuality of Isis, if there is a feminine presence it is ultimately without agency. The bride, as subaltern, is left behind after the ritual consummation, and only the groom continues on to be 'resurrected' in Egypt as the hawk-headed sun god Horus. Instead of representing the healed and balanced hero, hiding in Horus is the insecure and over-inflated male ego – it is he who has risen and not the fully unified self.

In stark contrast to the powerful presence of the 'The Risen', which seems to suggest a fully actualized self at the mandala's centre so far from the fragmented Crow, 'Walking Bare' suggests an alternative centre – a mystical centre – the self truly healed and free from the insanities of the wounded ego and delusions of an artificial life. The bird of 'The Risen' is huge and all-powerful – 'He stands, filling the doorway / In the shell of earth' (*CP* 439). The poem is rife with allusion – Christ rising from the tomb; Janus standing at the doorway; the burning bush of Moses; the 'World Egg' – and ends with the alchemist at his furnace. Changing base metals to gold, the alchemist, 'In the wind-fondled crucible of his splendour / The dirt becomes God'. Following

Hughes's line of thought, the hero of 'The Risen' represents the fully actualized and integrated man. However, like Faust, Hughes overreaches here; the
apotheosis reflects a fundamental flaw in the mythology. The alchemist's
goal, going all the way back to the inception of alchemy in ancient Egypt,
was to become one with God, not to become God. The Egyptian god of
alchemy was Thoth, the scribe of the gods (inventor of writing) and, most
importantly, the Ibis-headed god of equilibrium who weighed the hearts of
the dead to determine if they were to be admitted to the paradise of the
underworld.

In 'Walking Bare', the purged soul passes into the underworld stripped of
everything and at peace, waiting for Thoth to pronounce his verdict: 'What is
left is just what my life bought me / The gem of myself. / A bare uncertainty,
without confection' (CP 436). The mineral imagery of 'gem' reflects the
elemental nature of the transformation made possible through the alchemical
fires of the 'blowtorch'. The self is perfectly balanced on Thoth's scales, 'I rest
just at my weight', with 'just' alluding to 'justice' and 'justified'. The poem's
emphasis is on the insubstantial: 'Lightness beyond lightness releasing me
further'. This is the final emptying of the self and the gravity of the ego: 'A one
gravity keeps touching me'. The closing two couplets attest to the healing and
liberating power of the centreless centre:

> For I am the appointed planet
> Extinct in an emptiness
>
> But a spark in the inhalation
> Of the corolla that sweeps me.   (CP 437)

Like D. H. Lawrence's 'Not I, not I, but the wind that blows through me',[17]
these lines assert their power through the total relinquishing of the power of
presence and authority: 'extinct', or a mere 'spark'. The sacred is selfless.

In the trade edition, 'Walking Bare' is followed by three more poems: 'Bride
and groom lie hidden for three days', 'The Owl Flower', and 'The Risen', plus
the 'Finale'. In the folio edition, 'The Owl Flower' is the only poem that
follows 'Walking Bare', leaving the reader with a more gracious, fluid and
subdued closing than 'The Risen' – perhaps ultimately too soft for Hughes.
'The Owl Flower' reminds us of how far the shaman has come in Cave Birds
in terms of self-healing and hope. The resurgence of life in the flush and rush
of the poem represents the rebirth and resurrection of the purged and
balanced self at one with the world: 'Wet with nectar / The dead one stirs'
(CP 439).

While there are many ironies in the book, the one noted in the 'Finale' – that
the healing is temporary and will have to be repeated – is unavoidable. The
reality for Hughes is that the vast majority of people will never follow the

shaman, manifest in the poet or holy man, and never know the biblical 'peace that passeth understanding' as we walk bare through the world. It all depends on trusting the Goddess, the feminine principle, and getting back in touch (if we ever were) with nature and our natural wholeness. Hughes believed that hearing the right stories at the right time and reading the right poems in the right place could heal us and motivate us to do the right thing. Following the labyrinthine narrative from the outer circle in *Crow*, down through *Gaudete* and into *Cave Birds*, shows us one way to survive the crazy world. The mythic is an Other mode of being and a means by which Hughes taps the elemental powers of primordial places and people. Hughes uses myth, the myths of peoples outside the empire and often outside the modern Western world, to construct creative psychic spaces and places that super-charge his imagination. Myth gives Hughes spontaneous access to creative spaces he could not otherwise reach; it should shock the reader's imagination and start the healing process, allowing them to break through to the other side. Myth was the strongest medicine Hughes could find, and it worked for him. Temporarily healed, he would head back into history, culture and nature in *Remains of Elmet* and the later poems.

NOTES

1. Ted Hughes, *Crow* (London: Faber and Faber, 1972), p. 11.
2. *LTH* 614. This phrase appears in a note citing Tom Paulin's review of *SGCB* in the *London Review of Books* (9 April 1992). Many of the reviews critical of the book echoed Paulin's critique, which essentially summarized the general concerns of Hughes's use of myth as a way of understanding history. Some reviewers were not as accommodating as Paulin. See Terry Eagleton's 'Will and Ted's Bogus Journey', *Guardian* (2 April 1992).
3. See Hughes's comments on W. B. Yeats as a poet/shaman liberator in *WP* 270–3.
4. See also 'The Burnt Fox' in *WP* 8–9.
5. For example, Sean O'Brien, *The Deregulated Muse* (Newcastle upon Tyne: Bloodaxe, 1998), p. 37.
6. Friedrich Nietzsche, 'On the Uses and Disadvantages of History for Life', in *Untimely Meditations*, trans. R. J. Hollingdale (Cambridge: Cambridge University Press), 1983.
7. Ted Hughes, quoted in Ekbert Faas, *Ted Hughes: The Unaccommodated Universe* (Santa Barbara: Black Sparrow Press, 1980), p. 204.
8. Marvin Harris, *Cows, Pigs, Wars, and Witches: The Riddles of Culture* (New York: Vintage, 1974), p. 245.
9. *Ibid.*, p. 245.
10. Most notably Jacqueline Rose in her book *The Haunting of Sylvia Plath* (London: Virago, 1991).
11. C. G. Jung, *Mandala Symbolism* (Princeton: Princeton University Press, 1972), p. 5.
12. Hughes says he left Crow in hell when the project was aborted, *LTH* 297.

13. *LTH* 581.
14. See *LTH* 383.
15. See *WP* 6–7.
16. Keith Sagar and Stephen Tabor, *Ted Hughes: A Bibliography 1946–1995*, 2nd edn (London: Mansell, 1998), p. 79.
17. D. H. Lawrence, 'Song of a Man Who Has Come Through', *The Complete Poems of D. H. Lawrence* (New York: Penguin, 1962), p. 250.

6

TERRY GIFFORD

Hughes's social ecology

In Chapter 2 Paul Bentley argues that part of the shock of Hughes's first two books arose from his conception of 'nature' as what Bentley calls 'social and even political'. In Chapter 3 Chen Hong shows how Hughes's early animal poems were actually offered as challenges to human nature. By the time of *Remains of Elmet* (1979) Hughes had come to regard human culture as nature – industry, farms and people not only embedded in nature in the Calder Valley of West Yorkshire, but suffering the same processes of growth and decay: mill chimneys 'flower' before 'they must fall into the only future, into earth' (*CP* 457); over the generations mill workers become 'four-cornered, stony' as the local stone, itself 'conscripted / Into mills' (*CP* 463); scattered moorland settlements decay as 'the fragments / Of the broken circle of the hills / Drift apart' (*CP* 485). What is striking is that culture is so deeply embedded in nature that nature can also be represented as culture. Beyond the separations of simile, there is also metaphor working both ways: 'the silence of ant-warfare on pine needles / is like the silence of clogs over cobbles' (*CP* 456); the sky is a millstone 'Grinding the skin off earth' (*CP* 474). A natural silence is like the historical absence of workers' clogs, but also, just as mill chimneys 'flower', weather slowly grinds the earth's skin off. What is left of that skin are the fragments of gritstone outcrops that, in the final lines of the poem 'Heptonstall', can stand for both nature and the fragments of half-abandoned villages. Both outcrops and villages 'drift apart' in a geological timescale that changes circles of geography and history in a completely natural cyclical process.

Of course, also embedded within the covers of *Remains of Elmet* are references to Hughes's family – Hughes and his older brother Gerald in 'Two', his mother in 'The Angel', his Uncle Walt in the untitled epigraph poem and his father in all the references to memories of the First World War. His mother's extended family, together with Hughes's first wife Sylvia Plath, are all there in 'Heptonstall Cemetery'. These are the remains of what was the initial impulse for the book as an autobiography, as Hughes explained to Fay

Godwin, which stalled because 'nothing connected' (*LTH* 378). I remember Fay Godwin telling me, when *Remains of Elmet* had long been out of print, that Hughes was determined to persuade Faber to reprint it, which they eventually did in a form that was closer to his initial desire for a celebration of his family's strong connections to place, if not exactly as a localized poetic autobiography as in his original conception. This later book, *Elmet* (1994), is a much more peopled publication which was partly made possible by the deaths of family members. (Hughes avoided writing about named living people.) It includes the story of 'Walt' in the First World War, pinned down by a sniper in a shell-hole, who spent a day in his imagination on a long circular walk linking the villages and beauty spots between Mytholmroyd and Hebden Bridge: 'All that day he lay. He went walks' (*CP* 770). The local dialect form of 'went walks' is part of the intimacy of this shared landscape: in the poem his uncle is telling the poet this story at an actual location – 'I got this far'. When Walt then looks up to towards the skyline, 'towards all that was left', as the poet puts it in the final line, it is as though in some way a responsibility – for the story and for the landscape – has been passed on, 'left' now to the poet in 'all' its layers of nature and culture, geology and history, moors and memories. In many ways, four years before his death, Hughes was fulfilling that responsibility in *Elmet*.

For Hughes, nature and culture are not only interlinked but indistinguishable in this landscape. An understanding of nature in the Calder Valley requires a sensitivity to its particularly local forms of perception, appropriation and communication. Similarly, an understanding of culture around this moor-rimmed valley requires an awareness of how it has been shaped by weather and geology. A sense of such an intimate, symbiotic relationship is fundamental to an appreciation of Hughes's poetic responsibility for an ecology that enfolds both human culture and more-than-human nature, what might be called, borrowing a term from the American social theorist Murray Bookchin, 'social ecology'.[1] Bookchin argued that there is a 'deep-seated continuity between nature and society',[2] that to exclude humans from a conception of nature was to reduce the usefulness of the term 'nature', and that the localized modes of social interaction with nature formed a localized construction of nature. This is precisely what is being poetically explored in Hughes's work following the embodied and deeply symbolic marriage of humans and nature in the poem at the crux of *Cave Birds* (1978), 'Bride and groom lie hidden for three days', discussed by Rand Brandes in Chapter 5.

Although the poem 'Walt' was included in *Elmet*, it had appeared five years earlier in the collection *Wolfwatching* (1989) as the first part of a two-part poem of the same title.[3] Published ten years after *Remains of Elmet*, and at a time when it must have seemed unlikely that this book would be reprinted, *Wolfwatching* contains eight poems out of its twenty-one that would be included in what was to become *Elmet*, most of them the poems about Hughes's family members that would ingrain nature in *Elmet* with cultural memory. What these poems do to *Wolfwatching* is to complicate its central concern with environmental responsibility with what ecocritics now call 'environmental justice' – the idea that environmental issues are also social issues, just as issues of human rights are often implicated in concerns about exploitation of natural 'resources'.[4] Much nineteenth-century literature, for example, can now be read as linking environmental health with human spiritual, mental and physical health.

So what is it that links 'Walt' with 'Wolfwatching', the First World War with a caged wolf, the degradation of both humans and nature and their potential resilience? Hughes appeared to be asking the same question when he suggested that readers of *Wolfwatching* ask, 'why consult just these familiars at just this time?'[5] Concern for familial and environmental loss seems to be the answer. The title poem is four pages of outrage at the spirit and knowledge lost in a young wolf in London Zoo whose eyes are 'like doorframes in a desert / Between nothing and nothing' (CP 757). This poem is preceded by one about the emptiness of Hughes's father's life returning from the First World War and is followed by 'Telegraph Wires' which carry 'the tones / That empty human bones' (CP 757). Similarly 'The Black Rhino', which is accompanied by a long note about its decline and the poem's role in raising funds for protection, is preceded by 'Anthem for Doomed Youth' and followed by a poem about his mother collecting 'Leaf Mould', weeping 'for her girlhood and the fallen'. The poet in her womb came to mourn, in his turn, for 'Paradise and its fable' located in that place of his childhood (CP 768). This poem is followed by the third protest at the human treatment of nature and carries the name of a famous racehorse: 'Manchester Skytrain'. What begins as a reminiscence about gambling, draws attention to the breeding of 'a top-heavy, twangling half ton / On the stilts of an insect' to be kept in stables that are 'asylums / Of these blue-blooded insane' (CP 769). This poem is followed by 'Walt', thus maintaining the collection's pattern of intertwining and juxtaposing concerns for human and more-than-human nature that exemplifies Hughes's social ecology.

This culminates in a poem of environmental justice that sees the treatment of mining communities and their environment following the 1984/5 miners' strike as parallel to that of the Native Americans 'On the Reservations' as the poem's title has it. Here Hughes is engaging with the environment around Mexborough, South Yorkshire, to which his family moved when he was eight. In a letter to the French scholar Joanny Moulin, Hughes explained that the dedicatee of this poem, Jack Brown, is an ex-collier, who lives in Barnsley (centre of the coal-belt – the 'reservations' in which the unemployed colliers now find themselves imprisoned). The whole poem was a belated response to various requests for me to write something about the Miner's Strike and the resulting destruction of the Coal Mining Industry in the North of England (the watershed of the River Don in South Yorkshire) – where I went to school (most of my schoolfriends were sons and daughters of colliers). Jack Brown became an active Labour campaigner. A very talented writer himself – but not much published. Because of an unfortunate thing in our social history, the 'industrial masses' in England feel themselves to be a slightly different nation from those who employ and govern them. Different in education, privileges, expectations, allegiances. And those who employ and govern them also tend to regard them as such – a different nation. The unexploded bomb in British society ... The epigraphs from the Americas are there merely to touch my overall metaphor (that the whole population of unemployed miners was dealt with as the US Govt dealt with tribes) into context. The colliers literally demanded 'work' – for themselves and as they said 'their sons': the tribes refused to do any 'work', ever. The colliers didn't know what to do with doing nothing – the rich, large-scale, sophisticated spiritual life of the tribes was cultivated out of 'doing nothing'. Dreaming.[6]

The strength of feeling expressed here at the mistreatment of the miners by Mrs Thatcher's government is every bit as strong as that against the treatment of animals in the three poems earlier in the collection. The reference to the location of the South Yorkshire coalfield as a 'watershed' is not only typical of Hughes's way of thinking about place as nature (with rivers to the fore of his consciousness), but emphasizes, as does *Elmet*, that human lives are formed by, and dependent upon, place: social history is natural history; environmental ecology is social ecology. The pollution of the rivers of Hughes's childhood – first the Calder in West Yorkshire and then the Don in South Yorkshire – reflects, literally, an industrialist society's stance towards both nature and people. New evidence reveals that a concern for both people and rivers underpinned the apparently celebratory poetry of the collection *River* (1983) which was largely concerned with the rivers of Hughes's third and final home in Devon.[7]

In the same year as the publication of *River* Hughes contributed to a book titled *West Country Fly Fishing* (1983) an overview of the history of the fishery on two Devon rivers, the Taw and the Torridge. Although Hughes is celebratory in this essay, of sea trout night fishing, for example – 'the least touch can be anything from half a pound to seven or eight – which is the difference between a swallow and a tiger ... This ... leaks an especially high-quality adrenalin into the blood – which is no doubt the drug we are hooked on'[8] – Hughes moves towards an account of the dramatic decline of the trout and salmon fishery in these rivers. An indication that the subtext of this essay was really about water quality is revealed in a section of a letter to Keith Sagar omitted from *LTH*:

> Did you see my piece in *West Country Fly Fishing*? . . . The hoteliers on the two rivers are friends of one sort or another. So the essay is an attempt to glorify the rivers while suppressing the knowledge that they are going down the drain. Even twenty years ago they produced 1/3 of all salmon in the West Country. Last year only 43 salmon were caught on the Torridge. (It used to be a thousand to 1500.) It's become a farm sewer.[9]

This last phrase gives a hint of a little-known practical and political concern that underlies the poetry of *River*.

In his Introduction to his selection of Hughes's essays, *Winter Pollen* (1994), William Scammell attempts to anticipate criticism of certain intellectual positions repeatedly taken by Hughes in these essays and reviews. Scammell identifies two contentious assumptions commonly found in *Winter Pollen*:

> The tendency to equate civilization with repression, for example, and reason with rationalization, might be countered by quoting Chekhov's observation that there is more love for humanity in electricity and a hygienic water supply than in any amount of spiritual breast-beating.　　　　　(*WP* xiii)

Scammell's reference to water quality here touches upon a concern Hughes expresses elsewhere in *Winter Pollen* in a 1970 review of Max Nicholson's book *The Environmental Revolution*, in which Hughes cites, as an example of the need for the public to pressure for government intervention, 'the industrial poisoning of the water-systems in and around England' (*WP* 131). As it happens, from the 1980s onwards Hughes himself was very active in a campaign for 'a hygienic water supply' in the south-west of England, writing a reasoned campaign statement for a public enquiry and helping to found a pressure-group that has expanded into a national research and monitoring organization concerned with water quality in the nation's rivers. Whatever general tendencies Hughes observed in the uses of reason in the culture, he certainly supported his lyrical celebration of the life of rivers in his poetry with carefully reasoned discourse in his activism that was based upon reading the latest scientific evidence available. We can now see how, in Hughes's life, science informed the art, and reasoned discourse attempted to influence public policy in a manner that might provide a model for our times.

Hughes was named Poet Laureate in the year following the publication of *River*. At least two Hughes scholars believed that this collection was the height of the poet's achievement at the time they wrote their books on his work.[10] In his second book on the work of Hughes Leonard M. Scigaj wrote: '*River* will one day be recognised as one of the central literary masterpieces of the world; it should be required reading for all humans on our planet to help them attain responsible adulthood.'[11] More recently Keith Sagar has argued that *River*, the ninth major collection, is the apotheosis of Hughes's poetic career, the only collection to finally achieve Blake's four-fold vision.[12]

The iconic figure of that relationship in *River* was the most primitive – the fisherman hunter, but in his most self-conscious twentieth-century mode, as the poet himself. Just as fishing had always been a part of Hughes's life, so too had a river. Although the two rivers of his childhood – the Calder, then the Don – were so polluted that they contained few fish, as a child Hughes fished in the canal alongside the River Calder ('big, but rare trout') and in an oxbow lake beside the River Don until the first silage made in the area killed all the fish (*TB* 184). In Devon, where the poet lived for most of his adult life, Hughes's town, North Tawton, takes its name from the River Taw, one of the rivers flowing from Dartmoor that he wrote about for *West Country Fly Fishing* and that also appears in *River*. Hughes's belief in the symbolic value of a river as a 'vein' in the life of the 'sea-spirit' that regulates our globe had already been established in the poem 'December River' in *Season Songs* (1976). So the *River* collection was, for Hughes, about more than simply his most intimately known part of our environment.[13] It was also about a key indicator of the state of our relationship with it. Hughes's sense of social ecology came to be focused on the issue of water quality and its implications for human responsibility for all the life – human and non-human – that depended upon it.

When I asked Ted Hughes to tell me the story of his 'greening' as a poet he linked his reading of an article about marine pollution in the journal *The Nation* in 1959 when he was in America, and then Rachel Carson's exposure of the damage done by pesticides, *Silent Spring* (1962), with his experience of the rivers of his childhood: 'So my greening began you could say with everything that lay about me in my infancy.'[14] The plight of the fish in those rivers of his childhood, as much as in those of his adult life, is, Hughes explained, an unrecognized indicator of human self-destructiveness. In an interview Hughes said:

> Most people I talk to seem to defend or rationalise the pollution of water. They think you're defending fish or insects or flowers. But the effects on otters and so on are indicators of what's happening to *us*. It isn't a problem of looking after the birds and bees, but of how to ferry human beings through the next century. The danger is multiplied through each generation. We don't really know what bomb has already been planted in the human system.[15]

For Ted Hughes, his poems about rivers and fish are also clearly about the links between water quality and public health. What has not been known by readers and critics of his poetry, and of *River* in particular, is the extent to which this ecstatic poetry was informed by practical political action on behalf of the rivers in the south-west of England. The Hughes archives in Britain and America can reveal the link between the poet's activities in a range of discourses for a variety of forms of intervention concerned with water quality and health for all its dependants.

The first poem Hughes offered as Poet Laureate was about the rivers of Devon and appeared under the title, 'Rain-Charm for the Duchy, A Blessed, Devout Drench for the Christening of His Royal Highness Prince Harry'. In fact, this poem had originally been intended for the *River* collection.[16] The poet's unpublished correspondence reveals that there was actually an environmental agenda behind this poem and that the poem had some effect on local politicians:

'Surprising what effect the Poet Laureate label has,' Hughes wrote to Keith Sagar.

> The line [in 'Rain-Charm for the Duchy'] about the pollution (quite mild and domestic) of the Okement caused great agitation in Okehampton (responsible for the refuse) – might even affect the Council's laissez faire. These are the perks.
>   Pity I didn't leave in the lines about the Torridge – they were
>   'And the Torridge, that hospital sluice of all the doctored and scabby farms from Welcombe to Hatherlea to Torrington
>   Poor, bleached leper in her pit, stirring her rags, praying that this at last is the kiss of the miracle,
>   That soon she'll be plunging under her sprays, splitting her lazar crust, new-born,
>   A washed cherub etc'
>   But I thought it might seem in poor taste.[17]

Of course, Hughes was a well-known fisherman, so his concern for water quality in rivers is understandable at a personal level. But a closer look at what Hughes actually argued reveals a more complicated concern for all water users. In a long letter to *The Times* in 1985 his concern had been for the effects upon 'the employment and economy of their home rivers' of the 77,000 returning salmon caught by the Northumbrian driftnet fishery.[18] Hughes wrote a letter to me in answer to my enquiry about his justification for fishing (*LTH* 658–60),[19] but in a letter to me written the previous day that is marked 'unsent' in the Emory University archive Hughes points out that it is the fishermen, rather than the water authorities, who are most active in their concern: 'All the river renovation down here has been initiated by fishermen – I mean the actual cleaning of waterways. At least, in the early nineteen eighties it was – before it became politically OK. (And in fact, the political r[e]sistance was unbelievable – to a degree still is).'[20]

The documents in the archives reveal an impressive commitment of time and thought in attending committee meetings, site visits, reading scientific reports (with titles like 'The effects of surfactants in the Rivers Exe and Creedy')[21] and writing in various modes – letters, notes, speeches, satirical poems for campaigning colleagues – that go beyond the poet's concern for water quality as a fisherman. Indeed, despite the economic significance of the riparian business in the south-west of England, Hughes realized that perceived self-interest in a 'hobby' would undermine any arguments concerning water quality brought forward by riparian interests. In a letter to *Trout and Salmon* in July 1998 Hughes charted the history of campaigns for improved water quality in Devon's rivers since the early 1980s, including the 1983–5 Bideford estuary campaign, in which he took a leading role, but noted that 'a river that is nothing but a fishery has a poor prognosis'. 'Larger, social – in other words political – issues' had to be engaged by the riparian industry, he wrote. In the archive there is a long note headed: 'A NEW NAME FOR RIPARIAN ASSOCIATIONS' which indicates the intensity of Hughes's thinking about political strategy in the water politics of Devon. He has obviously been stung by the fact that

> a big chief of the Water Company attending the Taw AGM ... made the comment; it's wonderful to see what lengths a lot of old buffers will go to for their private hobby ... meaning 'elitist hobby, pursued by rich snobs who want to keep the fishing to themselves'. We are stuck with an image problem ... the bad effects are seen every time the Riparians try to defend the Sportsfishery against some damage [... and] have great difficulty getting their case taken seriously.

Hughes suggests 'Taw Fishery Cooperative' before continuing,

> Suddenly the cider works at Winkleigh wouldn't be occasionally brushing off its nose end the fly-like thought of the Taw Riparian Association – that amiable gang of 'silly old buffers'. It would suddenly be contemplating the idea of a group of businessmen intent on developing ... a multi-million pound business of immense benefit to the whole of North Devon [... and] everybody else would be in a different frame of mind.[22]

So it is significant that when I began researching Hughes's environmental political activity Carol Hughes drew my attention to her husband's being instrumental in founding the Westcountry Rivers Trust.[23] What had begun with Hughes's involvement with the Torridge Action Group, formed in 1983 to tackle a specific issue, led to his proposing the formation of the Westcountry Rivers Trust with Ian Cook in 1993. This was the first River Trust in England which was instrumental in eventually forming, with thirty other Rivers Trusts, the national water watchdog organization, the Association of Rivers Trusts.

In the Emory archive are a holograph draft and a typed copy of plans for legal action against the South West Water Authority, which is accused of having 'failed in its statutory duty to improve and maintain the fishery'. The notes begin, 'A crisis committee has been formed to explore the possibilities of Legal Action in defence of the Rod Fishery of the River Torridge.'[24] This is followed by eight and a half pages of holograph notes charting the decline of the Torridge fishery from the 1920s to 1984. The Torridge Action Group was formed to call for a public enquiry about the implications for the estuary and rivers that would follow from the particularly inadequate 'fine screening' sewage works proposed for Bideford that would still discharge sewage into the estuary, but below the town. In this it was successful, and Hughes was asked to represent the Action Group by making a representation to the enquiry in September 1985, the text of which is in the Emory archive. Hughes summarized the concerns of the Torridge Action Group in a letter to Keith Sagar in 1984:

> I've been involved in a local battle, of sorts, over Bideford Sewage system. The Water Authority, mightily leaned on by local building interests, are putting in a type of sewage system that merely screens the sewage (takes out 20% 'solids' – mostly cardboard, plastic etc ... 1600 new houses go in immediately.[25]

But a year later the depth of his involvement as he prepared for the enquiry was telling on Hughes as he wrote to Sagar:

> I made the mistake of becoming too involved in the battle over the River Torridge – fairly pointless. The battle is between the Water Authority and the Riparian Owners and fishermen. The Riparian Owners have lost collectively the best part of three million pounds and Albion will probably lose its run of salmon in the Torridge. But the whole business is perhaps mostly busyness and lies. I'm quite sick of it, but I don't see quite how to extricate myself.[26]

Fortunately he didn't extricate himself and he made a brilliant speech at the inquiry, of which Bideford campaigner Monica Pennington says, 'You could hear a pin drop and there were no questions. It was clear that he'd done his homework. But the fine screening plant was approved by the Inspector after the enquiry.'[27] But although this campaign failed,[28] for social ecologists the significance of Hughes's speech is that it expresses as much a concern for the health of local people and tourists as it does for the salmon population, drawing on a range of scientific evidence from both the human and the fish research into the consequences of raw sewage being discharged into the Torridge estuary that, according to Hughes's research, 'takes 12 days to change itself completely'. An indication of the concern for the effects on the human population can be seen from this part of Hughes's presentation to the enquiry:

> A local doctor has been heard to say that of all the holidaymakers who stay here for a few days canoeing and windsurfing and using the estuary for similar sports, 75% contract an ailment that needs treatment. [Nine doctors from the Wooda Surgery in the Bideford area had expressed their concern with the present situation.] Bideford Chemists prepare for the tourist season as if for a campaign. The chemist in Mill St displays a window sign, advertising his cure for diarrhoea. And in spite of their conditioning the local population does not escape. In general, they complain of an endless grumbling epidemic of throat and chest complaints and stomach disorders. In the 1984 tourist season 200,000 visited Bideford . . . The effect of the estuary's pollution on the state of mind of the local residents, is subjective and elusive. However, this depression is very real. Local people can feel in their bones that the whole situation is depressing . . . And this depression accumulates. But it can be picked up quite quickly. You do not have to be a superclean German or American to decide, after one good look at the sludge, that the Torridge Estuary is no place for a holiday.[29]

Here is a poet and storyteller presenting vivid, detailed and elusive material as evidence at a public enquiry in a mode of writing that was not formerly known to be part of his discourse. Yet the self-inflicted human ailments recorded here – transmitted by water, but also symptomatic of human pollution of earth and sky – surface in the poem 'If' that was later included in the *River* section of *Three Books* (1993): 'If you have infected the sky and the earth / Caught its disease off you – you are the virus.' The poem's final line catches the inescapable ecological pervasiveness of human water pollution: 'Already you are your ditch, and there you drink' (CP 740).

Ten years later, following Hughes's realization that a new name and a wider remit was needed, a press release dated 2 June 1995 for the formation of the Westcountry Rivers Trust states its aims more generally as 'concern about pressures on natural water resource' in the west of England and it intends to meet its aims through a broad range of activities, including education – 'the trust has already acquired an area of suitable river, allowing free access and fishing to children'. Ted Hughes was a founding trustee.[30] Of course, one of Hughes's most powerful and educational interventions on behalf of water quality and public health was the children's story *The Iron Woman* (1993). In a letter to his editor at Faber and Faber Hughes wrote, 'We could send John Major a gold-backed copy. Present all the chieftains with one, maybe ... And all the cabinet.'[31] In 1992 Hughes was a very visible supporter of Ian Cook's court case against South West Water for their failure to regulate water quality on a stretch of the River Creedy in Devon which Cook owned. The foam on the river, which had a sewage works upstream, was likened by Judge Cox to 'the face of a beautiful woman scarred by disease' (the presence of a poet in court obviously improving judicial language). Hughes was quoted as saying outside the courtroom, 'It's an important case, an historical case because it's reactivated the power of common law in this terrific issue of water quality in rivers.'[32] South West Water contributed £5,000 for a research grant for the Institute of Freshwater Ecology to investigate the effect of the detergents on the River Exe. This led to the alarming discovery that chemicals in the river were changing the sexual characteristics of fish, with dangerous implications for human health.[33] Here was another example of practical involvement, active concern, bringing about changes to river quality that would be unknown to readers of *River*.

The view of science expressed by Hughes in his 1976 essay 'Myth and Education' was that scientific objectivity excludes ethical and subjective aspects of experience to the extent of holding 'the human element' in contempt: 'The prevailing philosophies and political ideologies of our time subscribe to this contempt, with nearly a religious fanaticism, just as science itself does' (*WP* 146). Whilst this has clearly been true for the scientific development of pesticides that led to Rachel Carson's writing *Silent Spring*, for example, when Hughes needs to inform himself about what he calls 'the chemistry of the Torridge Estuary'[34] it is to the latest available objective science that he turns, as we all must today to reduce our various forms of pollution. Effective activism from a figure such as Hughes requires a wide range of discourses to raise questions about the variety of experiences for which we need to take responsibility in making our informed environmental choices. The dualities that have contributed to the development of the environmental crisis – separations of ways of knowing and communicating such as science and humanities, activism and art, speech-making and poetry – can now be seen to have been brought together in the reconnective practice of Hughes's social ecology.

The poet's obsession with rivers, which began beside the Calder and the Don and matured beside the Taw and the Torridge, took him to Iceland with his son in 1979, and to Alaska in 1980, where Nicholas eventually worked as a fish biologist. In the Alaska poem 'That Morning', with which Hughes concluded the later *Three Books* version of *River*, looking down on parallel lines of salmon reminds him of looking up in South Yorkshire during the war at a sky 'hung with the drumming drift of Lancasters' on their way to bomb the cities of Germany (*CP* 663). In one of his most ecstatic poems of ecological integration, which celebrates fishing beside bears, among lupins and salmon 'hung in the cupped hands of mountains / made of tingling atoms', where all is so 'alive in the river of light', Hughes begins by evoking human self-destruction and ends by standing 'among the creatures of light, creatures of light': 'So we found the end of our journey', father and son, poet and scientist, social ecologist and scientific ecologist (*CP* 664). It is in poems such as this that Hughes's imagination enacts, as he says of the imagination of each new child, 'nature's chance to correct culture's error' (*WP* 149).

NOTES

1. Murray Bookchin, *The Philosophy of Social Ecology: Essays on Dialectical Naturalism* (Montreal: Black Rose Books, 1990; 2nd edn 1995).
2. Murray Bookchin, *The Modern Crisis* (Montreal: Black Rose Books, 1987), p. 59.
3. Some of the material on *Wolfwatching* in this chapter appeared in an earlier form in Terry Gifford, 'The Ecology of Ted Hughes: *Wolfwatching* – The Final Poetic Statement', in Ronald Schuchard (ed.), *Fixed Stars Govern a Life* (Atlanta: Emory University, the Academic Exchange, 2006), pp. 37–45.
4. See Joni Adamson, Mei Mei Evans and Rachel Stein, *The Environmental Justice Reader: Politics, Poetics, and Pedagogy* (Tucson: University of Arizona Press, 2001).
5. *The Poetry Book Society Bulletin* 142 (Autumn 1989), p. 3.
6. TH to Joanny Moulin, 6 April 1995, Mss 644, Box 54, ff. 3, Emory.
7. Some of the material on *River* in this chapter appeared in an earlier form in Terry Gifford, 'Rivers and Water Quality in the Work of Brian Clarke and Ted Hughes', *Concentric* (Taiwan) 34:1 (March 2008), pp. 75–91.
8. Anne Voss Bark (ed.), *West Country Fly Fishing* (London: Batsford, 1983), p. 36.
9. 14 December 1983, Add 78757, f. 139, BL.
10. Craig Robinson, *Ted Hughes as Shepherd of Being* (London: Macmillan, 1989), p. 205; Leonard M. Scigaj, *The Poetry of Ted Hughes* (University of Iowa Press, 1986), p. 290. For a discussion of Robinson and Scigaj's critical comments on *River* see Terry Gifford, *Green Voices: Understanding Contemporary Nature Poetry* (Manchester: University of Manchester Press, 1995; 2011), pp. 133–5.
11. Leonard M. Scagij, *Ted Hughes* (Boston: Twayne, 1991), p. 133.
12. Keith Sagar, *Ted Hughes and Nature: 'Terror and Exultation'* (www.keithsagar.co.uk, 2009), p. 53.
13. It is significant that the bulk of Hughes's one-page will, written in his own hand, is taken up with the detail of distributing his ashes, 'scattered on Dartmoor at a point between the sources of the River Taw and the East Okement – a point selected by Ian Cooke [sic] of Weircliffe, Exeter. If a point roughly equidistant to the sources of the Teign, the Dart, the Taw and the East Okement can be found, that would be ideal.' Copy of Hughes's will kindly supplied by Ian Cook, 3 October 2006.
14. Gifford, *Green Voices*, p. 132.
15. Blake Morrison, 'Man of Mettle', *Independent on Sunday* (5 September 1993), pp. 32–4.
16. TH to Keith Sagar, 21 January 1985, Add. 78757, f. 150, BL.

17. *Ibid.*
18. *The Times* (13 August 1985).
19. See also Terry Gifford, '"Go Fishing": An Ecocentric or Egocentric Imperative?', in Joanny Moulin (ed.), *Lire Ted Hughes: New Selected Poems 1957–1994* (Paris: Editions du Temps, 1999), pp. 145–56.
20. 15 January 1994, Mss 644, Box 54, ff. 2, Emory.
21. W. A. House, 1 March 1993, published by the Institute of Freshwater Ecology, Natural Environment Research Council.
22. 16 June 1993, Mss 644, Box 54, ff. 1, Emory.
23. Letter to T. G., 10 September 2005.
24. Mss 644, Box 166, ff. 1, Emory.
25. 9 March 1984, Add. 78757, f. 143, BL.
26. 7 June 1985, Add. 78757, f. 152, BL.
27. Interview with Monica Pennington, 9 July 2009. See also Ed Douglas, 'Portrait of a poet as eco warrior', *Observer* (4 November 2007), Review section, pp. 10–11.
28. Although it was built, the system was ultimately adapted to discharge Bideford's sewage, not in the estuary, but in the sea off Westward Ho! Interview with Monica Pennington, 9 July 2009.
29. Mss 644, Box 170, ff. 1, Emory.
30. The recently retired Chair of WRT, Michael Martin, writes: '[Ted] was a huge support to me both intellectually and emotionally as we struggled to put W.R.T. together.' Letter to T. G., 9 August 2006.
31. 26 January 1993, Mss 644, Box 54, ff. 1, Emory.
32. *Guardian* (16 April 1992).
33. 'Ted and I were convinced that there was an unusually high level of industrial detergent being discharged. We were right and both Ted and I met with Professor John Sumpter of Brunel University who was conducting experiments with oestrogen mimicking chemicals that were suspected of feminising fish in rivers. Male fish were developing female characteristics [with] implications for human development especially in foetal development.' (Letter from Ian Cook to T. G., 9 August 2006.) In 1994 Ian Cook helped publicize this research which linked discharges in the Dart to cancer clusters in the human population of the Torbay area (*Observer*, 21 August 1994).
34. Mss 644, Box 168, ff. 7, Emory.

7

TRACY BRAIN

Hughes and feminism

To couple Ted Hughes's name with feminism may seem surprising. As Nathalie Anderson says, 'That a chill exists separating Ted Hughes from the feminist community . . . scarcely needs documenting.'[1] Largely, this arises from controversies concerning Sylvia Plath's life[2] and work.[3] Hughes explains in a letter to his son Nicholas, 'The incessant interference of the feminists and everything to do with your mother's public fame made it impossible for me . . . everything I did was examined so minutely . . . I thought, let the feminists do what they like . . . let your mother's Academic armies of support demolish me' (*LTH* 712–13).[4]

Despite the tensions between them, feminism and Ted Hughes share powerful concerns about relationships between men and women. Both explore the politics and negotiations – particularly domestic – of how men and women live together. Through a male view and sensibility, Hughes explores 'feminist ideas without labelling them as such'.[5] He is interested in female creativity, though this is rooted in assumptions about naturalness as well as archetypal masculine fears of women. I want to pick my way through all of this to explore what a sympathetic feminist reading of Hughes's poems reveals.

Can Hughes only create positive portrayals of women when they embrace traditional, biologically rooted, feminine roles? When at work, the protagonist of 'Secretary' 'hurries among men, ducking, peeping'. She darns and cooks 'For father and brother'. The implication is that she would be happier doing this instead for a husband and children. The evidence for this is in her aversion to social, emotional and sexual contact, 'Hiding her lovely eyes until day break', and causing the poem's male speaker to think that she would 'shriek' and 'weep' if he touched her (*CP* 25). Hughes provides a sensitive critique of a male world where women occupy an uneasy place, and lose some crucial part of themselves as a result. There is a suggestion that there is a reciprocal loss – of the woman herself – to the poem's speaker.

In 'Emily Brontë' the female persona's commitment to her poems – here reflected in the moorland landscape with its Romantic isolation – replaces social and sexual life. Emily Brontë's lover can only be the 'wind' whose 'kiss would was fatal'. Her baby can only be the 'stream' that 'bit her breast' instead of suckling there. Her pregnancy can only be the 'curlew' that 'trod in her womb' or a 'stone' that 'swelled under her heart' (CP 485–6). 'Secretary' and 'Emily Brontë' differ in tone, but, like the mathematician in Plath's 'Two Sisters of Persephone', the personae go 'graveward with flesh laid waste, / Worm-husbanded, yet no woman'.[6] These poems explore the difficulties women have in functioning outside the home as creative beings, rather than anticipating the later backlash in which 'Feminism came to mean denigrated motherhood, pursuing selfish goals and wearing a suit.'[7]

'Witches' is concerned with the disappearance of magic from a world dominated by a 'science' and 'Small psychology'. While mysterious and uncontrollable female power is fearsome, 'Witches' mourns its loss, wondering if women's witchery will resurface, or even if it is still in their possession, unknown to them and dangerously hidden: 'who's to know / Where their feet dance while their heads sleep?' (CP 80) This last line – spoken from a first-person-plural male viewpoint, expresses a mixture of hope and trepidation that such inexplicable power and creativity still exist.

Deeply influenced by Robert Graves's *The White Goddess*, Hughes thought that to resist biological archetypes of male and female behaviour was to deny nature. He says of Peter Redgrove's and Penelope Shuttle's *The Wise Wound*, 'What it opens to women (libbers or not) is ... the kingdom where they rule by right of their sex ... the very thing they have been persuaded to relinquish, the very thing they most intimately know ... is after all pure gold – with historical, physiological proof' (LTH 392). To Hughes, creativity – and this could take many forms – was equally the sphere of men and women, and essential to the nature of both.[8] The poems concern themselves with impediments to its expression, and stem from a feminist question: 'Has there ever been a revolution that restored a goddess religion – or ... didn't move from "irrational dependant mystery" toward "rational masculine autonomy"?'[9]

Like many of Plath's poems, Hughes's 'Lines to a Newborn Baby' explores what women 'most intimately know', in this case breastfeeding. Plath gives us, 'I stumble from bed, cow-heavy and floral ... Your mouth opens clean as a cat's'.[10] Hughes gives us, 'your mother's milk already / Toughens you and prepares you' (CP 96). The poem admires the good of what breastfeeding does, its special female power.[11] A later poem, 'The Womb', is influenced by Plath's iconography of the reproductive female body, confirming her proto-feminist belief that this subject matter should be central to poetry. The poem's conceit, with its 'Dreaming rituals of moon-religions', is of the reproductive organs: the 'still empty' uterus; the 'dark tree' and 'dark world / Hanging' on it, with its 'bud of hunger' and 'flower', that evoke ovaries and ovum and fallopian tubes. The opening lines, 'The Womb / Ponders / In its dark tree', echo those of Plath's 'Childless Woman': 'The womb / Rattles its pod, the moon / Discharges itself from the tree with nowhere to go'.[12] So does its sympathy for infertility; the 'salty drops of pain' (CP 580) mean there is no baby, and suggest both tears and menstrual blood.

'Creation of Fishes' in *River* expresses reservations about the force of women's reproductive drives. Here, the female moon tricks the male sun into drowning their children, the stars. Thereby she gains custody of them all each night as their children can no longer live out of water, near the sun's intense heat. The poem allegorizes the male fear of a woman's compulsion to have children and the deviousness she will exercise to get them, as well as anxieties about being deprived of paternal contact: 'He fished up his quickest, youngest daughter . . . She died in his fingers. // Flaring, his children fled through the river glooms. // Fingers dripping, the Sun wept in heaven. // Smiling, the Moon hid' (CP 656). 'Sketch of a Goddess' from *Flowers and Insects* allegorizes a similar fear. An iris flower doubles as a woman whose sexual and reproductive drives are all-consuming and deadly: 'She's lolling her tongue right out . . . Her uterus everted – // An overpowered bee buries its face / In the very beard of her ovaries. // It deafens itself / In a dreadful belly-cry – just out of human hearing' (CP 722).

In *Tales from Ovid* 'Venus and Adonis (and Atalanta)' seems full of imaginative compassion for a woman who must give birth without being able to move or scream. Is the poem feminist in its sympathetic sensibility, or voyeuristic in its detailed observation of what she endures? Obsessed with her father, Myrrha tricks him into sleeping with her and becomes pregnant. Her transformation into a tree is described as a violent rape: 'The earth gripped both her ankles as she prayed. / Roots forced from beneath her toenails'. The assault continues: 'The gnarling crust has coffined her swollen womb. // It swarms over her breasts'. Unable to speak or move, 'she weeps, // The warm drops ooze from her rind' (CP 953).

This rivals *The Bell Jar*'s depiction of nightmarish childbirth, characterized by the woman's immobility and inability to communicate pain.[13] 'Myrrha's cramps are clamped in the heart-wood's vice. / Her gagged convulsions cannot leak a murmur . . . // The trunk erupts, the bark splits, and there tumbles // Out into the world with a shattering yell / The baby Adonis. . . . They wash him // With his mother's tears' (CP 954). The only sound Adonis makes is this 'shattering yell', as if on behalf of his voiceless mother. Otherwise, he listens silently to Venus's tale, then ignores its lesson and is killed by the boar: 'dagger tusks in under his crotch / Then ploughed him with all its strength as if unearthing / A tough tree's roots' (CP 963). It is circular: the tree from which Adonis is born foreshadows his 'death-agony'; his suffering recalls Myrrha's. Mother and son are punished violently for failing the objects of their love.[14] There is a sort of democratic equality in the consequences visited upon men and women both here.

Such equality of consequences operates in other poems that explore the possibility of reciprocity between men and women, and in Hughes's arguably feminist revisions of the story of the fall. Blame is not Eve's alone in 'Apple Tragedy'. Enflamed by the fruit that Hughes wittily turns to cider, each character acts out his or her own vice: the serpent's for mischief and pleasure (he 'had a good drink / And curled up into a questionmark'), Adam's for 'rage' (CP 250) and violence, Eve's for sex and lies. Hughes revisits the fall in 'Genesis of Evil'. Eve's original sin becomes an enchanting thing that mesmerizes Adam: storytelling itself. She tells her stories each night like Shaharazad, so 'Adam could hardly wait' for the 'next instalment / Of the snake's bloody love-thriller / From Eve's lovely lips' (CP 268). What the serpent, and the fruit, teach Eve, is intoxicating narrative itself. The implication is that communication, and mutual interest, are vital to a successful relationship. The poem celebrates female creativity as a happy fall – for Hughes the best part of any feminine nature.

'Lovesong' considers the sexual politics of love and its destructive perversity. The male and female personae – equally subject and object – take turns as the lines alternate between stereotypically gendered forms of cruelty and suffering. Hers are manipulative and entrapping, his violent: 'Her love-tricks were the grinding of locks ... His promises were the surgeon's gag'. The poem begins, 'He loved her and she loved him' (CP 255), but in the end, they become what the other most detests: 'In the morning they wore each other's face' (CP 256).

In 'Folktale', the lovers take turns declaring what they want, one thing each. Her needs soon exceed his, disrupting the sequence of seemingly fair exchanges. Two of her 'wants' in a row are stated, and a third is added with a conjunction: 'She wanted only shade ... She wanted a love knot ... And a child of acorn'. Reciprocity cannot be sustained, though neither persona is objectified. Hughes provides the antithesis to 'Cinderella's' happy ending. Instead, 'their fingers met / And were wrestling, like flames / In the crackling thorns / Of everything they lacked – // as midnight struck' (CP 788).

In 'The Lamentable History of the Human Calf', the destruction of love through intimacy is not mutual responsibility, but primarily caused by the woman's systematic and inexhaustible neediness. Secondarily, it stems from the male speaker's repeated mistake of trying, impossibly, to satisfy this. Driven by pre-emptive jealousy and possessiveness, she asks for every bit of him – nose, ears, legs, heart, liver, tongue, lungs, eyes, brains, arms – to feed to her dog. The poem ends, 'Now I live with a bitch an old sour bitch now I live with a bitch / a bitch a bitch so I live with a bitch an old sour bitch and / there was a maiden a maiden a maiden' (CP 301). With comic seriousness, the maiden has turned into a bitch, but one the man creates. This is no simple literalization of the male anxiety that women will eat them up. Rather, it confronts the uncomfortable idea that men's and women's desires produce exactly what they do not want: for him a bitch (a pun also, suggesting an overbearing, spiteful woman); for her, a bodiless man who is stripped of the masculinity that first attracted her.

'The Lamentable History of the Human Calf' is probably a response to Plath's 'The Courage of Shutting-Up', where the woman, rather than the man, loses her body parts. These become male trophies. The dismemberment strips her of key communication skills: her tongue for telling stories and talking back; her eyes for observing and expressing. Hughes signals this dialogue not just through content, but also by echoing Plath's repetitions – like a needle caught in a record's scratch – especially of body parts. As if complicit with the man who wants to take them, or trying to manipulate him into thinking that he does not really need them, Plath's speaker asks, 'But how about the eyes, the eyes, the eyes?'[15] Hughes's speaker is told by the woman, 'I want your heart, your heart, your heart', and 'Give me your tongue, your tongue, your tongue' (CP 300).

Hughes might be discussing his own poems, as well as Shakespeare's plays, when he describes the latter as 'experimental attempts to separate ... the beloved female from the delusions that make the hero see her as a witch'.[16] 'Witch' rhymes with 'bitch', but it is the negative that Hughes calls the 'delusion'. It would be a mistake to condemn poems that examine male fears of women's deadliness as 'tirades of seeming misogyny' as Hughes describes some passages by Shakespeare.[17] They are not simple messages about what men think, or Hughes himself thinks, when looking (to cite from a book Plath owned) 'through the black or rosy spectacles which sex puts upon his nose'.[18] In 'Eclipse', the spider's 'gentle / Sinister dance' (CP 348) is of murderous seduction: 'Is she devouring him now?' (CP 350). 'Thomas the Rhymer's Song' is also a warning to men: 'When you are old enough to love, / You'll be taken prisoner'. Thomas tells his own story: 'A Lady with a knife of flame, / Oh there he met love's pain! / As she stripped the flesh from his bones, / And nailed his heart to a tree' (CP 628–9). Yet such poems are not mere exaggerations of the *vagina dentata* myth, in which the man's desire empowers the woman to eat him, body and soul.

Jacqueline Rose writes of the need 'to allow the coexistence of complicity and critique – the exposure, in Hughes's case, of ... the worst of male fantasy which he lays bare, endlessly returns to and repeats'.[19] Simultaneous 'complicity and critique' may more helpfully be applied to Hughes's reflection of traditional patriarchal social and mythical views of women, set against his deliberate analysis of, and resistance to, these views. Hughes does not shy away from representing truths that are not pretty or flattering to his male persona, and we should not assume that 'the worst of male fantasy' reflects his own views and desires. One might say that he demonstrates courageous honesty, and an admirable lack of the shame that Rose elsewhere says 'relies on the art of exposure, even if exposure is what it hates most'.[20]

Nathalie Anderson writes, 'Hughes's disquieting presentation of women is part of a larger indictment – ultimately of a society which represses not only ... a female principle within the psyche, but actual women as well'.[21] Terry Gifford is helpful, too, here, arguing that throughout his work 'Hughes is himself critiquing the male origins of grotesque images of the feminine'.[22] Rather than seeing negative portrayals of women in the poems as evidence of Hughes's own misogyny or pathology, we might see them as an exposure of powerfully felt fears and established archetypes that can only be understood and eradicated if they are acknowledged and examined, from different angles, over time.

'She Seemed So Considerate' also examines the woman's transformation from maiden to bitch. It pre-empts 'The Hidden Orestes', where the Electra/Plath figure's peasant husband, in colloquial, humorous phrases, 'can't make out / What's eating his wife'. Further, 'he's alarmed / By the uncanny masculine voice / That now and again ... Bursts from her lips / With a demonic snarl' (CP 1175). Early in Cave Birds there appears a depiction of a nightmare relationship in 'She Seemed So Considerate' ('My solemn friends sat twice as solemn / My jokey friends joked and joked') (CP 421). Set against it is one of the collection's last poems, 'Bride and groom lie hidden for three days', another poem about reciprocity. The man and woman build each other, taking pleasure in each other, body part by body part. They take turns in a characteristically gendered manner, but instead of the nightmare ending of 'Lovesong', the lovers here 'bring each other to perfection'; neither triumphs over the other. The poem is Hughes's response to the 'many different accounts of the Creation of Man & Woman'. Any gendered debate that asks 'Did she give most, or did he?'[23] cannot be resolved. She 'smooths', 'gives', 'stitches' and 'inlays'. He 'assemble[s]', 'connects', 'sets' and 'oils' (CP 437–8). Each makes the other exactly what they desire: he is the epitome of idealized masculinity, and she of femininity. It is a rare moment of mutual love and pleasure between a man and woman, though in admittedly reified circumstances.

There is nothing idealized about the relationship Hughes depicts in his two versions of 'Actaeon'. The first originally appeared in *Cave Birds*, but Hughes replaced it with 'She Seemed So Considerate',[24] which is also concerned with the great cost of a man's sudden recognition that a woman is not what she first appears to be. 'Actaeon's' story is of arch masculinity coming unexpectedly upon ultra femininity, and being destroyed by it. Hughes's versions are marked by sympathy for both sides, and, as we see often in his work, a transposition of myth or fairy tale into a domestic landscape.

Diana's strangeness is reconfigured as a wifely familiarity that Actaeon takes for granted: 'her voice ... was a comfortable wallpaper'; 'the blank of his face / Just went on staring at her / Talking carpet talking hooverdust'. It is not clear, syntactically, whether it is Actaeon or Diana who is talking, domestically, of carpet and hooverdust. Are the words muffled, or so boring that the person who should be listening instead tunes them out? In either case, it is dangerous not to look and listen, and then to do so; Actaeon thereby misses the cues and incites, suddenly, unexpected rage. 'The jigsaw parts of her face ... / Began to spin', only to become the 'zig-zagging hounds' (*CP* 558) that tear Actaeon to pieces. It is myth, and it is a woman's ordinary marital fury.

Twenty years later, Hughes returned to the story of Actaeon's blundering into female anger. Here, it is not just the anger of one woman that presents grave danger, but of multiple women banding together in a very female setting: 'what he saw were nymphs, their wild faces // Screaming at him ... crowding together / To hide something' (*CP* 938). The implication is that communities of women are dangerous to men. Feminism has often explored the difficulty of articulating female subjectivity within male-dominated cultures. Actaeon's story reverses this: a man loses his voice in the face of great female power. 'No weapon was to hand – only water. // So she scooped up a handful and dashed it / Into his astonished eyes, as she shouted: / "Now, if you can, tell how you saw me naked."' It is as if a husband interrupted his wife's bath, only to be faced with a fury so great he is left speechless: 'No words came. No sound came but a groan' (*CP* 939).

'Only when Actaeon's life / Had been torn from his bones, to the last mouthful' (*CP* 941) by his own hounds, 'Only then / Did the remorseless anger of Diana, / Goddess of the arrow, find peace' (*CP* 942). In a typescript, instead of 'find peace', Hughes writes 'become quiet' and then 'become calm'.[25] Both phrases rely on an external observation of Diana. In the published version, with the words 'find peace', the poem gets close to inhabiting Diana's point of view, or at least knowing her intimately enough to describe her thoughts and feelings, which it does sympathetically. This might be a surprising emotional resonance to end with, given what she has inflicted on Actaeon, who has disappeared by this point, not just as a body and life, but as the poem's central figure and sensibility, more evidence of Diana's triumph, after the poem's previous closeness to his viewpoint. It is a marked change from the narrative strategy that concludes the earlier 'Actaeon', where Actaeon's viewpoint is maintained to the last line, which highlights the paradox of his voice continuing 'Even though life had ceased' (CP 559).

The ending of 'Actaeon' seems to evoke Plath herself. 'Goddess of the arrow' alludes not just to the bow and arrow of the goddess of hunting, but also to the famous lines from Plath's 'Ariel': 'I / Am the arrow, // The dew that flies / Suicidal'.[26] Hughes writes, 'Sylvia's poems & novel hit the first militant wave of Feminism as a divine revelation from their Patron Saint' (LTH 719). Elaine Showalter tells us, 'Hughes could not escape ... "the Fantasia about Sylvia Plath" ... her iconic status with feminists ... and the anger directed at him as her betrayer'.[27] In this light, the second 'Actaeon' becomes a metaphor for Hughes's attack by crowds of angry feminists – with Diana as their leader. The poem suggests that they will be satisfied with nothing less than Actaeon's – and Hughes's – silence and death.

Hughes saw Jacqueline Rose's study of Plath as representative of such attacks. He describes The Haunting of Sylvia Plath as a

> merely specious argument about the result of my editing Ariel. Her entire book was a feminist fantasia – incriminating me for somehow depriving women of this, that and the other, in SP's work. In fact ... the Roses of this world – got everything, every line of SP's verse ... But you know all about the stupidity of malice (or is it the malice of stupidity?) ... I can't stop readers thinking J. Rose and her disciples are orating from the Mount.[28]

Sarah Churchwell argues that the critical reception of Birthday Letters created an inversion: 'earlier accusations that Hughes silenced Plath' underwent a 'transformation ... into a reading of all feminists as aggressive, masculinized speakers who attack the nobly silent Hughes'.[29] The accuracy of Churchwell's observation is ironic, given the fact that Hughes is not silent about feminism in Birthday Letters. Several poems allude to feminist aggression and misinterpretation of Plath's work, though the word 'feminism' does not appear in the book.

In 'Blood and Innocence', the unspecified 'They', who make increasingly outrageous demands for the details of Plath's life, encompasses general readers, fans, biographers, academics and feminists. 'Brasilia' also refrains from specific identification of those who prop up Plath's 'Empire' with their relentless attention to her 'effigies' and 'portraits' (CP 1158), and their indifference to the real consequences suffered by the 'We' – Hughes and her children – who are 'dragged into court' (*CP* 1157) as a consequence of what happens in her books.[30] 'The City' works through a topographical conceit of Plath's poems as 'a dark city centre' surrounded by the 'suburbs' of 'Your novels, your stories, your journals'. 'The hotels are lit like office blocks all night / With scholars, priests, pilgrims' (*CP* 1179), who, like evangelical academics and overzealous fans, are blind to the real Plath.[31] Interested only in their own theories, 'They ignore you … And they all surge past you' (*CP* 1180).

'The Dogs Are Eating Your Mother' operates through a specific analogy between academic feminists and 'dogs' or 'hyenas'. To some, it may seem in keeping with 'over-simplified and pejorative representations of feminism'.[32] A fairer reading would see the poem not as engaging with feminism as a set of ethical and political ideas, but rather as a dramatic representation of a particular set of events. The analogy is associative, depending on the reader's knowledge of the controversy concerning Plath's gravestone.

This began when the stone was defaced 'by a feminist who objected to the imposition of the name Hughes'.[33] Hughes explains, 'Sylvia Hughes … was her legal name[34] …] I took it into my head to insert the Plath after Sylvia because I knew … what she had brought off in that name, and I wished to honour it … The mason … informed me that the letters of her married name had been levered off' (*LTH* 555). The vandalism was repeated four times (*LTH* 555). Numerous supporters wrote to Hughes, disparaging his antagonists as 'feminist',[35] a word Hughes himself never uses in his official letters on the subject,[36] perhaps because he did not see these actions as genuinely representing feminism, or perhaps because he did not wish to inflame things further by naming it.

'The Dogs Are Eating Your Mother' makes Jacqueline Rose wonder, 'Why then does Hughes once again represent with such unremitting anger those who have responded to Plath's writing …?'[37] The question seems deliberately to miss the very material point of what angered Hughes. 'We arranged / Sea-shells and big veined pebbles … But a kind / Of hyena came aching upwind. / They dug her out. Now they … Even / Bite the face off her grave-stone, / Gulp down the grave ornaments, / Swallow the very soil'. This refers directly to the desecration of Plath's grave, but also, metaphorically – and this is what seems to upset Rose – to what Hughes sees as the exploitative use to which Plath's words are put by self-interested academics: 'Let them / Jerk their tail-stumps, bristle and vomit / Over their symposia' (*CP* 1169). It is difficult to read the poem and not recall earlier associations in Hughes's work between women and dogs – or bitches – as we saw in 'The Lamentable History of the Human Calf' and its images of dismemberment and devouring. A key difference in 'The Dogs Are Eating Your Mother' is that women are cannibalizing another woman: Plath, and the children to whom the poem is addressed, are the victims – not a man.

Hughes says of those who write about Plath, often without 'an interest in' her: 'They ... construct hypothetical realities ... for the empty spaces that lie between [facts]. These hypotheses are supercharged with their own "subjectivity" – effects of feminism pretty obvious in many places, etc. But often just the lust to imagine the worst – you know, as in ordinary gossip.'[38] This echoes the poems, where Hughes does not use the word 'feminism', but evokes it through words and ideas that have an associative relation to the vocabulary of the letter: 'supercharged', 'subjectivity', 'lust to imagine the worst ... as in ordinary gossip'. Generally, 'gossip' resonates as a misogynist term. The subtext of the poems is that a perverted version of feminism operates in the behaviour of Plath's so-called female 'friends' – just as it operates in the work of some feminist academics. In both cases, the infusion of their own subjectivity blocks any real interest in Plath herself, and with dire consequences. Hughes asks, 'As for your venturings into what SP made of certain events – well, are you doing more than stir the darkness?'[39] It is the very question the poems ask of her friends.

It is a fundamental feminist principle that female solidarity and activism are crucial if women are to navigate themselves through a male-dominated world, let alone change it. In 'Visit', women are rivals and enemies. Apparently Hughes's 'Girl-friend / Shared a supervisor and weekly session / With your American rival and you. / She detested you' (CP 1047). In 'The Hidden Orestes' Electra's husband says of her, 'Every woman / Who sits in their home, no matter how friendly, / She hates' (CP 1175). Sisterhood is frequently turned into the most damaging form of gossip. In the early uncollected poem 'Bad News Good!' a 'lady here, under crow-possession, / Will pluck out her evil tidings / From your eye's lightest confession, / Then flap off with the evidence bleeding'. Prompted by idiocy or envy, and certainly by a 'Lust to rend and to derange', she will not stop 'Till every word that wounds be buried / Where it comes closest to kill' (CP 107). Hughes often converts things into this allegorical language of animals, so that any particular instance of an animal reference becomes more complicated than it seems to be on its own. Crows and foxes are his most totemic animals, and seldom female as they are here. To talk about women as crows evokes animal vitality, survival instinct and cunning. Like the female hyenas in 'The Dogs Are Eating Your Mother', they are pack animals, and creatures that kill weaker animals as well as feeding opportunistically on corpses.

In 'The Laburnum', published in the last year of his life, the Hughes speaker talks to Plath about the interventions of her female friends after their marriage breakdown, when their 'words sawed at you ... Chipped at you. They wanted you to know ... About what they had heard' (CP 1176). Female friendship and support are a mask for poisonous gossip, a pretext for hurting the person they pretend to help. 'They consoled you / With howls from their own divorce, with the revenge / You could not find in yourself, with a future / You could not find in yourself'. Female solidarity, founded on personal experiences of sexual politics, might resemble feminism, but in this poem is deadly: 'They almost laughed / To show you your grave'. Equally so is the lie, 'Who else dare / Tell you this truth?' and the false claim 'We are your true friends' (*CP* 1177).

'Howls & Whispers' extends this idea, alluding to the vindictive and destructive advice of Plath's mother and female analyst, and then the woman friend who brings Plath distorted – and painful – information about what Hughes, in his words, 'was said to have said, / Was said to have done'. This pernicious group of supposed sisters grows: 'And her friends, the step-up transformers / Of your supercharged, smoking circuits, / What did they plug into your ears / That had killed you by daylight on Monday?' These women wear 'masks' (*CP* 1179) of female solidarity, the supposed foundation of feminism, but according to Hughes their true faces are of naked self interest and self-righteous importance. On a proof page, Hughes scored out the line 'Essences of mouldy experience',[40] but its import remains in the final version. Rather than thinking of Plath, these women revisit their own stale, bitter pasts – with terrible consequences.

Hughes's changes to *Birthday Letters* may reflect his unease about the incendiary nature of 'The Laburnum' and 'Howls & Whispers'. In an early typescript of the full manuscript, they were companion poems; the penultimate was 'Cries & Whispers'[41] and the last was 'The Laburnum'.[42] He removed both,[43] instead reserving them for the limited edition *Howls & Whispers*.[44] Thereby he abandoned the idea of ending *Birthday Letters* on this note of anger towards extraneous enemies. Instead he closed it with 'Red', bringing the collection's focus back, lovingly, to Plath herself.

It can be difficult, in the end, to reconcile such opposing trends in Hughes's writing. There is his clear – and in human terms, understandable, even if sometimes unfair – antipathy to some aspects of feminism. Yet it does not seem to be an antipathy to feminism on any intellectual or political level, but a reaction to certain events that, it might be argued, were only tangentially to do with feminism anyway. It is not clear how those who dug up Plath's grave were acting out of any substantial feminist philosophy, even if they thought they did this in its name.

There is his careful, systematic examination of the sexual politics between men and women, and his sustained attempts to explore creative possibilities, and limitations, for women, in ways that are feminist in their sensibility. In the body of his work, women are not merely victims, or simple objectified objects of male desire or male fear. The poems search for reciprocity between men and women, and mutual love and desire, however hard they may be to find, or however uncomfortable we may feel about the circumstances in which they can exist.

If an individual poem operates through a Madonna/whore binary opposition, its overall message is seldom, if ever, to freeze women at one of these poles, or to see the alternation between them as an inevitable fate. A single poem tells a misleading story. The body of Hughes's work provides a different narrative, where echoes, patterns and shifts emerge; questions become meaningful within a larger context. Each poem must be seen as part of an elaborate and complex story, told over a long writing career.

NOTES

1. Nathalie Anderson. 'Ted Hughes and the Challenge of Gender' in Keith Sagar (ed.), *The Challenge of Ted Hughes* (London: Macmillan, 1994), p. 91.
2. See Ryan Hibbett, 'Imagining Ted Hughes', *Twentieth Century Literature*, 51:4 (Winter 2005), p. 414.
3. See Lynda K. Bundtzen, 'Mourning Eurydice', *Journal of Modern Literature*, 23:3/4 (Summer 2000), p. 456.
4. Hughes writes of 'ardent feminists trying to find somebody to stick the Gestapo Swastika onto'. TH to Leonard Scigaj, undated, Add. 88918, f. 7, BL.
5. Pamela Aronson, 'Feminists or "Postfeminists"?', *Gender and Society*, 17:6 (December, 2003), p. 905.
6. Sylvia Plath, *Collected Poems* (hereafter *SPCP*) (London: Faber and Faber, 1981), p. 32.
7. Nancy Gibbs, 'The War against Feminism', *Time* (9 March 1992), p. 52.
8. Hughes and Plath took turns with writing and childcare: *LTH* 518, and Sylvia Plath, *Letters Home* (London: Faber and Faber, 1975), pp. 387 and 416. Hughes encouraged Assia Wevill's art (TH to Assia Wevill, 16 February 1965, Mss 1058, Box 1, ff. 28, Emory; 19 February 1965, Mss 1058, Box 1, ff. 31, Emory; undated, Mss 1058, Box 1, ff. 50, Emory).
9. TH to Peter Redgrove, 6 February 1984, Mss 876, Box 1, ff. 6, Emory.
10. 'Morning Song', *SPCP* 157.
11. Hughes writes of his daughter's birth: 'she met her mother ... / Propped up in the bed, weeping with joy'. 'She's forgotten her Mummy's breast, that nursed her for over a year / Because it wanted to give her / Everything that could be given, then more'. TH to Frieda Hughes, 2 October 1997, Mss 1014, Box 1, ff. 80, Emory.
12. *SPCP* 259.
13. See Sylvia Plath, *The Bell Jar* (London: Faber and Faber, 1963), pp. 67–9.
14. Hughes writes, 'Violence is what Venus inflicted on Adonis. She called it Love.' Add. 88918/7/3, BL.
15. *SPCP* 210.
16. TH to Leonard Scigaj, 7 June 1985, Add. 88918/7/1, BL.
17. *SGCB* xi, 1993 edn.
18. Virginia Woolf, *A Room of One's Own* (London: The Hogarth Press, 1978), p. 124.

19. Jacqueline Rose, *The Haunting of Sylvia Plath* (London: Virago, 1991), p. 160.
20. Jacqueline Rose, *On Not Being Able to Sleep* (London: Vintage, 2003), p. 1.
21. Anderson, 'Challenge of Gender', p. 92. See also Elizabeth Bergmann Loizeaux, 'Reading Word, Image, and the Body of the Book', *Twentieth Century Literature* 50:1 (Spring, 2004), pp. 18–58.
22. Terry Gifford, *Ted Hughes* (London: Routledge, 2009), p. 136.
23. Add. 88918/7/1, BL.
24. Mss 644, Box 63, ff. 60, Emory.
25. Mss 644, Box 135, ff. 1, Emory.
26. *SPCP* 239–40.
27. Elaine Showalter, 'Who Remembers Ted Hughes?', *Chronicle of Higher Education* 54:27 (14 March 2008), B5–B6.
28. TH to Keith Trivasse, 4 February 1997, Add. 88918/134/3, BL.
29. Sarah Churchwell, 'Secrets and Lies', *Contemporary Literature* 42:1 (Spring 2001), p. 120.
30. See *LTH* 559–60.
31. 'The scholars want the anatomy of the birth of the poetry; and the vast potential audience want her blood, hair, touch, smell, and a front seat in the kitchen where she died.' *WP* 164.
32. Amber E. Kinser, 'Negotiating Spaces for/through Third-Wave Feminism', *NWSA Journal* 16:3 (Autumn 2004), p. 135.
33. Mss 644, Box 149, ff. 9, Emory. See Julia Parnaby and Rachel Wingfield, 'In memory of Sylvia Plath', *Guardian* (7 April 1989).
34. 'Sylvia Hughes' appeared on her British driving licence, smallpox vaccination record, US passport (Mss 644, Box 180, ff. 20, 21, 22, Emory) and a letter to Marcia Plumer, 4 February 1963 (Smith College Rare Book Room).
35. Mss 644, Box 149, ff. 10, Emory.
36. See *LTH* 552–61.
37. Rose, *On Not*, p. 67.
38. TH to Susan Hileman, 5 February 1997, Add. 88918/134/3, BL.
39. *Ibid.*
40. Add. 8918/1/39, BL.
41. The original title of 'Howls & Whispers'.
42. Add. 8918/1/12, BL.
43. Perhaps they were ineligible for *BL* because of their full revelations. See Jo Gill, *The Cambridge Introduction to Sylvia Plath* (Cambridge: Cambridge University Press, 2008), p. 112.
44. Leonard Baskin refers to 'An Addendum of Letters' as an early title for *HW*. This suggests Hughes wanted the book viewed as a subsequent addition to *BL*. The manuscripts reveal they were nonetheless tangled in composition. 28 February 1998, Add. 8918/1/40, BL.

8

VANDA ZAJKO

Hughes and the classics

Hughes's engagement with classical texts was not that of the 'lapsed classicist' whose formal acquaintance with Greek and Latin literature provided a privileged frame of reference throughout his life, nor was he a self-declared 'outsider' for whom the appropriation of the classical constituted a defiant political gesture.[1] Hughes's interest in ancient literature was distinctive precisely because it formed part of a much wider interest in the narrative repositories of the past and did not treat material from Greece and Rome with particular reverence. His preoccupation with what he described as the 'mythic' quality of writers led him to construct a poetic genealogy within which Aeschylus and Euripides took their place alongside Milton, Coleridge, Keats and Yeats, and to value the work of both ancient and modern poets as much for what eluded expression as for their words. On Hughes's reading, classical authors were oriented away from their place in the literary canon and re-evaluated for the part they play in rendering visible archaic matter, the productions of the collective mythic imagination, now dimly remembered by an aggressively modern world as dream.

If a concept of myth provides one entry point for examining Hughes's take on the classical, translation provides another. Beginning with a rendering of Homer for the radio and ending with adaptations of Greek tragedy for the stage, via an iconoclastic version of Seneca's *Oedipus* and the much-fêted *Tales from Ovid*, Hughes moved between ancient languages and artistic contexts with the freedom of the highly literate. And yet his trajectory was far less conventional than this description implies. From an early age he was interested in the particular qualities of the Yorkshire dialect and its relation to conventional poetic forms. The exuberantly rich linguistic texture of his output throughout his life testifies to his ongoing activity as translator between different registers of his native tongue. Although competent only in French, he translated works from all the main European languages, as well as Hungarian, Serbo-Croat, Hebrew and Latin and Greek. He also experimented with the creation of a new language when working with Peter Brook on the *Orghast* project. His relation to his source texts varied, then, considerably, and it has been suggested that when working with contemporary poetry he adhered to 'a principle of literalness' that did not usually concern him when working with the classics.[2] Although he had a strong sense of tradition and of the multiple poetic legacies he inherited, he was not obviously intimidated by the literary past and rejected the provincialism of the generation of British poets who preceded him. Susan Bassnett has recently argued that translation is a key term for the understanding of Hughes's oeuvre because so many of his diverse activities involve processes that can effectively be described as translational.[3] In particular, she makes the connection between his linguistic forays into alien cultures and the 'crossing over' of the shaman, the figure identified by Hughes with the poet, who moves between real and symbolic worlds in order to proffer healing to fractured communities. This dynamic conflation of the sophisticated poet/translator with the isolated visionary of primitive religion captures something of the paradoxical quality of Hughes's attitude towards the texts of the classical past.

Hughes's revitalized sense of the term 'mythic' and its relation to more conventional usage is explored extensively in *Shakespeare and the Goddess of Complete Being*. Here Hughes argues that Shakespeare uses myth in three broadly distinctive ways: as decorative reference, as structural device and as a mechanism, secreted within a plot, which, although fully secularized and stripped of narrative detail, nevertheless still functions to give a story its metaphysical power (*SGCB*, 1993 edn).[4] It is this third use of myth that explains the ongoing appeal of the mythic work of art whose appreciation involves the mining of 'crypts and catacombs' rather than familiarity with the 'upper architectural marvels' that more commonly find cultural favour (*SGCB* 39). It is not enough for a play or poem to be 'about' a mythical figure at the narrative level for it to be granted mythic quality:

> Nobody to my knowledge has defined the term 'mythic' satisfactorily, but in these poems, and in poetry generally, most of us know well enough what it means. It does not necessarily mean that the subject matter of the poem is taken from the mythology of some historical culture, but that it constitutes an image of a particular kind ... Obviously many poems take myths as their subject matter, or make an image of a *subjective* event, without earning the description 'visionary', let alone 'mythic'. It is only when the image opens inwardly towards what we recognize as a first-hand as-if religious experience, or mystical revelation, that we call it 'visionary', and when 'personalities' or creatures are involved, we call it 'mythic'.
> (*SGCB* 35-6)

This exacting definition of the mythic text denies a classical work the automatic status sometimes afforded to it simply because it is from the 'historical culture' of ancient Greece or Rome: classical texts, like all others, are valued for their unselfconscious preoccupation with 'the life and death urgency of their business', a quality that is hard to describe in limiting, rationalist language but which is recognized (in the case of Shakespeare) as 'a charisma strobing from everything the characters say and do – a radiant medium in which they move' (*SGCB* 37).

Hughes's large-scale project in *Shakespeare and the Goddess of Complete Being* is to demonstrate that underpinning Shakespeare's mature plays is a prototype plot model drawn from two living myths, those of the Great Goddess and of the Goddess-destroying god. Although the details of the myths do not appear in the finished plays any more than 'the mathematics (without which it would have been unthinkable and impossible) appear in the nuclear reaction and the flash of the bomb' (*SGCB* 2–3), it is from drawing on their specific resources that the plays derive their power. Whether or not one accepts this overall argument with regard to Shakespeare, there are two aspects of the detailed discussions which illuminate Hughes's response to the classical, at least to the extent that is represented by myth: first, it is apparent that a certain myth may have a particular resonance for a writer such that it forms an 'umbilical link' between the structure of the mythic imagination and the author's own psyche (*SGCB* 39); second, once a myth has been assimilated fully by an author, its realistic trappings may be removed and its presence felt within a play or poem solely by means of its effects. When we examine these propositions in the context of Hughes's own creativity, we are provided with the means to trace his fascination with individual myths beyond the works where they are explicitly named.

If Hughes is sceptical about the pedagogic use of myth – the kind of self-conscious reference to a mythical character he belittlingly describes as 'illustrative, clever metaphor' – he is emphatically persuaded by the power of certain images to exert a hold over those with a poetic calling (*SGCB* 42). For Shakespeare, it was the nexus of images associated with Venus and Adonis that had this effect; for Sylvia Plath, it was the myths of Phaeton [sic] and Icarus. In these cases, and others like them, the 'mythic personality' of the author seizes on an image and obsessively reworks it, in a mysterious process not entirely within his or her control. As Hughes explains:

> The imprinted image complex can have propitious implications or sinister ones, presumably because the mythic personality, in choosing its image, finds what corresponds to its own character – which includes its fate. The mythic works of art which it then projects in the sign-language of that image, throughout life, are 'self-portraits' of the successive stages of that unfolding.   (*SGCB* 40)

The involvement of the mythic personality elevates a work into the realm of the symbolic, even if the realist details are all that most readers see (for Hughes, the pressures of the rationalist, secular world militate against the recognition and appreciation of the mythic). When it comes to Hughes's own corpus, the myths that dominate are those of Dionysus and Prometheus. The former, representing both the pre- and anti-rational world, is an intoxicating antidote to the limitations of culture; the latter is a scapegoat figure whose endurance, even of the most extreme travails and suffering, provides longed-for hope of eventual rebirth.[5] If we engage seriously with the idea of 'the fit' between a writer and a mythic image, and follow Hughes's lead in allowing some sense of autobiographical truth to become part of our critical vision, it is possible to develop a mode of reading whereby the progressive sense of intimacy with these figures illumines both poetry and life, the latter itself becoming a truly mythic work in the case of Hughes.

It is only relatively recently that Hughes's translation of *The Odyssey* V. 382–493 has attracted critical attention because it was not available prior to the publication of the *Collected Poems* in 2003. Commissioned for the radio, it was broadcast in 1960 as part of a series of translations of Homer by contemporary poets and so belongs to the period of Hughes's work dominated by the early collections *The Hawk in the Rain* and *Lupercal*. The episode describes the rescue of Odysseus from the sea by Athene, after he had been shipwrecked by Poseidon and spent two days and nights at the mercy of the waves, and the subject matter might be thought, in a general way, to have been appropriate for Hughes, given his well-known appetite for depicting the brutality of nature. In fact, the selection was made by Louis MacNeice, one of the editors of the radio series, and it is impossible to reconstruct from it any preference by Hughes. In the first detailed consideration of the translation, Stuart Gillespie describes its emphases as follows: 'Physical struggle is prominent. There is violence. A number of gods are invoked or otherwise mentioned. But none of these things is so central as a more fundamental subject still: the existential plight of man.'[6] Gillespie offers little to substantiate this reading, but he does refer by way of context to the poem entitled 'Everyman's Odyssey' in the *Lupercal* collection, a poem which, given its title, does seem to provide a key to interpreting the translation. Beginning as a direct address to Odysseus's son, the opening lines urge the young man to recall a particular period in his past life.

But in the course of the final stanza, the particular situation of the addressee is revealed as one known personally to the writer, the subtlest of grammatical indicators transforming its import from one moment in the mythological past to the broadest of possible presents and futures:

> I would hear
> How the father arrives out of the bottom of the world.
> I would see one of the beggars that brawl on my porch
> Reach hands to the bow hardly to be strung by man –   (CP 60)

It is this transformation, along with the poem's title, that presumably enables Gillespie to take the line that he does and position Hughes among the many commentators on the *Odyssey*, both ancient and modern, who have chosen allegory as their dominant interpretive mode. There is nothing controversial here as his reading does seem to cohere with our sense of Hughes's general predilections and his partiality for seeking out where possible deeper, generalized meanings.[7] But, as we have seen above, an overt reference to a named myth is not, for Hughes, the most satisfactory way of tapping into the power of a story. If we return to the idea of 'the poet's myth' it is possible to offer a different sense of the influence of the classical in *Lupercal*, an influence recognizable not from any 'dip into the myth-kitty' (*SGCB* 41) but from the omnipresent authority of Dionysus.

We do not know when Hughes read Euripides's play the *Bacchae* for the first time. (Recently Keith Sagar has suggested implicitly that it was around the time he went to Cambridge.)[8] But we do know that he had read it by 1958, when in a letter to his friend Lucas Myers he notes, jokingly, that 'in my next work – in progress – the son enters with the head of the father (thinking it the head of a lion, as Agave does hers). You see, I have read Hamlet, as Euripides had not' (*LTH* 117). In any case, beyond the remit of that particular play, Hughes was undoubtedly familiar with the idea of the Dionysian in a wider cultural sense. In another letter, this time to Sylvia Plath's mother and brother in 1960, he offers an allegorical interpretation of one of his own works, *The House of Aries*, elsewhere described as 'a tragi-farcical melodrama in verse' (*LTH* 167) in which individual characters are described as representing different aspects of 'the Self'. Here his description of the conflict between 'Morgan' and 'Elaine' serves as his version of the conflict between Apollonian and Dionysian principles made famous by Nietzsche. In the following passage he spells out the terms of the opposition and shows what has been at stake in the privileging of one term over the other:

> But ... a big BUT ... discoursive [sic] intelligence has become what it is, helped by the labours of the various thinkers and taught so to each succeeding generation, only by ridding itself of everything unpredictable, obscure, mysterious, ambiguous and emotional. In other words, a division has been created in the Self, between a briskly busy discoursive thought-process, logical, with an air of infallibility and precision, arrogant because it thinks it works according to eternal rational laws, and the whole emotional animal life of consciousness

which is on the whole impressionable, passive, and only positive in its intuitions. (*LTH* 174–5).

For Hughes at this time, poetry is obviously situated on the side of Dionysus, but his attitude to drama is less clear-cut. He criticizes his own dramatic endeavour above as being 'fairly fantastic' but then goes on to query the alternatives:

> Because it moves in a super-real dimension, a sort of dream dimension, it seems over emotional & over-eloquent, but there's no poetic drama in any other dimension as far as I can see. Normal people don't speak like that, but the stresses that break them down from within are trying to get things expressed in even more violent & complete language. Realistic drama seems to me to leave the reality unexpressed & I mean also unsuggested. (*LTH* 167)

Towards the end of his life, Hughes came to regard ancient Greek drama as providing a register for expressing emotional truths in dramatic form without the need for overblown rhetoric or hysteria, but in his early work the struggle to express this material occurs mainly in relation to his poems. The 'founding myth of his poetic career',[9] the famous account of the burnt fox entering his room at Cambridge to stop him writing critical essays, provides a memorable image of the damage meted out to the poetic imagination by overly critical processes. The 'bleeding fox' can be regarded as a literalization of the Dionysian metaphor, and its appearance is not an isolated incident since Hughes took seriously the manifestations of his dream-work and commented upon them often in his letters and critical writing.

Another such example is the bull who 'just wandered up' in a dream and compelled him to finish the poem 'The Bull Moses' from *Lupercal* (*LTH* 129). This bull appears in the poem, impervious to irritants, passive, self-contained, with a quiet source of knowledge born of another world: 'something / Deliberate in his leisure, some beheld future / Founding in his quiet' (*CP* 75). Within the landscapes of ancient Greek myth, the bull is a well-known symbol of Dionysus and it is surely not pressing the case too far to see in this representation the presence of the god whose aspect may not be always visible amongst the upper architectural marvels of the early collections, but who nonetheless haunts their deepest catacombs.

Given his wariness concerning realistic drama, it is perhaps not surprising that Hughes's first foray into the theatre was in collaboration with the experimental director Peter Brook, with whom he worked on a version of Seneca's *Oedipus* in 1968. Brought into the company late on in the creative process, Hughes described Brook's directing as being 'like prolonged group-analysis of everyone concerned' and relished the intensity of the whole experience (*LTH* 281).

Writing in the introduction to the eventual published text, his comments on the choice of Seneca's employment of the story rather than Sophocles's show the extent to which the two men shared a vision:

> I was in complete sympathy with Peter Brook's guiding idea, which was to make a text that would release whatever inner power this story, in its plainest, bluntest form, still has, and to unearth, if we could, the ritual possibilities within it. Sophocles' *Oedipus* would not have been so suitable for this experiment as Seneca's. The Greek world saturates Sophocles too thoroughly: the evolution of his play seems complete, fully explored and in spite of its blood-roots, fully civilized. The figures in Seneca's *Oedipus* are Greek only by convention: by nature they are more primitive than aboriginals . . . The radiant moral world of Sophocles is simply not present here. Seneca hardly notices the intricate moral possibilities of his subject. Nevertheless, while he concentrates on tremendous rhetorical speeches and stoical epigrams, his imagination is quietly producing something else – a series of epic descriptions that contain the raw dream of Oedipus, the basic, poetic, mythical substance of the fable, and whatever may have happened to the rhetoric, this part has not dated at all. For everybody must answer the sphinx. (SO 7–8)

Many of the elements here are by now familiar: the emphasis on embedded structure rather than on narrative detail; the preference for the primitive over the so-called 'civilized'; the focus on the mythic imagination of the poet; the attribution of universal meaning. Under this description, Hughes's Seneca is very much more the poet who sensationalizes the effects of passion than the Stoic advocate of reason, and the rhetorical ostentation, so often perceived as a key feature of Senecan style, is regarded as something to be stripped away, an excrescence delimited by time. It would be easy to conclude from this that Hughes was not interested in Seneca's use of language but only in his subject matter, and it is certainly the case that he did not try to reproduce it in any straightforward way. But he was challenged sufficiently by the project to struggle day after day with 'finding a simple language and tone for a supercharged theme' (LTH 618) and this preoccupation with how to use the limited resources of language to convey extreme sensation is one he shares with Seneca. The distinctive feature of Hughes's *Oedipus* is its compression, an effect achieved, in Neil Roberts's words, 'not by condensing syntax but by doing away with complex sentence structure and writing in a series of ejaculatory phrases, punctuated (in the form of spaces in the text) on the basis of speech rhythm rather than grammar'.[10] In the passage that follows, Teiresias's daughter, Manto, describes the abnormal physiology of the sacrificial victim in terms which also function metaphorically or analogically to describe the unnatural state of affairs in Thebes. The chilling description of nature's gore evokes horror at the perversion of the flesh

revealed, at Oedipus's torment to come and, in a more far-reaching way, at the
inevitable mortality of us all:[11]

>   something is wrong   no membrane to contain the
>   entrails and the intestines quake   father what can
>   this mean   usually they quiver a little but these are
>   twisting   shuddering look how they shake my arm
>   as if they had a separate life   (SO 28)

On the printed page, the lack of punctuation and uncapitalized sentences are
more obvious than they would have been in performance, and the novelty of
the idiom, at least for Hughes, is striking. Brook's innovative working prac-
tices, combined with the awareness that Senecan tragedies may not in their
own time have been designed as performance texts, may have liberated
Hughes from what he perceived to be the formal restrictions of the conventional theatre, and the shamanistic potential of this scene, in particular, may
have resonated with his own understanding of the performative. But there are
ways in which this work can also be described as highly literary, because, in
the same way that Seneca drew upon his predecessors in his reworking of
mythic tales, Hughes draws upon literary giants such as Shakespeare and T. S.
Eliot in his. 'Therein lies a point of principle,' as John Talbot instructs:
'effective criticism of Hughes's classical translations depends as much on
attention to his use of mediating English sources as of the ostensible classical
sources themselves.'[12] *Oedipus*, then, is a translational work in the broad
sense referred to by Bassnett involving linguistic skill, the negotiation of
cultures and imaginative engagement with forces beyond the rational.

It was nearly thirty years before Hughes returned to writing for the theatre
and when he did, as we shall see, he was reconciled to its conventions, to the
Dionysus of the Great Dionysia. This process of reconciliation took place in
the wake of a ferociously difficult period in Hughes's life, when he grappled
with the after-effects of the deaths of Sylvia Plath and of Assia Wevill and her
daughter Shura, and many have commented on the shift in focus of Hughes's
work at this time. However one chooses to characterize this shift (as the result
of a shamanic journey, as a creative working through of personal trauma, as
the product of a specifically masculine guilt), in *Crow*, *Gaudete* and *Cave
Birds*, there is a marked intensification of the mythological qualities of his
poetry. Another theatrical venture with Brook, the hugely ambitious *Orghast*
project undertaken in 1971 for a theatre festival at Persepolis, involved,
amongst other things, a dramatization of the Prometheus myth using an
invented language, and during this period Hughes also undertook an explicit

poetic reworking of the same myth, published in 1973 as the series *Prometheus on His Crag*. Recalling Hughes's own discussion of the creative process in *Shakespeare and the Goddess of Complete Being* cited above, it is hard not to think of these compositions as the result of a mythic personality obsessively reworking its chosen image, as mythic works of art, 'projected in the sign-language of that image', as 'self-portraits of the successive stages of that unfolding' (*SGCB* 40). The mythic image in question at this stage of Hughes's life is undoubtedly Prometheus, and so another way of explaining the shift in focus of his work might be as a reorientation away from Dionysus, the capricious and predatory god, towards Prometheus the Titan, who pays the price for understanding through intense and prolonged suffering.

It would be wrong, however, to offer too mono-dimensional a reading of such an eclectic poet. Writing about the aftermath of *Crow*, Susan Bassnett observes that 'what also starts to become apparent from this period onwards is Hughes's fascination for the ancient world, for the Latin and Greek foundation texts that had provided part of the bedrock upon which English literature had been built'.[13] Mythology continued to be important for Hughes, as it had always been, but the literariness of his sensibility also made its presence felt and the symbolic resonance of literature infused by myth persisted in fascinating Hughes both as reader and writer. The introduction to the 1997 *Tales from Ovid* shows how in the *Metamorphoses* Hughes found an ancient text that satisfied both his intellect and imagination and that his interest was provoked in part by its enormous influence on the later English writers he admired. His remarks here demonstrate an acceptance of the formative role played by classical literature that is less confrontational than earlier references to the 'myth-kitty' might have led us to expect:

> During the Middle Ages throughout the Christian West [the *Metamorphoses*] became the most popular work from the Classical era, a source-book of imagery and situations for artists, poets and the life of high culture. It entered English poetry at a fountainhead, as one of Chaucer's favourite books, which he plundered openly, sometimes – as with the tale of Pyramus and Thisbe – in quite close translation. A little later, it played an even more dynamic role for Shakespeare's generation – and perhaps for Shakespeare in particular.
>
> ... Different aspects of the poem continued to fascinate Western culture, saturating literature and art. And by now, many of the stories seem inseparable from our unconscious imaginative life. (*TO* vii)

Hughes has not abandoned his commitment to the world of the imagination but there is here, perhaps, a greater sense of ease with the trappings of 'high culture' than demonstrated before. One of the episodes in *Tales from Ovid* deals with the conflict between Pentheus and the Roman version of Dionysus,

Bacchus, from book 3 of the *Metamorphoses*. We might have expected Hughes to exploit the opportunity the episode presents and play up the dire implications of ignoring Bacchus/Dionysus. But instead it is one of Pentheus's speeches that Hughes elaborates most fully, giving the unrepentant sceptic some seventy extra lines and a memorable, vitriolic eloquence in abuse of the god and his followers:

> But you have surrendered the city
> Not to war's elemental chaos
> And heroes harder and readier than yourselves
> But to a painted boy, a butterfly face,
> Swathed in glitter.
> A baboon
> Got up as an earring
> In the ear of a jigging whore.   (CP 995)

In the final years of his life, Hughes wrote extensively for the theatre, translating, in swift succession, Wedekind's *Spring Awakening*, Lorca's *Blood Wedding* and Racine's *Phèdre*, as well as Aeschylus's *Oresteia* and Euripides's *Alcestis*. Both classical works were produced posthumously (in 1999 and 2000 respectively) and so, unlike *Oedipus*, they did not derive from a process of collaboration with actors and directors. Lorna Hardwick has argued that this lack of symbiosis results in the emergence of a polarity between the poetic and dramatic aspects of a performance text,[14] and it is certainly the case that both trilogy and play have tended to be evaluated textually, rather than in terms of their impact on an audience. Given that at the same time as he was working on these plays, Hughes was writing *Birthday Letters*, a significant context for this evaluation has proved to be the relation of his choice of project to the events of his life and much has been made, for example, of his transformation of the *Alcestis* into 'an essentially positive play' whose final word is 'hope'.[15] One reviewer went so far as to suggest that Hughes's version of the play is a 'cleanup job', the purpose of which is to shift the blame for Alcestis's death to the god Apollo and exonerate Admetus, her husband.[16] Another strand of criticism has endeavoured to trace the creative interplay between these last translations and Hughes's own poems with the result that the former are made to 'fit into the development of Hughes's own writing rather than standing outside the rest of his output'.[17] Although this might have had the effect of mainstreaming Hughes's classically inspired work, for many critics the drama of Hughes's relationship with Plath has eclipsed the poetic achievement, and the plays have been read, not for their own value or how they might illumine their source texts, but for the light they shed on Hughes's domestic situation.

For those with an overly restricted sense of Hughes as a poet of nature, the choices he made as translator and adaptor at the end of his life may seem counter-intuitive or partial. But the trajectory of his engagement with the mythic, as we have seen, suggests that the moment was finally ripe for an encounter with Greek tragedy. The god Dionysus, terrifying when ignored, was honoured by the Athenians with a theatre festival that allowed for an exploration of the extremes of the human condition at the heart of their civic space, a triumph for the fragile synthesis of intellect and emotion. Aeschylus's trilogy, often acclaimed as the world's first dramatic masterpiece, enacts a similar process of delicate reconciliation, allowing rationality to triumph, but simultaneously honouring the primal and the savage. This striking ancient alternative to the model of repression was perfect for Hughes and he rose to the challenge magnificently, neither intimidated nor overpowered by its dense metaphorical language or its status as canonical text.

Michael Silk has celebrated Hughes's version as relatively respectful to the significant qualities of the Greek, arguing that it 'presents an idiom – or, as usual, a range of idioms –acceptably, if sometimes elusively, in touch with the bold elevatedness of the Greek'.[18] As the following examples show, this flexibility of idiom enables Hughes to do justice to the variety of different voices in the play, whilst maintaining a finely judged control over escalating imagery. This is his translation of the final words of Cassandra before she enters the palace, where she knows she will be murdered:

> This was life.
> The luckiest hours
> Like scribbles in chalk
> On a slate in a classroom.
> We stare
> And try to understand them.
> Then luck turns its back –
> And everything's wiped out.
> Joy was not less pathetic
> Than the worst grief.   (O 65)

If we compare this to the versions by Robert Fagles and Michael Ewans respectively below, we see that Hughes breathes life into the image of the 'sponge' and extends it, focusing a moment's attention on the childlike quality of the powerlessness of human beings when confronted by whimsical fate (*Agamemnon* 1327–30, Oxford Classical Text):

Oh men, your destiny
When all is well a shadow can overturn it.
When trouble comes a stroke of the wet sponge,
and the picture's blotted out. And that,
I think breaks the heart.

Oh the fate of human beings! When prosperous
they're like a shadow; if misfortune strikes,
one stroke of a wet sponge destroys the picture.
I pity this more even than our pitiable fate.[19]

In the following extract Hughes again develops an image, this time the famous depiction of Agamemnon caught in Clytemnestra's murderous spider's web from a passage of lament by the chorus (*Agamemnon* 1492–6, repeated at 1516–20, Oxford Classical Text). The last two lines here are interpolations by Hughes who conflates the thought-pictures of the two modes of death (web and blade) to give us the breathtaking final image of a pinned-down fly:

He was killed
By his treacherous wife.
The spider's web
Swaddled him helpless.
Then a bronze blade
Came out of nowhere.
A great King died
Like a spinning fly. (O 74–5)

Again, this time in a passage from the *Libation Bearers* spoken by the Nurse Cilissa (749–62), Hughes interpolates two images (of flowers and a kitten) into the description of the baby Orestes and takes advantage of a lacuna in the Greek to summon up both the sweet smell of the infant and his animal helplessness:

But now – Oh, Orestes,
Orestes is dead! Orestes!
I took him fresh from his mother's womb,
Fragrant as an armful of flowers.
It was my milk he drank,
Like a blind kitten.
It was me he cried for.
Night after night, it was me
He wore out with endless wants.
Through whole nights I held him,
Rocking his sleeping trust in my arms –
He was my life.

> And I was his life.
> A baby is helpless at both ends.
> I understood the dumb cries
> Of his two needs.   (O 126–7)

Fagles attempts a more prosaic translation, presumably to denote the colloquial speech-pattern of the Nurse: 'Red from your mother's womb I took you, reared you ... / nights, the endless nights I paced, your wailing / kept me moving – led me a life of labour, / all for what?'. And Fagles leaves the lacuna, an interpretative move that some may feel accurately preserves the Greek. But one can choose to leave a gap, or allow a gap to speak, the latter being a metaphor that captures something of Hughes's translational practice beyond the limited sense of the words that appear on the page. There can be little doubt that the *Oresteia* is a mythic text in the demanding Hughesian sense and in the final play of the trilogy we sense that its images opened inwardly for Hughes towards a first-hand experience both optimistic and transformative:

> Let your rage pass into understanding
> As into the coloured clouds of a sunset,
> Promising a fair tomorrow.
> Do not let it fall
> As a rain of sterility and anguish
> On Attica.   (O 184)

NOTES

1. 'Lapsed classicist' is the self-description of Michael Longley in *Living Classics: Greece and Rome in Contemporary Poetry in English*, ed. S. Harrison (Oxford: Oxford University Press, 2009), pp. 97–113. In his chapter, 'Contemporary Poetry and Classics', in T. P. Wiseman (ed.), *Classics in Progress* (Oxford: Oxford University Press, 2002), p. 5, Oliver Taplin contrasts 'the iconoclastic, anti-monarchist' Tony Harrison with 'the royalist, male-sympathising' Ted Hughes.

2. Neil Roberts, *Ted Hughes A Literary Life* (Basingstoke: Palgrave Macmillan, 2006), pp. 179–80.

3. Susan Bassnett, *Ted Hughes* (Tavistock: Northcote House, 2009), pp. 82–3.

4. All subsequent references are to the revised paperback edition (1993).

5. I have written elsewhere about the anthropological aspects of the Prometheus myth and its relation to Hughes's work. See Vanda Zajko, '"Mutilated towards Alignment?": *Prometheus on His Crag* and the "Cambridge School" of Anthropology', in Roger Rees (ed.), *Ted Hughes and the Classics* (Oxford: Oxford University Press, 2009), pp. 100–19.

6. Stuart Gillespie, 'Hughes's First Translation: "*The Storm* from Homer, *Odyssey*, Book V"', in Rees (ed.), *Hughes and the Classics*, p. 37.

7. See, for example, the discussion in 'Myths, Metres, Rhythms' in *Winter Pollen*, where, in discussion of the image of the wren, he decries 'that kind of sharp focus on

the contextual particularities, the natural history, in realistic terms' which 'precludes any casting of the chosen bird in a mythic role within a pattern of deeper shared understandings relating to group life'. *WP* 316.

8. Keith Sagar, 'Ted Hughes and the Classics', in Rees (ed.), *Hughes and the Classics*, p. 3, where it is referred to, after Graves's *The White Goddess*, as Hughes's 'next holy book'.

9. Roberts, *Literary Life*, p. 19.

10. *Ibid.*, p. 183.

11. Charles Segal expands on this in his essay 'Boundary Violation and the Landscape of the Self in Senecan Tragedy', in J. Fitch (ed.), *Oxford Readings in Classical Studies: Seneca* (Oxford: Oxford University Press, 2008), pp. 136–56. See especially p. 155.

12. John Talbot, 'Eliot's Seneca, Ted Hughes's *Oedipus*', in Rees (ed.), *Hughes and the Classics* p. 63.

13. Bassnett, *Ted Hughes*, p. 47.

14. Lorna Hardwick, 'Can (Modern) Poets Do Classical Drama? The Case of Ted Hughes', in Rees (ed.), *Hughes and the Classics*, p. 58.

15. So Robert Macfarlane, reviewing the translations of the *Oresteia* and the *Alcestis* in the *Independent on Sunday* (31 October 1999): 'For all its calamitous potential, and despite the grim echoes of his own situation, Hughes turns *Alcestis* into an essentially positive play.'

16. See Daniel Mendelsohn in the review essay 'Not an Ideal Husband', *New York Review of Books* (11 May 2000).

17. Bassnett, *Ted Hughes*, p. 93.

18. Michael Silk, 'Ted Hughes: Allusion and Poetic Language', in Rees (ed.), *Hughes and the Classics*, p. 252.

19. Aeschylus, *Oresteia*, translated by Robert Fagles (1977) for Penguin Classics and by Michael Ewans (1995) for Everyman.

9

NEIL CORCORAN

Hughes as prose writer

'The prose-style of poets'

'I have but an indifferent opinion of the prose-style of poets: not that it is not sometimes good, nay, excellent; but it is never the better, and generally the worse from the habit of writing verse,' says William Hazlitt, with characteristic pugnacity, at the opening of 'On the Prose-Style of Poets'.[1] Composer exclusively of prose and not of poetry, Hazlitt has his own axe to grind here, but his strictures about the prose of the Romantics which follow in this essay and his opposing recommendation of the virtues of another exclusive writer of prose, Edmund Burke, are still worth attention in the way they suggest that poets can easily forget the strengths prose needs. Even if we have long since learned to admire the varied virtues of, say, *Biographia Literaria* and the preface to *Lyrical Ballads*, it is salutary to attend to Hazlitt on the magnificence of a prose style which differs from poetry 'like the chamois from the eagle'. A poet's style, craving 'continual excitement' and therefore always aspiring to the condition of the eagle, may have scant respect for the necessary agility, persistence and level-headedness of the chamois, in for the long haul.

Necessarily, however, such strictures are less appropriate to a post-Romantic period ushered in by Ezra Pound's recommendation that poetry be at least as well written as prose; one in which by far the dominant form of poetry has become free verse, not metre; in which successive 'ages of criticism' have flourished; and in which poets have varyingly – sometimes intimately – accommodated themselves to or even, in the cases at least of T. S. Eliot and William Empson, moulded the forms and styles of the literary-critical academy. As a consequence, we are likely to be sceptical about what may well now seem Hazlitt's prescriptivism, and to admire rather than derogate a prose developed from or dependent on the habit of writing verse. We may even admire a prose congruent with a poet's verse, in which a poem may be discovered in gestation, or the motive or movement of mind or sensibility necessary to a poem may be found compellingly acknowledged. Such diverse instances as Wallace Stevens's *The Necessary Angel*, by turns pellucid and resisting the intelligence almost successfully; passages of meditative near-entrancement in Seamus Heaney; and the spiritedly acerbic camp, both comically throwaway and genuinely self-explanatory, of Frank O'Hara's 'Personism: A Manifesto' are all ungainsayable adjuncts to the muse's diadem.

In such a context it becomes possible to say at least neutrally but even admiringly that Ted Hughes's prose is often poetry by other means. Here are four examples, from what are normally considered quite different types of prose writing.

In one of the *Tales of the Early World*, a children's book, Woman wants a playmate and God tries to fathom what she has in mind. She wants it to be 'beautiful and exciting', she says, 'like the sea'. God gets the idea and plunges into the ocean, creating 'a white commotion':

> And as he rode up into the breakers a huge shaggy head reared out of the water ahead of him. She saw its deep-sea staring eyes. It reared a long neck, draped with seaweed ... Then its shoulders heaved up, and as the great comber burst around it, it turned. She saw its long side, like a giant white-silver shark. For a moment, it seemed to writhe and melt, as if it were itself exploding into foam, and the next thing God was rolling up the beach, battered by foam.[2]

God, by the process of accident and approximation which characterizes his creative endeavours in these tales, has generously attuned himself to Woman's desire and made her a horse. This is an event in nature but, simultaneously, in language. The horse is created by the similitude of shape which the rising and arching wave, the excited behaviour of the sea, shares with a horse's head, that similitude which, in a mode of back-formation, brings the expression 'white horses' into the language. It is also created out of what Woman perceives elsewhere in this passage as 'the sea's hoarse, constant roar'. God creates, that is, by means of a pun. Woman's own similitude, in which the sea's metamorphosis is first perceived as a 'white-silver shark', has to be re-educated as God's new animal simultaneously enters the world, language and her cognition, all of which are themselves writhing and melting in this virtuoso passage of enthusiastic imagining.

In 'Sylvia Plath and Her Journals', one of the many places in which Hughes's prose accompanies his poetry's enduring engagement with the writer and her work, he evokes her essential quality by adducing Shakespeare's Ariel and Plath's own – 'Ariel' was the name of her horse and *Ariel* the title of her most famous volume – as a combinatory metaphor to distinguish her from 'the normal flowering and fruiting kind of writer'. Plath is one whose work is 'roots only':

Almost as if her entire oeuvre were enclosed within those processes and trans-
formations that happen in other poets before they can even begin, before the
muse can hold out a leaf. Or as if all poetry were made up of the feats and shows
performed by the poetic spirit Ariel. Whereas her poetry is the biology of Ariel,
the ontology of Ariel – the story of Ariel's imprisonment in the pine, before
Prospero opened it.[3]

The Ariel metaphor acts almost as an electrification of what might otherwise
seem a slightly precious organicism in this, conveying with justness the sheer
scale of Plath's difference from other writers; of, that is, her exceptionalism,
which is implicitly made to echo or even rival Shakespeare's, and which
Hughes registers in everything he writes about her. His prose here seems
virtually a form of cohabitation with the deep structures of her verse and is
almost biomorphically definitive. Present in its few sentences too is a view of
Plath intimated throughout the course of Hughes's writing about her. She is a
poet of an heroic but ultimately unwinnable struggle against overwhelming
psychological odds; but she is attuned always to a plot of mythical articulation and transformation, in the single long poem of which her individual
poems are component, sometimes warring, parts, and not at all an exponent
of confessional discourse, as she has frequently been (disastrously) misread.

When Hughes discusses his own poems in his prose it can be interpreta-
tively transformative. On 'The Thought-Fox' in *Poetry in the Making* and 'In
the Likeness of a Grasshopper' in *Winter Pollen* he is mesmerizing. It is almost
as though he is back in the creative place itself, setting an illuminating lamp of
prose beside the poem's original manuscript, inserting a second co-creative
self between poem and reader in a uniquely sympathetic form of close reading; reading, as it were, from the inside out. Despite such performances
polished for publication, what he says briefly of 'Thistles' in a little note to
his sister Olwyn shortly after he had first published it is as valuable in the way
it turns one of his greatest poems in an altogether unanticipatable light. This
prose is not so much mirror or lamp as, in a metaphor he himself deploys
elsewhere, the laser light of a radically experimental modernism:

> Thistles was a sort of Picasso thistles – the plant, you see, from an academic
> point of view, being the nucleus of associations on the whole more important in
> the piece than the plant. Also a sort of Walt Disney thistles, and Klee thistles.
> Not really thistles. Their plume isn't red, each has several plumes, etc. It's a
> scherzo, not very serious. The idea of the decayed Viking was really the main
> one – the one I'd had before & been amused by.[4]

A scherzo and not really serious, maybe, but only as Picasso, Disney and Klee
are not really serious in their playful (or popular) forms of attention; and a
scherzo serious enough to open this poet's greatest single volume, *Wodwo*.

Wodwo stays unmanageable, disconcerting and plain weird in all sorts of ways, but is, since the publication of this letter, at least the kind of thing we might almost expect from a poet who finds the idea of a decayed Viking amusing, and tells his sister so.

Letters not written for publication always to some extent put us in the position of voyeurs, hardly knowing how to position ourselves in relation to the prurient interest they permit or provoke. This is intensely so with some of Hughes's letters since his biography has, in some of its detail, been the subject of such extensive, often melodramatic speculation. In fact, in Christopher Reid's selection the profile of Hughes which emerges is at least as much that of a father as it is of a lover and husband, and we must think hard about a man left alone with the daunting prospect of bringing up young children. The letters to his son Nick are admirable: in the patient dedication of their paternal concern and counsel; in their delighted apprehension of shared interests; and notably in the strength of their readiness to discuss the thing father and son share of absolute necessity, Sylvia Plath and her memory. Even very deep affection between fathers and sons is often, I think, expressed only through irony. Ted Hughes's letters to Nick are not like that. This brief passage, written towards the very end of Hughes's life, in a letter in which he eventually accounts for *Birthday Letters*, his volume of poems addressed to Plath, makes vibrantly articulate between father and son both vulnerable human necessity and the fundamental necessity for a writer of the act of writing out of – in both senses – that vulnerability:

> What I was needing to do, all those years, was deal with what had happened to your mother and me. That was the big unmanageable event in my life, that had somehow to be managed – internally – by me. Somehow through my writing – because that's the method I've developed to deal with myself. In Ireland, I did find a way of dealing with it – not by writing about it directly, but dealing with the deep emotional tangle of it <u>indirectly</u>, through other symbols, which is the best and most natural way.[5]

This needs little comment, except to note that the 'method' defended here is also the one Hughes identifies and defines in Plath herself; and that something else, externally now, between father and son, rather than internally, is also being managed – very well – here.

Poison and cure

These four passages focus aspects of Hughes's prose which I want to touch on in this essay: his work for children; his observations on poetry; and the new thing added to our conception of this poet by the publication of his letters. But first Hughes's deep ambivalence about writing prose at all needs to be considered. This is peculiar, since the prose is remarkably extensive, including five books of children's stories; a collection of radio talks for children; a large volume of literary and other essays which omits a considerable amount of published material but includes the outstanding essay on English versification, 'Myths, Metres, Rhythms', which I discuss extensively elsewhere;[6] a vast, controversial study of Shakespeare; the stories originally published together with poems in *Wodwo*, reprinted along with others as *Difficulties of a Bridegroom* (1995); and Christopher Reid's selection from what appears to be a huge archive of letters. In addition, prose of a highly charged, sometimes lineated, kind – 'rough verse', Hughes calls it – constitutes the form of *Gaudete* (1977).[7]

Two other works, in which poetry and prose are interdependent, are also relevant to a consideration of Hughes's ambivalence: the Ur-Crow, in which the poems eventually published in 1970 as *Crow: From the Life and Songs of the Crow* were to have been plotted into a prose narrative;[8] and his Laureate poems, some of which are freighted with mythological and arcane reference and extensively annotated in lengthy, essayistic and opinionated footnotes, in a way possibly owing something to David Jones, whom Hughes admired. Although *Rain-Charm for the Duchy and Other Laureate Poems* (1992) is not often considered seriously by people who write about Hughes, it could be argued that its relationship between poem and prose emblematizes an essential in Hughes's work, since some of the Laureate poems are virtually incomprehensible without their notes. The prose is therefore essential to the poems' semantic survival, although whether the notes justify the opacity of the poems is another matter. Hughes's letters suggest that prose was similarly vital, if not exactly in this way, to the survival of his poetry, even that he regarded his poetry and prose as in some sense sharing a symbiotic relationship. The letters also offer an arresting chronology, making it plain that Hughes was, in fact, at work on children's stories prior to the publication of his first volume of poetry, *The Hawk in the Rain*, in 1957.

Writing to Olwyn as early as 1956, he says he has discovered his 'secret': that he can write poems only when he is busy with prose at the same time.[9] This early perception of prose as poetic enablement is maintained in a letter to his brother in 1957 in which, while admitting the financial benefits of children's stories for a freelance writer, he still insists that they 'come to me absolutely naturally so I'm not prostituting my imagination', and he hyperbolically envisages writing about 5,000 of them.[10] To John Montague, also a writer of short stories as well as verse, he says in 1961 that prose stories 'help me write verse – get the machine going unself-consciously, very necessary in my case'.[11] And in 1969 he is telling Richard Murphy that the *Crow* poems 'make more sense with the prose story', clearly then regarding the work as an integral entity of prose and poetry. As such, it would have further developed the dual form initiated by *Wodwo*, itself possibly prompted by Robert Lowell's revolutionary 1959 volume, *Life Studies*. Our knowledge of its original conception means that *Crow* must have, even for its admirers, what Hughes's subtitle may imply and what he says Coleridge's 'Ballad of the Dark Ladie' actually does have, 'an amputated kind of completeness'.[12] This is an oxymoronic notion but, transferred to the way the poems of *Crow* seem provokingly both fragmentary and at the service of an occulted teleology, it has persuasive hermeneutic power.

Nevertheless, prose is also for Hughes, and from the beginning too, a kind of catastrophe. At issue here is prominently but not exclusively the prose of speculative or argumentative discourse rather than fictional narrative. Hughes makes a point of preserving in *Winter Pollen* his often reiterated undergraduate dream of a smouldering, bloody-handed, anthropoid fox which convinces him to change his degree from English to Archaeology and Anthropology because, the fox says, the writing of critical prose is 'destroying us'.[13] Even if this seems too perfect a Hughesian-mythical fit, another kind of 'story', to be entirely credible as an actual dream, the letters are, corroboratively, frequently negative about prose. In 1983, disparaging in humorously crude terms his long essay on Leonard Baskin, Hughes registers extreme exasperation, saying he'll write no more prose and claiming that he cannot recognize himself in it.[14] A decade later, he explains that he abandoned writing stories for adults because those in *Wodwo* turned out to be 'prophecies about my own life' and in subsequent attempts the prophetic element was even plainer.[15] This is eerie and also tantalizing: but the apparent ability of these stories to tap into an obviously terrifying authorial uncanny could hardly have been more powerfully expressed than by Hughes's decision to stop writing them; which must have been a form of death for a writer who has regarded prose as necessary to verse composition.

This self-protective self-denial consorts with Hughes's feelings about the vast prose effort represented by *Shakespeare and the Goddess of Complete Being* (1992). In a letter to Seamus Heaney in 1998, the last year of Hughes's life, he raises the symbiotic interrelationship between his poetry and prose in a form especially piercing because self-doubting when he says, 'I sometimes wondered if that Shakes [sic] tome wasn't the poem I should have written – decoded, hugely deflected and dumped on shoulders that could carry it.'[16] Some readers of the *Goddess* have wondered not this exactly, but the obverse: whether the book wasn't, by other (prose) means, the poem which he did in fact write as virtually his life's work, in extended sequences which discover alternative ways of both approaching and deflecting a single, inescapable node of distress and finding new codings for it, a distress whose simplest name is Sylvia Plath. That these sequences acted in part therapeutically is what he admits in the letter to Nick which I quoted above. It is the distress of writing the cognate Shakespeare prose, though, which prompts the harrowing negativity of letters in which Hughes blames it for destroying his 'immune system'.[17]

By preventing Hughes from writing English essays, the fox of his undergraduate dream had presumably prevented a community of dream-foxes from being killed: but, by backsliding so catastrophically into prose, Hughes had, he appears to have thought at the end of his life, virtually killed himself. It may seem heartless to say so but there must be fantastication, even of a melodramatic kind, in this. Nevertheless, it is clear that, for Ted Hughes, prose is simultaneously obligation and exacerbation, essential to his life as a poet and at the same time dangerous to his life as a man. It may even be said that prose is, for this writer, a kind of *pharmakon*, the Greek word meaning both poison and cure which Jacques Derrida famously discussed as an almost vertiginously endless play of irresolvable signification.

Stories

As cure, Hughes's prose is prominently associated with children. Although children's stories were there from the beginning for Hughes, as I have said, their importance has not always been recognized by those who write primarily about his poetry, although it is always recognized by poets who write for children and by children's writers. Some of Hughes's stories engage riches of anthropological material of the kind which also fuel a great deal of his poetry; and his 'creation tales', eventually collected in *The Dreamfighter* (1995), may be contemporary 'just so' stories on the Kipling model, but they are also continuous with the mythical and metaphysical effort and effects of some of his poetic sequences. In particular, the figure they identify as 'God' almost scandalously diverges from the figure so named in the Bible, to the extent, I assume, of making some of these stories extremely problematical for Christian or quasi-Christian classrooms. They appear to subvert the narrative of Genesis or, at the very least, to relativize its truth value. Even in a largely post-Christian, or even post-religious, culture the word 'God' continues to carry high valency. José Saramago wonders in *The Gospel According to Jesus Christ* whether one of the things wrong with God is that, unlike everyone else, he shares his name with no one; in Ted Hughes he does.

Hughes's is an anthropomorphic God subject to nightmare, for instance, and to a hectoring mother who, like Hamm's parents in their dustbins in *Endgame*, lives submerged under rubbish. Far more significantly, this is a

God for whom Creation is not the serene authoritativeness of a seven-day plan but a matter of frustrated accident and happenstance. He therefore bears a strong family resemblance to the figure named 'God' in *Crow*; and in this context the original prose-and-verse conception of that sequence takes on an added significance. Neil Roberts tells us that 'Earth-Moon', which was published as a children's poem, was originally written for *Crow* and that Hughes once, 'perhaps provocatively', described *Crow* as a children's story.[18] Anyone who remembers Hughes's readings from the book in the 1970s, with their combinations of verse and apparently partly improvised prose, will find this tantalizing. His beguiling voice had the paradoxically almost assuaging power necessary to a bedtime story; and *Crow* does, in fact, include a poem called 'A Bedtime Story'. For all its bleakness, *Crow* is not entirely unlike Hughes's children's stories, which are unsparing of children's emotional aptitudes as they are conventionally, perhaps sentimentally, conceived. The stories frequently engage forms of sadness and distress without anxiety or condescension: in this story of creation such things just are. An exhaustion with life may lead to thoughts of suicide, for instance; and one haunting moment figures the bee's labour of pollination as the carrying of a demon's tears in his veins. He needs the sweetness of flowers to make him happy, but 'When he is angry and stings, the smart of his sting is the tear of the demon'.[19] The tears of things smart and sting in these stories too.

Hughes appears to have possessed and nourished an intimate rapport with children probably unusual in a man of his generation. His prose for children is profoundly at one with the elements of wonder, mystery and amazement which may also be read out of some of the poetry. This is in part a romantic indebtedness, a keeping of the imaginative lines of communication open by keeping them attuned to the virtue of originary impulse and the poignancy of its falling-off; and Hughes is in this sense, after Yeats (and Lawrence), another of the last romantics, given that 'romanticism' seems, as literary history advances, a term less relevant to chronology than to individual temper. Hughes's prose for children grows, though, at least as much from anthropology as from aesthetics, and specifically from the belief expressed epigrammatically in the essay 'Myth and Education' that 'Every new child is nature's chance to correct culture's error'.[20]

Culture's error

One of Hughes's most compelling, if eccentric, prose pieces is a contribution to a sixtieth-birthday *festschrift* for William Golding in 1986. Entitled 'Baboons and Neanderthalers' and nominally taking *The Inheritors* for theme, the essay displays knowledge of the anthropological theories of

Eugene Marais, which Hughes finds credible, even compelling. People, says Beckett's Estragon, 'are bloody ignorant apes'. Quite the contrary, thinks Marais, according to Hughes: people are over-intelligent apes; premature baboons, in fact, miscarried at a developmental stage when intelligence far outran affective and instinctual capacities. Hughes's unforgettable figure for Marais-man is thus 'a jittery Ariel among the Calibans'; and this is appropriately Shakespearean since what *Shakespeare and the Goddess of Complete Being* calls 'the Shakespearean moment' is, in one of its aspects, 'the inevitable crime of Civilization, or even the inevitable crime of consciousness'.[21] Art and culture are to be understood as compensation for the repression in the unconscious of the consequences of baboon miscarriage which produced humans suffering a tragic misfit between intelligence and instinct.

As far as I know, Marais's theory is held in no repute by contemporary science, and its undoubted poetry is at least as comic as it is tragic. But its view of human nature as animal perversion, and of art's compensatory necessity, account for a great deal in Ted Hughes: notably, for his valorizing of the identity between animal intelligence and instinct as the very ground of his poetic endeavour and its occasions, and his interest in anthropological accounts of the way the curative powers of shamanic figures work in so-called 'primitive' societies. The effort of some of Hughes's prose has itself a quasi-shamanic function: its diagnostic attention is engaged as thoroughly as it is because it attempts to draw the poison of civilization and consciousness; and any potentially curative capacity it might have involves its author in the risk of being, himself, poisoned. However far-fetched this may seem, some such view of the urgency of his prose occasions does appear to underwrite the engagements of his later career.

In *Shakespeare and the Goddess of Complete Being* the crime of consciousness finds a local habitation in the mapping of Shakespeare's agonized sexuality onto the religio-political crisis of his time. The long essays on poetry and poets written in the latter part of Hughes's life – written, we might say, against time – are racked by comparable efforts of identification. They make comparable demands of attention on their readers too when Hughes almost naively trusts that reiteration, microscopic attentiveness, variations of perspective and, occasionally, a Lawrentian resort to exclamatory enthusiasm and hyperbole will supply for conventional discursive argument. Secure architectonic control is not a Hughesian virtue in these long pieces; and we might well find ourselves returning in exhaustion to Hazlitt's relevant praising of the chamois.

'Sylvia Plath: The Evolution of "Sheep in Fog"', 'The Poetic Self: A Centenary Tribute to T. S. Eliot' and 'The Snake in the Oak', on Coleridge, all derive ultimately, as *Shakespeare and the Goddess of Complete Being* does, from

Yeats, who is, in all sorts of ways, the originary poet for Hughes. The Shakespeare book declares its Yeatsian inception in its epigraph:

> The Greeks, a certain scholar has told me, considered that myths are the activities of the Daimons, and that the Daimons shape our characters and our lives. I have often had the fancy that there is some one myth for every man, which, if we but knew it, would make us understand all he did and thought.[22]

Hughes's essential effort in these essays is, consequently, to identify the single myth in these poets – which might in fact be syncretic, as when Plath is discovered combining Phaeton and Icarus – and to unravel, with a species of agonistic patience, the way this is a 'daemonic' given which the poet must first locate and then work through in the accumulating individual poems of an entire life. These poems therefore become, for Hughes, phases of self-knowledge and self-development, 'chapters in a mythology' as he calls them in relation to Plath. Poems have what Hughes calls, also apropos of Plath, 'inexorable inner laws' which must be obeyed under penalty of emotional and artistic disintegration. They are the symbolic representation or projection of the very struggle to constitute psychological and emotional equilibrium, or the confession of an ultimate inability to do so.[23]

The human risk of poetry is therefore almost appallingly high: the cost is potentially not less than everything. In these essays, then, Hughes is not so much a literary critic as both the intuitive diviner and the practised investigator of the occult secret of the individual oeuvre. For all that his archetypal mythologizing has an avatar in Jung, his procedures sometimes resemble Freud's in his case studies, the Freud immersed in Conan Doyle; and he can evince too a comparably almost unnerving assurance in both his procedures and their results. Sometimes, as in the Plath essay, this assurance dazzles with illumination and Hughes is unignorable; at others, notably with Eliot, it illuminates no poet of that name recognizable to me. Unjustified assurance comes to seem therefore, as it always does, presumptive, and leads only to our questioning the grounds on which judgement and discrimination are being made. Hughes's method is manifestly intended as its own justification, as much a form of medical as of literary diagnosis; and one cannot help but think that an invitation is implicitly being extended to explicate the single myth of Hughes's own oeuvre.

Hughes's valuation of poems is, then, something other than aesthetics. In attempting to trace the contours of the activities of the daimons, 'the powers in control of our life, the ultimate suffering and decision in us', these late, nominally literary essays share some of the occult interests which disconcerted some otherwise appreciative reviewers of the letters. This is an unignorable aspect of Hughes's prose, in which such matters as astrology, witchcraft, superstition, shamanism and occult neo-Platonism often arrest and sometimes consume his attention. Disconcertion is probably inevitable unless one shares at least some of Hughes's idiosyncratic beliefs; and the letters in particular manifest the obsessive-compulsive in this regard, notably when their recipients appear to be uncritical admirers. The idiosyncrasy, however, is at root a suspicion of the reflex assumptions of rationality, a hostility to scientism, and an underwriting of the ecology apparent throughout Hughes's life and writing and rendered parabolic in *The Iron Woman* (1993). It is one of the paradoxes of Hughes's prose therefore that it relishes contemporary scientific terminology. This is probably best read as the register of a combative desire to appropriate and make differently usable, as part of an alternative epistemological and even ontological effort, the language of error. Nevertheless, it can disconcert often enough too, as the shaman dons the antiseptic gloves of the laboratory.

Shadowy tenants

The poisoned chalice of Ted Hughes's prose is elevated effortfully, then, above error; and the effort, I have suggested, sometimes shows at the levels of style and argument. It's a relief, always, to turn to the grace and subtlety of those simply memorable statements made more casually about poets he admires.

On Keith Douglas: 'inside each line an entirely fresh melody starts up, forges a quick path against our expectation, and leaves the line as a trace of its passage, while a quite different melody, from some unexpected angle, inscribes another flourish beneath it, followed by another just as surprising'.[24] Hughes here demonstrates a talent for the closest of close reading, in both the accuracy of sympathetic analysis and the specificity of aural attention. He suggestively evokes the almost aleatory nature of Douglas's music, which many have found difficult to hear at all. He conveys its ultra-modern restlessness, appreciating the risky adventure of a rhythm subverting itself in the very act of articulation. In addition, forging a path and leaving a trace could be implicitly military metaphors and therefore empathetically appropriate to the poet of such work as 'How to Kill', who was himself killed at twenty-four, leaving his angular lines as the trace of his own passage.

On Emily Dickinson Hughes writes that, despite her poetry's trust in the life she loves, her poems constantly approach 'almost a final revelation of horrible Nothingness ... Remaining true to this, she could make up her mind about nothing. It stared through her life. Registering everywhere and in everything the icy chill of its nearness, she did not know what to think.'[25] This turns Dickinson inside out in the way the poems sometimes reverse themselves, carrying what initially appears to be warmth to a sudden freezing point, or opening gaping chasms in what had seemed solid ground. The scepticism of what Hughes thinks her sense of Nothingness prompts her to – 'she could make up her mind about nothing' – is so intrinsic to her poems that we might think of it as forming both the rationale of her (lack of) punctuation and the reason for her vast productivity. Hughes phrases this with a little flicker of ambiguity: she did not know what to think about anything, or she knew exactly what to think about nothing, since she thought about nothing else. And he reads that response as itself an act of attention virtually religious in its devotion, producing the (eventually) published liturgy of an intense privacy, a negative revelation.

On Dylan Thomas in his letters: 'Somewhere inside his head was a minia-ture replica of the world, with heavens and hells to match, in a brilliant radiance, slightly caricature, but quite real: it tumbles through his prose.'[26] This characterization of Thomas's microcosmic representation of an actual world which, by the vivid light of peculiar and peculiarly artful imagination, becomes alternatively actual, itself brilliantly replicates in critical prose the brilliant replications of its subject, even while intimating an element of critique. Then, meditating further on the way Thomas's letters form 'the best introduction to the way his poetry ought to be read', Hughes says: 'Everything we associate with a poem is its shadowy tenant and part of its meaning, no matter how New Critical purist we try to be.'[27] The general-ization, made against a critical orthodoxy – *the* critical orthodoxy of the Cambridge syllabus which this critic had himself rejected – is all the more compelling because of the proof just given of this critic's own competence within the terms of that very orthodoxy. It is compelling in other ways too: and the phrase 'shadowy tenant' vividly summons the material – biographical or historical, for instance, the stuff of letters, or mythical-psychoanalytical, the stuff of Hughes's readings – which critical dispensations less narrow than the New Critical might lure from its resident dark corners in poems.

In Hughes's remarks on living poets in his letters there are varieties of both acuity and generosity of the kind we find elsewhere in the letters too. Generosity is outstandingly present in the unenviously complimentary letter to Seamus Heaney when he won the Nobel Prize in 1995.[28] But there is also occasionally an acerbic humour, expressed with excellent comic timing. Eliot's smile, for instance, is 'like someone recovering from some serious operation'; and, of Neruda, 'he read torrentially for about 25 minutes off a piece of paper about 3" by 4". Then he turned it over, & read on', where the comma is deliciously placed, and the ampersand appropriately and surely satirically urgent.[29]

With regard to Eliot, however, whom, 'The Poetic Self' makes plain, Hughes revered above all other moderns – indeed, it appears, above all other poets except Shakespeare – the satire is subdued to awe: 'when he spoke, I had the impression of a slicing, advancing, undeflectible force of terrific mass. My image for it was – like the bows of the Queen Mary.'[30] The 'image' here – for earned authority and absolute singularity of aim – is itself made use of in a memorial poem by Seamus Heaney, to whom Hughes had presumably said something similar in conversation. In 'Stern' in *District and Circle* (2006) the prose-style of a poet therefore becomes, fittingly, a new poem by another poet. A private conversation between poets turns into the public conversation of literary history, the register of a continuity of poets – Eliot, Hughes, Heaney – vigilantly looking out for one another, in several senses, as Heaney conceives of himself 'standing on a pierhead watching him / All the while watching me as he rows out'.

NOTES

1. William Hazlitt, *The Fight and Other Writings*, ed. Tom Paulin and David Chandler (London: Penguin Books, 2000), p. 393.
2. Ted Hughes, *Tales of the Early World* (London: Faber and Faber, 1988), p. 80.
3. *WP* 178.
4. *LTH* 170.
5. *Ibid.*, 711–12.
6. See Neil Corcoran, *Shakespeare and the Modern Poet* (Cambridge: Cambridge University Press, 2010), pp. 183–99.
7. For his definition of *Gaudete*, see Ted Hughes, *Difficulties of a Bridegroom: Collected Short Stories* (London: Faber and Faber, 1995), p. ix.
8. A version of the narrative is recovered from various sources in an appendix to Keith Sagar's *The Laughter of Foxes: A Study of Ted Hughes* (Liverpool: Liverpool University Press, 2000), pp. 170–80.
9. *LTH* 34.
10. *Ibid.*, p. 108.
11. *Ibid.*, p. 189.
12. *WP* 496–7.
13. *WP* 9. Carol Hughes confirms that the contents of *Winter Pollen* were selected collaboratively by Hughes and William Scammell.
14. *LTH* 474.
15. *Ibid.*, p. 644.
16. *Ibid.*, p. 704.
17. See, for instance, *LTH* 719.
18. Neil Roberts, *Ted Hughes: A Literary Life* (Basingstoke: Palgrave Macmillan, 2006), p. 168.
19. Ted Hughes, *The Dreamfighter and Other Creation Tales* (London: Faber and Faber, 1995), p. 50.
20. *WP* 149.
21. John Carey (ed.), *William Golding: The Man and His Books* (London: Faber and Faber, 1986), p. 166; *SGCB*, 1993 edn, p. 47.
22. W. B. Yeats, *Essays and Introductions* (London: The Macmillan Press, 1961), p. 107.

23. *WP* 205.
24. Keith Douglas, *Complete Poems*, ed. Desmond Graham, with a new introduction by Ted Hughes (Oxford: Oxford University Press, 1987), p. xxi.
25. *WP* 158.
26. *Ibid.*, 79.
27. *Ibid.*, 81.
28. *LTH* 683.
29. *Ibid.*, pp. 159–60, 247.
30. *WP* 645.

10

JONATHAN BATE

Hughes on Shakespeare

Oscar Wilde remarked that criticism is the only civilized form of autobiography, while Virginia Woolf believed that all Shakespearean criticism is as much about the critic's self as the dramatist's plays. Shakespeare is a mirror in which serious readers and spectators see sharpened images of themselves and their own worlds.

Shakespeare was the absolute centre of Ted Hughes's sense of the English literary tradition. The plays were a major influence on his own poetry, in terms of both linguistic intensity and thematic preoccupation. The world of Hughes's verse is one in which, as Macbeth puts it, 'light thickens, and the crow / Makes wing to the rooky wood'.[1] More than any other poet, Shakespeare assaulted Hughes – one of the great literary *readers* of the twentieth century – with the shock of the as-if-new. An unpublished journal entry dated 22 January 1998 begins 'The idea of flamingoes. Of clam-dippers. Read with amazement: "Mine eye hath played the painter and hath stell'd" as if I'd never seen it before'.[2] This is what Hughes did throughout his life: read Shakespeare with amazement, as if he had never read him before. The key to Shakespearean acting is to speak each line as if it were being spoken for the first time, as if it were new minted from the thought-chamber of the character who utters it. In this regard, Hughes – who was fascinated by actors and the process of making theatre – read Shakespeare as if he were an actor playing all the parts. Which is probably how Shakespeare wrote Shakespeare.

Encouraged by his intellectual mentor, his older sister Olwyn, Ted Hughes read the whole of Shakespeare when he was a teenager, working his way through a battered copy of W. J. Craig's double-column, small print Oxford edition, originally published in 1891. In the summer of 1957, having moved to America with Sylvia Plath, he told his Cambridge friend Lucas Myers that he was rereading all the plays in what he considered to be their order of composition. He showed particular interest in the late collaborations with Fletcher, *Henry VIII* and *The Two Noble Kinsmen*: 'The Shakespeare in it is incredible in that it seems at first better than Shakespeare–but the rest, a great deal, is Fletcher. "Late Shakespeare" gets the blame for a lot of Fletcher' (*LTH* 105). In distinguishing between the styles of Shakespeare and Fletcher, he revealed the ear for the movement of Shakespearean verse that went along with his appetite for a big-picture understanding of the plays.

Shakespearean characters are prominent in the pantheon of Hughes's presiding deities. A poem in *Lupercal* (1960) is written from the point of view of 'Cleopatra to the Asp'. A verse sequence drafted in the 1980s under the title *Court Cards* offers readings of works ranging from *Venus and Adonis* to *The Tempest*, by way of the major tragedies and the relationship between Hal and Falstaff in *Henry IV*, partially published in 1987 as *A Full House* (*CP* 731–6). The dead Sylvia Plath makes one of her earliest entrances into the corpus of Hughes's poetry via 'Ophelia', first published privately in *Orts*, then revised in *River* (*CP* 655). 'Setebos' in *Birthday Letters* casts Sylvia as Miranda, Ted as Ferdinand, Aurelia Plath as Prospero, Ariel as the aura of creativity shared by the lovers and Caliban as their dark secret inner life. An unpublished poem among the *Birthday Letters* drafts refracts Plath's anger against her father through Timon of Athens's rage against the world.[3] One of the very last poems Hughes published was entitled 'Shakespeare, drafting his will' (*CP* 1193).

Although his responsiveness to Shakespeare in both verse and prose was lifelong, it was only in 1969 that Hughes began to write systematically about the plays. An exchange of letters with his publisher, Charles Monteith at Faber and Faber, explains the origin of a project that would consume Hughes for well over twenty years, almost until his dying day. In 1968 he had edited *A Choice of Emily Dickinson's Verse* for a Faber series. Monteith asked him to undertake a similar volume of Emily Brontë, a poet close to his heart. Hughes replied that he would think about it, but that what he really wanted to do was a selection of Shakespeare's verse for the series. He suggested that it would be novel and interesting to treat Shakespeare's plays as poetry, not as drama. Monteith was extremely enthusiastic, immediately seeing a ready market. The Faber archive reveals that he proposed a decent advance (£150 on delivery) and a royalty of 10 per cent on the hardback, 7.5 per cent on the paperback. Hughes could do the Brontë as well, but the Shakespeare was infinitely more important.

Ted Hughes set to work. But the coming three months, March to May 1969, were among the most traumatic of his life. First his lover, Assia Wevill, gassed herself and her daughter Shura. Then, just seven weeks later, on 14 May, Hughes recorded in his journal that he had woken at one o'clock in the morning with the absolute conviction that his mother was dead. He was still shaken when he got up. He wrestled over the introduction for the anthology ('dismay and disapp[ointment] with it') until the phone rang at 10.15. It was his sister Olwyn, who told him that 'Ma died last night'. He always believed that it was the shock of the news of Assia's death that killed his mother.[4]

Despite all this, he managed to deliver the typescript of A *Choice of Shakespeare's Verse* to Monteith on 23 June 1969, explaining in a covering letter that he had written a long introduction, but was sending a short one. He was not satisfied. Throughout the summer and autumn, he reworked both the selection and the introduction. On 3 December, from Lumb Bank in Yorkshire, he sent Monteith a new version 'with minute introduction (the cancelled efforts fill a small suitcase)'. At the same time, he dispatched 'my collected Crow pieces–35 or 40'.[5] He had been working on crow poems for years. On Assia's death, he had stopped writing new ones, but continued revising old ones and changing his mind about how many, and which, to include in a published sequence.

The Shakespeare project, then, had its origins in a time not only of extraordinary personal trauma but also of thinking about his first major poetry collection since *Wodwo* (published in 1967, but mostly written before Sylvia Plath's death in 1963). Years later, Hughes would introduce public readings of the *Crow* poems by explaining that Crow's quest was to meet his maker, God. But every time he met Him, it was a Her, a woman, an incarnation of the goddess. Each time, Crow was unsatisfied and had to move on to another encounter.[6] Hughes read Shakespeare's career in the same way that he read his own *Crow*: the argument that begins to emerge in the introduction to *A Choice of Shakespeare's Verse* and that is articulated at enormous length in *Shakespeare and the Goddess of Complete Being* (1992) is that Shakespeare's developing art unfolded through a series of encounters with this same goddess.

The wellspring of this idea takes us back to Hughes's teenage years. The desire to read Shakespeare more profoundly was one of the forces that led him to apply for a place to study English at Pembroke College, Cambridge. As a 'going up' present, his school English teacher, John Fisher, gave him a copy of Robert Graves's *The White Goddess*.[7] The best account of the importance of this book to Hughes, and its formative influence on the way in which he read Shakespeare, is a letter to Nick Gammage written over forty years later (*LTH* 679–81). Here, Hughes recalled that he felt a little resentment on his first reading of *The White Goddess*, since Graves had taken possession of what he considered to be his own 'secret patch'. The book's argument was that the same goddess who presides over birth, love and death was worshipped under different names in the mythologies of the Greeks and the Egyptians, the Irish and the Welsh, and countless other ancient cultures. Beautiful, fickle, wise and implacable, she later becomes the Ninefold Muse, patroness of the white magic of poetry. Shakespeare, Graves mentions in passing, 'knew and feared her': we see playful elements of the goddess in Titania, a more serious approach in Lady Macbeth and Cleopatra, and her ultimate manifestation in the absent but forceful deity of Sycorax, Caliban's mother in *The Tempest*.[8] Graves's syncretic method – his yoking of Middle Eastern material with Celtic – was already familiar to Hughes from his own researches in arcane mythology, which had begun in his early teens. What really struck him in the book were 'those supernatural women. Especially the underworld women'. He'd already begun to work out a relationship with a chthonic female deity in 'Song' (*CP* 24), which he always considered to be his first important poem.

Gammage asked Hughes whether *The White Goddess* had been his first exposure to the religious context in which Shakespeare's imagination was formed. He replied that he was not sure how clearly or consciously he saw the pattern at the time, but that the idea of 'Goddess-centred matriarchy being overthrown by a God-centred patriarchy' was indeed most likely something that he first really grasped in the Graves. 'In giving me that big picture fairly early, yes, The White Goddess had a big part – and it was the Graves maybe that made the link directly to that lineage in English poetry – from the Sycorax figure to La Belle Dame [of Keats] and the Nightmare Life in Death [of Coleridge's 'Ancient Mariner']. Made it conscious and obvious' (*LTH* 681). Woman and goddess, sex and death, the underworld and the hidden current of nature worship in opposition to patriarchal monotheism – this was the network of associations that Hughes took from Graves and brought to his reading of Shakespeare.

He knew that such associations would raise the eyebrows of academic Shakespeare experts. On New Year's day 1970, he wrote again to Monteith, explaining that the introduction to the anthology was the consequence of his having been 'bitten fiercely by my hypothesis bug'. Monteith had to understand that it was 'an imaginative idea rather than a scholarly idea, so it may take time to plant its fifth columns and get some acceptance, especially as Shakespeare scholars are such a jealous lot'. Disarmingly, Hughes added that he hadn't read any Shakespeare criticism, except for A. C. Bradley long ago.[9]

Because of various complications and delays at Faber, together with anxieties over the timetable for publication of a series of titles in different genres by the ever-prolific Hughes, the Shakespeare anthology did not appear until the autumn of 1971. It was overtaken into print not only by a privately printed text of the Introduction accompanied by a quietly self-revelatory poem called 'Crow's Song about Prospero and Sycorax' (*CP* 576), but also by an American version of the entire book with a variant title – foisted on Hughes by the publisher – that took the form of a quotation from *Cymbeline*: *With Fairest Flowers While Summer Lasts*.

The Shakespearean whose opinion Hughes valued most highly was the director Peter Brook. It was Brook, he later wrote in the dedication to *Shakespeare and the Goddess of Complete Being*, who 'provided the key to the key'. It was for Brook that he had worked on Seneca's *Oedipus* at the Old Vic, his seminal exposure to the making of powerful theatre, and for whom he had been asked to write a *King Lear* screenplay (never completed). Hughes made a point of sending Brook the American as opposed to the British version of the anthology. Faber had decided to tuck most of the Introduction, to which he had devoted so much effort through so many difficult months, away at the back of the volume. The extended American version had the virtue of presenting it up front.

The Introduction to *With Fairest Flowers While Summer Lasts* remains the most lucid and economic summary of Hughes's hypothesis about the key to Shakespeare's imagination. In reading Shakespeare, he proposes, we periodically come upon passages of white-hot poetic intensity. When he extracted these passages and put them together in an anthology, he discovered that many of them had a structure of feeling in common, a 'strong family resemblance'. They were all hammering at the same thing, 'a particular knot of obsessions'.[10] By reading them as short, self-contained lyric poems, we simultaneously 'look through them into our own darkness'[11] and find ourselves 'plucking out Shakespeare's heart' – which, we discover, 'has a black look'.[12]

'The poetry has its taproot,' Hughes claims, 'in a sexual dilemma of a peculiarly black and ugly sort.'[13] Belittling as it might seem to boil Shakespeare down to a single idea, if the idea is big enough it can prove itself the key to his imagination. After all, for all his vaunted variety and impersonality, Shakespeare was finally 'stuck with himself'. The works are the expression of his own nature. The greatest passages constitute Shakespeare's recurrent dream. In them, his imagination 'presents the mystery of himself to himself'.[14] Wilde and Woolf would no doubt say at this point that the heart, the nature, the dream, the imagination, into which Hughes was gazing as he wrote this were not Shakespeare's but his own.

In the early 1590s, during a period when the theatres were closed because of plague, Shakespeare wrote two narrative poems, *Venus and Adonis* (goddess of love attempts to seduce reluctant virginal male youth who is more interested in hunting and ends up being gored to death by a boar) and *The Rape of Lucrece* (king's son Tarquin attempts to seduce, then rapes, virtuous woman Lucrece, who commits suicide, such is her shame). Here, 'where nothing but poetry concerned him', argues Hughes, Shakespeare produced two versions, one light and the other dark, of his core fable.[15] The same structure can, however, be seen in many of the plays, for instance in 'the polar opposition of Falstaff and Prince Hal' in the *Henry IV* plays, or the encounter between Angelo and Isabella in *Measure for Measure*.[16] In each case, one figure represents the earth, submission to the body and the forces of desire, while the other stands for the heavens, purity of spirit and the repression of desire. Venus and Falstaff are figures of capacious and celebratory desire, embodiments of the 'goddess', while Tarquin and Angelo represent destructive sexual possessiveness turned against the goddess.

For Hughes, a great poet is, as Ben Jonson said Shakespeare was, the soul of the age. The opposition is accordingly read not only as Shakespeare's personal dilemma, but also as a perfect representation of 'the prevailing psychic conflict of his times in England, the conflict that exploded, eventually, into the Civil War'.[17] The repression of the goddess by the forces of radical Protestantism took its distinctively English form in the extirpation of the cult of Mary. Though the process was temporarily slowed by the cult of Queen Elizabeth as a kind of substitute Mary, the rise of Puritanism amounted to a dragging into court 'by the young Puritan Jehovah' of 'the Queen of Heaven, who was the goddess of Catholicism, who was the goddess of medieval and pre-Christian England, who was the divinity of the throne, who was the goddess of natural law and of love, who was the goddess of all sensation and organic life – this overwhelmingly powerful, multiple, primeval being'.[18] The forces that drive Hughes's own poetry – the implacable but vital law of nature, woman, sexual desire, sensation, organic life, sacramental royalty – are overwhelmingly those associated with the goddess.

For Hughes, Shakespeare's distinctive twist on the myth is his imagination of figures who attempt to 'divide nature, and especially love, the creative force of nature, into abstract good and physical evil'. Nature, being one (the goddess of *complete* being), will not let them do this, with the result that love returns in the destructive form of rape, murder, madness and the death-wish. An 'occult crossover' occurs, causing a 'mysterious chemical change' in which 'Nature's maddened force' takes over the brain that had rejected her.[19] This was what he called the Tragic Equation. In a single sentence of wild reach and energy, Hughes sketches how the equation operates as the key to the 'powerhouse and torture chamber' of Shakespeare's complete works:

> Hamlet, looking at Ophelia, sees his mother in bed with his uncle and goes mad; Othello, looking at his pure wife, sees Cassio's whore and goes mad; Macbeth, looking at the throne of Scotland, and listening to his wife, hears the witches, the three faces of Hecate, and the invitation of hell, and goes mad; Lear, looking at Cordelia, sees Goneril and Regan, and goes mad; Antony, looking at his precious queen, sees the ribaudred nag of Egypt betraying him 'to the very heart of loss,' and goes – in a sense – mad; Timon, looking at his loving friends, sees the wolf pack of Athenian creditors and greedy whores, and goes mad; Coriolanus,

looking at his wife and mother, sees the Roman mob who want to tear him to pieces, and begins to act like a madman; Leontes, looking at his wife, sees Polixenes' whore, and begins to act like a madman; Posthumus, looking at his bride, who of his 'lawful pleasure oft restrained' him, sees the one Iachimo mounted 'like a full-acorn'd boar,' and begins to act like a madman.[20]

In this passage, we see both the strength and the weakness of Hughes's reading of Shakespeare: yes, there is a recurrent pattern of madness or quasi-madness provoked by intensity of sexual and familial relations, but no, this cannot be the key to all of Shakespeare (it underplays comedy, self-conscious theatrical play and so much more). In trying to reduce all the dramas to a single force, there is inevitably something forced. Hence such giveaways as 'goes – *in a sense* – mad'. Yet the insights offered by the pattern are exceptionally rich. Richard III, Tarquin, Hamlet, Angelo, Othello, Macbeth – each of them is, as Hughes says, a 'strange new being', a 'man of chaos' (xvii). And it is the men of chaos ('from Aaron to Caliban') who speak the most memorable poetry, the passages that Hughes extracts and presents in his anthology. His selection has at its centre a great riff of nearly forty sequences of high-voltage poetic madness from Macbeth, Lear and Timon.

At various points in his Introduction, Hughes deploys phrases remembered from his undergraduate study of English at Cambridge: 'dissociation of sensibility' (T. S. Eliot on what happened to English poetry around the time of the Civil War), 'the Shakespearean moment' (Cambridge-influenced critic Patrick Cruttwell's phrase for the historical and cultural forces that came to a head in the 1590s, making it possible for Marlowe, Shakespeare and Donne to write the greatest poetry ever seen in the English language). Hughes redefines Eliot's 'dissociation of sensibility' as a rupture in English culture caused by the banishment of the goddess from the national psyche. He sees 'Blake, Wordsworth, Keats, Hardy, (Hopkins), Yeats and Eliot, to name the most obvious, as records – made at upheaval intervals – of Nature's attempt to correct the error, supply the natural body of things and heal the torment' (*LTH* 336). In this list, he is at once proclaiming a line of succession from Shakespeare to himself and offering a Gravesian reading of the Leavisite canon he studied for the first part of the Cambridge English Tripos, prior to his switch to Archaeology and Anthropology.

The copy of *With Fairest Flowers* that Hughes sent to Peter Brook was accompanied by a letter summarizing the argument that had shaped both selection and introduction, together with an outline for a possible dramatization that would set this argument, and Shakespeare's work, in the religious context of his age: 'Elizabeth and Mary Tudor go straight into the Venus lineage ... Then it could be brought forward, using Milton's Paradise Lost and Samson Agonistes as a continuation of Shakespeare's series.' There could be an epilogue in the style of the ancient Greek satyr play that followed a cycle of tragedies: rival politicians Edward Heath and Harold Wilson would be monkeys in the mask of Adonis and Tarquin, 'Lucrece would be Princess Anne, and Venus would be a schizophrenic female gorilla in Regent's park' (*LTH* 329).

Though eminently capable of self-parody of this kind, Ted Hughes was deadly serious about his great Shakespearean project. Undeterred by the lukewarm critical response to his anthology, in 1973 he wrote a poem called 'An Alchemy' for a celebration of Shakespeare's birthday (*CP* 279–82). In a letter to fellow poet Peter Redgrove (who would later visit Gravesian goddess territory himself in *The Wise Woman*, co-written with Penelope Shuttle, and *The Black Goddess and the Sixth Sense*), Hughes explained that 'An Alchemy' was a compacting of his anthology, in which he had sought to demonstrate how Shakespeare's own personal psychodrama embodied the historical development of the national psyche, even the entire Western tradition: 'Shakespeare recorded, somewhat helplessly, what was actually going on in the English spirit, which was the defamation, subjection and eventual murder of what he first encountered as Venus – the Mary Goddess of the Middle Ages and earlier ... So the poem [*Venus and Adonis*] sets up Shakespeare as the crucial record of the real inner story of the whole of Western History. But very abbreviated and in bagatelle style' (*LTH* 336).

Hughes told Redgrove that he did not want to burden himself with an entire book, which was why he had worked out the idea in the abbreviated form of anthology, introduction and then poem. But he couldn't let go of his desire to unlock the key to the plays. Eventually, in *Shakespeare and the Goddess of Complete Being*, he would tell the same story in unabbreviated form and in a style that was no bagatelle.

In 1978, inspired by Hughes's anthology, a Swedish actor and director called Donya Feuer put together a one-woman show called *Soundings*, which interlinked an array of Shakespearean soliloquies. She started up a correspondence with Hughes, leading him to write a long letter further developing his theory by way of a detailed reading of the play she went on to stage the following year, *Measure for Measure* (*LTH* 405–19). They remained in touch, by post and telephone. By now he believed that the fifteen plays of the second half of Shakespeare's career, from *As You Like It* in 1599 to *The Tempest* in 1611, formed a single epic cycle. In 1990, Feuer wrote to suggest that she might create a production that brought extracts from all fifteen together in a single narrative. Beginning on Shakespeare's birthday, 23 April, Hughes sent her in return a steady stream of immensely long letters, which he eventually worked up into the book that was published two years later. Obsessively, he devoted almost all his time to the project. The archives of his papers in Emory University and the British Library contain dozens of drafts, revisions, fragments, proofs, recordings of dictation, amounting to well over 10,000 pages of handwritten and typed material. Hughes later said that writing so much prose had destroyed his immune system, made him ill, almost killed him.

Faber agreed, with some scepticism, to publish the book. In the summer of 1991 it was put into the hands of a copy-editor, Gillian Bate. Each of her scrupulous and particular requests for clarification led Hughes to send great screeds of new material. Thus on 21 July 1991, in answer to a letter about routine copy-editorial matters: 'I'm sorry to be so long returning this, but I wanted to clear up one thing that has been a difficulty from the beginning. The business of Occult Neoplatonism. One can't just refer to this and assume that even Shakespearean scholars will understand and supply the rest. 400 years of cultural suppressive dismissal aren't going to be lifted' (*LTH* 596). Six weeks later: 'Thank you for the thousand improving suggestions. Don't be alarmed by the enclosed ...'[21] The next day: 'Dear Gillian, I've sent you the wrong note – in the text and as a spare copy – for page 344. By wrong I mean an early draft, a little unclear and missing the main opportunity. This is the most important note of all – clarifying every obscurity. Destroy the other one, so it can't creep back in.' A week after this: 'Also, is it possible to have a note to a note. For instance, on this page 18 I would like to add a brief note to "prodigiously virile" – 9th line from the bottom.' The note is then provided: 'As the son of an occasional Butcher, and the nephew of several farmers, Shakespeare's familiarity with pigs is not irrelevant to his myth. The imagination's symbols are based on subliminal perception. The male, aphrodisiac, pheromone scent spray, sold in modern sex-shops, is based on a hormone extract from the Wild Boar.' Another letter, the same day: 'How are you getting on? This isn't a new note, though it's new to you. It's an old note that I lost – and have now found. Could you tuck it in? I think it's a Note, don't you? If it were inserted as a para, at that point, it might be just a bit dissonant – in tone, in actual style. How does it appear to you?' Gillian Bate sent a calm postcard in reply: 'Dear Ted, Thank you for all your communications of this week. I am digesting them slowly and hope to be in touch middle of next week with any questions still remaining ... I have to return all to Fabers end of next week.'

Before the end of that week, another fat envelope dropped through her letterbox: 'Dear Gillian – "What, will the line stretch out to the crack of doom?" This is a *rewritten* note – just slightly lengthened. But it struck me that the original was confused and inadequate. Just slot it in' (16 September 1991).

Then on 3 November came a desperate plea: 'The last bubbles of the last gasp. I know you are onto other work, that Fagin and Fagin, as my friend Leonard Baskin calls them, have cut off any more payment, and that you are ready to scream if you see that dreaded red-hot iron albatross – the word Shakespeare – ever again, but I am happy to refund you for any time this now costs: and refund you treble ... Enclosed below are the last bits of wordage repair.'

On 18 November, Christopher Reid, Hughes's commissioning editor at Faber, put his foot down and said that they simply could not implement the latest set of changes. This did not stop Hughes from making hundreds more corrections in proof, before the typescript was finally sent to the printer at the end of the year.

Shakespeare and the Goddess of Complete Being was published on 9 March 1992. It was an attempt to read the whole of Shakespeare (though very much weighted towards the second half of his career) through the argument that had been aired in the Introduction to the anthology and expanded across Hughes's writings in prose and verse, on poetry and on myth, in the intervening years. 'The idea of nature as a single organism is not new,' he had written in a book review back in 1970, while the anthology was at press, 'It was man's first great thought, the basic intuition of most primitive theologies. Since Christianity hardened into Protestantism, we can follow its underground heretical life, leagued with everything occult, spiritualistic, devilish, over-emotional, bestial, mystical, feminine, crazy, revolutionary, and poetic' (WP 132). *Shakespeare and the Goddess of Complete Being* presents itself as an excavation of the occult, the underground, Shakespeare. It is an aria upon those aspects of Shakespeare's works that are most spiritualistic, devilish, over-emotional, bestial, mystical, feminine, crazy, revolutionary and poetic. Dipping one moment into Cabbala and Hermetic Occult Neoplatonism, Gnostic ritual and alchemy, the next into biographical speculation about Shakespeare's relationship with the Earl of Southampton, and the one after that into the historical clash of Catholic and Protestant – 'Shakespeare was a shaman, a prophet, of the ascendant, revolutionary, Puritan will (in its Elizabethan and Jacobean phase) just as surely as he was a visionary, redemptive shaman of the Catholic defeat' (SGCB 91) – it maps the Venus/Adonis/boar (sex/will/death) triad across the works, whilst also sketching a secondary theme of the Rival Brothers (another key Hughesian preoccupation, and one with autobiographical origins).

At several crucial moments, Hughes breaks one of the cardinal rules of twentieth-century Shakespearean criticism: he links the plays directly to the life. It is unimaginable, he suggests (though most previous critics had silently imagined the possibility), that when Shakespeare came to plot *All's Well that*

Ends Well he could have failed to recognize 'just how closely the story tracked his own domestic life, and particularly that most decisive move he ever made – his first flight from his wife (for whatever reason). And his continuing to stay away, except for those visits' (*SGCB* 116). Pursued by an infatuated woman, forced by her powerful guardian to marry her, haunted by her image when he thinks himself in an adulterous liaison with another woman: this is Hughes's reading of both Bertram in the play and William of Stratford in real life. 'When Shakespeare was writing *All's Well that Ends Well* the autobiographical secret sharer must have been breathing down his neck. To avoid it with a different plot, if he had wished to, would have been the simplest thing. But he must have searched out that specific plot for that specific reason – to deal in some way with that heavy breather' (*SGCB* 116–17).

Wilde and Woolf may come to our assistance again: this is Ted Hughes dealing with the heavy breather, the 'autobiographical secret sharer'. We have no way of knowing whether or not Shakespeare's flight from Stratford and Anne Hathaway some time in the mid or late 1580s was 'the most decisive move he ever made'. But we know for sure that the whole course of Ted Hughes's future life was decided by his flight from Sylvia Plath and Court Green in 1962.

Similarly with his account of the interplay of love and lust in the character of Troilus: 'this new factor, the larval or introductory phase of the hero's idyllic (idealistic) love, enables Shakespeare to connect his Mythic Equation to the impassioned enigma of his own subjectivity (as the *Sonnets* revealed it) in a way that is impossible to ignore . . . This helps to give *Troilus and Cresida* its autobiographical feel' (*SGCB* 179). A bomb is exploding here. In short, 'the loved and the loathed woman in the one body' (*SGCB* 183) is the beautiful, the desired, the unashamedly adulterous Assia Wevill just as much as it is Shakespeare's Cressida. Hughes has thought deeply, but above all feelingly, from experience, about heterosexual desire and its relationship to death in this play. He has less to say about the homoerotic dimension of the Greek camp – the question of same-sex desire is a conspicuous absence from nearly all Hughes's work, which cannot be said of Shakespeare's.

From *All's Well*'s Helen, the bold and fatherless traveller who prefigures Sylvia, Hughes's Shakespeare – or should we say Shakespeare's Hughes – has proceeded to the dark, complex figure of Cressida/Assia, at once seductress and victim, on an inevitable path to a terrible end. Later, with *King Lear*, comfort will be found in the form of a very different woman, younger, de-eroticized and above all discreet. One of the book's epigraphs is a quotation from Ann Pasternak Slater's *Shakespeare the Director*: 'Cordelia is the quiet absolute . . . her very silence is the still centre of this turning world' (*SGCB* xix).

Unsurprisingly, *Shakespeare and the Goddess of Complete Being* was condemned by most academic critics as an extended eccentricity. Professor John Carey of Oxford University set the tone in the *Sunday Times* of 5 April 1992:

> Most Hughes-ish of all is the book's enormous and glaring self-contradiction. For in its whole goddess-worshipping stance it purports to celebrate the female principle, fluid and fertile, as against the logical and scientific male ego, with its 'repetitive tested routines'. Yet Hughes, cramming the live flesh of each play into the straitjacket of his myth, is a positive demon for repetitive routines, and the pretentious scientific language he adopts throughout (comparing the plays to rockets, space capsules, nuclear power stations etc) clinches his similarity to the male ego he is supposed to be condemning. This same contradiction runs right through his poetry, pitting the designs his brain concocts against the anarchic welter of his imagination.
>
> Fortunately, his poetic dynamism does at one point break free from the rhapsodic muddle of Shakespearean exegesis that mostly entangles him. In a long footnote on page 11 he describes a huge matriarchal sow, gross, whiskery, many-breasted, a riot of carnality, with a terrible lolling mouth 'like a Breughelesque nightmare vagina, baggy with overproduction'. Although smuggled in as a hermaphroditic version of the mythic boar, this sow has absolutely nothing to do with Shakespeare, and everything to do with Hughes's violently divided feelings about women. A magnificent late-Hughes prose-poem, the footnote is worth all the rest of the book several times over.

Dr Eric Griffiths of Cambridge was moved to wonder whether Hughes had been rewiring his house, such was the profusion of imagery regarding Shakespeare's voltage, poetic current, flashpoints and the like. Griffiths concluded that there were '28 pages worth reading in this book (beginning at p. 129). In those pages, Hughes pays attention to what Shakespeare wrote. The effect is wonderful.'[22] The pages in question are indeed a masterclass in the close reading of a particular technique of Shakespearean verse, namely the rhetorical figure of doubling known as hendiadys. The analysis of one example from *All's Well*, 'the catastrophe and heel of pastime', is especially brilliant (*SGCB* 142–5).

Hughes was stung but not deterred. He penned an unpublished essay called 'Single Vision and Newton's Sleep in John Carey', which gave him the occasion to set off on his Gravesian mythical-poetic journey once more: 'my Crow is Bran of the Tower Ravens. Bran who was Apollo (a Crow God) plus his son, the Crow demi-god Asclepius the Healer (whose mother was the white Crow Goddess Coronis), was the god-king, a crow god, of early Britain, where he was also the Llud who was Llyr who was Lear. More mumbo jumbo to make [Carey] smile.'[23]

As for Griffiths, he was an academic. Hughes does not pretend to be – nor in his worst nightmares could have imagined himself as – such an aetiolated creature. He approaches the plays 'like an industrial spy, not for the purpose of discursive comment, but with the sole idea of appropriating, somehow, the secrets of what makes them work as fascinating stage events, as big poems, and as language, so that I can adapt them to my own doings in different circumstances'. So it is that 'Griffiths spends his days thinking and talking about scholarship and criticism. I spend my days, as I always have done, inventing and thinking about new poetic fables which, though vastly inferior to Shakespeare's in every way, as I do not need to be told, are nevertheless the same kind of thing.'[24]

The American edition, meanwhile, provided an opportunity to add some extra material, including a key sequence that Hughes had unaccountably forgotten to include for Faber, in which he worked out 'The Tragic Equation in *The Two Noble Kinsmen*' – taking him back to his early perception about the power and significance of that last play, written in collaboration with John Fletcher.

Twenty years after it was written, *Shakespeare and the Goddess of Complete Being* remains *sui generis*, and certainly cannot be recommended to students as an introductory critical study of the plays. But it does not now seem quite so eccentric in its entirety. Hughes always regarded the poet as shaman and prophet, and there is indeed something ahead of its time, something prophetic, about several aspects of the book. At the time he was writing, mainstream Shakespearean criticism was almost entirely secular. In subsequent years, there was a huge revival of interest in the playwright's engagement with religious questions and in the possibility of a hidden vein of Catholicism running through his imagination. Again, the proscription against biographical reading of the plays – shaped by Cambridge-style 'New Criticism' – began to break down in the early twenty-first century. Hughes's hunches about the possible autobiographical element in such plays as *All's Well* and *Troilus* anticipate a string of subsequent speculations in which critics and biographers have linked details in the plays to everything from Shakespeare's sex life to the social climbing suggested by his pursuit of a coat-of-arms to his political associations with the circle around the Earl of Essex. Thirdly, in a remarkable excursion linking the Tragic Equation to the differing impulses of left and right brain (*SGCB* 157–61), Hughes proves himself to be a John the Baptist heralding the advent of a new and very twenty-first-century genre: neurological literary criticism that benefits from developments in scanning technologies such as functional Magnetic Resonance Imaging in order to ask questions about what exactly might have gone on in Shakespeare's brain as he wrote, and what really happens in our brains as we read or listen to his extraordinary language.

Ultimately, though, on Wildean/Woolfian principles, the spectacle of Hughes reading Shakespeare is less interesting and important than that of Shakespeare reading Hughes. To return to the place where we began, the journal entry of 22 January 1998 was written in the immediate wake of the first appearance of *Birthday Letters*. Its main substance is a deeply searching account of the effect on Hughes's work of his suppression of those poems from print for so many years. Having quoted the first line of Sonnet 24, 'Mine eye hath played the painter and hath stelled', Hughes continues, 'What a peculiar piece! Started trying to get my mind back into Alcestis.' The translation of Euripides's *Alcestis*, to which he returned in the last summer of his life, was yet another of his attempts to bring a beloved wife back from the grave. In its light, and the light of *Birthday Letters*, the whole of sonnet 24 becomes haunted by the memory of Sylvia Plath that was printed so indelibly upon the heart of Ted Hughes:

> Mine eye hath played the painter and hath stelled
> Thy beauty's form in table of my heart,
> My body is the frame wherein 'tis held
> And perspective it is best painter's art.
> For through the painter must you see his skill
> To find where your true image pictured lies,
> Which in my bosom's shop is hanging still,
> That hath his windows glazèd with thine eyes.
> Now see what good turns eyes for eyes have done:
> Mine eyes have drawn thy shape and thine for me
> Are windows to my breast, wherethrough the sun
> Delights to peep, to gaze therein on thee.
> > Yet eyes this cunning want to grace their art:
> > They draw but what they see, know not the heart.

NOTES

1. *Macbeth*, ed. Kenneth Muir, Arden edition, 1964, III.2.50.
2. Add. 88918/1/2, BL.
3. Add. 88918/1/4, BL.
4. Add. 88918/128/1, BL.
5. Unpublished letter in Faber archive.
6. Personal recollections by John Billingsley of a reading in 1976 and Jonathan Bate of a reading at the Hobson Gallery, Cambridge, 27 February 1978.
7. Inscribed 'Edward J. Hughes, to celebrate "going up". October 1951, with all good wishes, John Fisher'. PR6013.R35 W58 1948 Hughes, Emory.
8. Robert Graves, *The White Goddess: A Historical Grammar of Poetic Myth* (London: Faber and Faber, 1948), p. 426.

9. Unpublished letter in Faber archive.
10. *With Fairest Flowers While Summer Lasts* (New York: Doubleday, 1971), viii.
11. *Ibid.*, p. v.
12. *Ibid.*, p. viii.
13. *Ibid.*
14. *Ibid.*, p. ix.
15. *Ibid.*
16. *Ibid.*
17. *Ibid.*, p. xi.
18. *Ibid.*, p. xiii.
19. *Ibid.*, p. xvii.
20. *Ibid.*
21. This and subsequent quotations from Emory Mss 844/105/7.
22. *The Times* (9 April 1992).
23. Add. 88918/6/8, BL.
24. *Ibid.*

II

NEIL ROBERTS

Class, war and the Laureateship

Hughes nailed his flag to the mast of the establishment when he became Poet Laureate, not just by accepting the post, but by reviving its most archaic and despised function, the celebration of royal birthdays, which had lapsed in the early nineteenth century. He joined the line of Shadwell, Cibber and Southey in being derided by other poets for his loyal efforts, and for his relations with members of the Royal Family. Reviewing *Rain-Charm for the Duchy and Other Laureate Poems* for the *Sunday Times*, Peter Reading described most of the poems as 'clumsily contrived, cringingly sycophantic hack-work', and speculated that 'the poet laureate has been superseded by the court jester'.[1] Becoming Laureate coincided with, and may have contributed to, a decline in Hughes's critical reputation. Yet he probably took his royal verses more seriously than any of his mediocre eighteenth-century predecessors. He was a lifelong monarchist and, while still at university, had composed a dialogue between Elizabeth I and Elizabeth II, in which the former scorns the latter's reduced role, saying,

> A king is the symbol of control over a nation which quite effectively does keep them in some sort of harmonic subjection and discipline, which is the only mood in which they can be happy or efficient. Under a leader every individual becomes a more disciplined cohesive unit in the national purpose ... Over centuries man's mind has accustomed itself under the image of a King, the passionately contemplated image of a national leader, to assemble and invoke all its deepest powers.[2]

Hughes echoed these sentiments forty years later in notes he wrote for a poem celebrating the Queen's sixtieth birthday. In this poem, he explains, the symbolic 'birds of the British Isles ... find their true selves (their spiritual selves) by finding the spiritual unity of the Islands, which is "the ring of the people", which is also the Crown' (*CP* 1218). Hughes was not a narrow and petty nationalist. He borrowed the phrase 'ring of the people' from the celebrated Sioux shaman Black Elk, for whom, Hughes emphasizes, 'it

150

embraced . . . all the different peoples of the earth, not only his own tribesmen' (*CP* 1217). However, his phrase 'spiritual unity of the Islands' casts a mystifying cloak over the conflicted history and diverse present aspirations of the problematic nation, or state, on whose behalf he attempted to speak.

Here we come to a crucial question, which links the diverse terms of this chapter's title. From what position is Hughes speaking as a representative of the nation in his Laureate poems? As it happens he has given us a direct answer to this question. Most readers agree that, apart from the title poem, which was actually written before he became Laureate, the verses collected in *Rain-Charm for the Duchy* are unworthy of their author's powers. That volume does, however, contain a resonant prose text, in the form of a 'Note' that Hughes wrote explaining his poem for the Queen Mother's ninetieth birthday, 'A Masque for Three Voices'. Although not a particularly distinguished example of Hughes's verse, this poem is perhaps the most interesting that he wrote as Laureate, being a review of major events of the twentieth century linked to the Queen Mother's life-line. As he puts it in the 'Note',

> My poem touches on the outlines of this period, seeing it as a drama from the British point of view, with the Queen Mother's role in the foreground. Seeing it, that is, from the point of view of the son of an infantryman of the First World War. This qualification defines the outlook of an offspring of that war, one for whom it was virtually the Creation Story, and such a shattering, all-inclusive, grievous catastrophe that it was felt as a national *defeat*, though victory had somehow been pinned on to it as a consolation medal. At least, it felt so in the tribal lands of the north. (*CP* 1219)

He goes on to explain that 'when the trial came with the Second World War, our sacred myth, the living symbol of a hidden unity, the dormant genetic resource, turned out the be the Crown', and specifically the Queen, as the Queen Mother then was.

There is a curious moment in the explanatory language of this passage, in Hughes's use of the phrase 'that is': 'from the British point of view, with the Queen Mother's role in the foreground . . . *that is*, from the point of view of the son of an infantryman of the First World War'. The sentence construction seems not to be further limiting, but rather defining 'the British point of view': a subject position, which the reader might feel to be a rather specialized one, is actually offered as definitive. In this rather long 'Note' Hughes comes close to presenting himself as someone through whom, by virtue of his generation, the history of the twentieth century has coursed: 'One who was born of the First World War, who spent his first nine years dreaming of the Second, having lived through the Second went on well into his thirties expecting the nuclear

Third and the chaos after' (*CP* 1210). But, as everyone who has read Hughes's poetry knows, the first of those three influences is by far the most powerful. As he writes in the poem for the Queen Mother, 'I died those million deaths. Yet each one bled / Back into me, who live on in their stead' (*CP* 825).

The subject position that he elucidates in the 'Note' is one not only of generation, but also of class. 'Infantryman' strongly suggests someone not of the officer class, as indeed Hughes's father wasn't. He was awarded the Distinguished Conduct Medal, only one level down from the Victoria Cross but, unlike the VC, marked by class: it had been instituted in the Crimean War as an equivalent to the Distinguished Service Order, to recognize bravery among the 'other ranks'. Expressions of class rancour are rare in Hughes, but one surprising and significant one concerns his attitude to Wilfred Owen. In a letter explaining his attitude to the war (as a member of his generation) to a younger correspondent, he follows his declaration of admiration for Owen's poetry with the confession that he has a reservation about him partly because he was an officer: 'Throughout the war my father as an infantryman and obviously an effective soldier . . . refused promotion. And told strange stories about officers (when he told any)' (*LTH* 594). He declares this to be a foolish reservation about Owen, and disowns it, but cannot banish it – a sign of the strength of the feelings about class and war that underlie it.

As Poet Laureate, both publicly and privately, Hughes writes about the Royal Family in a tone of reverential respect. He signs a letter to Prince Charles, 'Your loyal and humble servant' (*LTH* 651). But there was another side to his attitude to royalty. In 1974 he was awarded the Queen's Medal for poetry, and he wrote for his fourteen-year-old daughter Frieda a very funny account of his visit to the Palace to be presented with the medal. In this letter he confessed that he had felt an impulse to behave as a 'cheeky upstart' and get thrown out because he couldn't muster a sufficiently reverential attitude, except to the Queen herself, whom he liked personally.[3] No doubt Hughes developed more respect for individual royals when he got to know them better, but this letter is about his attitude to royalty as an institution, only a decade before he became Poet Laureate. And, as the phrase 'cheeky upstart' suggests, this attitude has something to do with his class background. In verses probably composed solely for his own amusement he declared there was 'Nowt to be sorry at' in being Poet Laureate and that 'the summit's / Summat.'[4] This fragment could hardly be more slight, but it suggests the attitude of an assertive Yorkshireman made good, rather than a reverential subject.

How important is class as an influence on Hughes's poetry? His espousal – indeed magnification – of T. S. Eliot's 'dissociation of sensibility' is well known, and in his earliest surviving reference to it he makes it explicitly a matter of class. Writing to Lucas Myers in 1959, he said that, being American, Eliot 'didn't perceive that the causes for this apparent dissociation of sensibility are in the inter-conflict of upper & lower classes in England, the development of the English gentleman with the stereotype English voice (and the mind, set of manners etc that goes with the voice) & the tabu on dialect as a language proper for literate men'. He adds that 'The only [English] poets speaking dialect since 1688 up to this century were Wordsworth, Keats & Blake' (*LTH* 146). This list suggests that what he means by dialect is some version of spoken English other than Received Pronunciation (though his omission of Tennyson is curious). This was not a passing preoccupation. Thirty-six years later he wrote in another letter of 'the hideous destructiveness of everything post-Restoration in Eng Lit' and all the other arts. Significantly he goes on to say that at Cambridge he had been 'made to feel all this as a personal sort of torment because, it is a fact, undergraduate life seemed to me modelled, in its exhibitionist manners and styles, and especially in its speech, on the Restoration fop' (*LTH* 680).

In his long essay 'Myths, Metres, Rhythms' (*WP* 310–72) Hughes extends his analysis of this conflict so that it rages through the whole history of the English language since the Conquest. The last fifty pages of this essay present a spellbinding analysis of the suppressed, unorthodox tradition of English metre, in which the Anglo-Saxon alliterative line is displaced by the courtly iambic, as a corollary to the imposition of a French-inflected 'King's English' as 'a language proper for literate men'. The Anglo-Saxon alliterative line, it is argued, still powerfully haunts the rhythms of Wyatt and is then excised by the dominant poetic tradition, resurfacing spasmodically in Smart, Blake, Coleridge and most decisively Hopkins. Hughes's starting-point is a review of *The Hawk in the Rain* by Roy Fuller, which declared the final line of 'The Horses' – 'Hearing the horizons endure' – 'unsayable'. Hughes is polite to Fuller personally and does not directly accuse him of imposing a 'tabu on dialect as a language proper for literate men', but his investigation of the history of English metre makes it clear that class conflict – or, more strongly, the conquest of poetic language by the ruling class – is a crucial subtext of his argument. When Richard Tottel published his *Miscellany* of verse specimens in 1557 his aim was to gather examples of 'the stateliness of the stile removed from the rude skill of common ears' (quoted in *WP* 347). In so doing he or his editors notoriously rewrote Wyatt's rugged metres to conform to the iambic norm. Hughes hears Tottel's class-inflected language echoing in the critical prose of E. M. W. Tillyard, who was still lecturing at Cambridge when Hughes was a student: 'The social implications of Tillyard's vocabulary are Tottel's, updated and correspondingly seasoned. He perceives a "transition from gross to refined irregularity" [in Wyatt] ... Using Tottel's courtly dismissive, he finds that "some of those [poems] written in the heavier metres ... are uncouth"' (*WP* 350).

Hughes calls this a poetic Civil War, but it is clear that for him the implications extend far beyond the literary:

> One the one hand, the class which inherited and constantly reasserted the Military Occupation's governing role, and with it that speech code of superior status, also constantly re-enforced the rule of strict metrical forms, which went on evolving as a poetic tradition rooted in the court-centred 'high' culture. On the other hand, though the Old English poetic tradition degenerated into stunted popular rhymes, the innate music of its 'sprung rhythm' survived and multiplied, underground, like a nationalist army of guerrillas, in the regional dialects of common speech.　　　　　　　　　　　　　　　　　　(*WP* 368)

There is no doubt which side Hughes is on in this war, and his language carries startling implications about how he conceives his role in it. One can almost hear him reciting Tony Harrison's resounding call to arms on behalf of the working class: 'So right, yer buggers, then! We'll occupy / Your lousy leasehold Poetry'.[5]

Hughes's hostility to the voice of the 'English gentleman' was not, of course, *merely* a matter of class. He believed that the standard form of educated speech which developed after the Restoration was incapable of expressing wholeness of being, and that 'English psychic life' became 'cut off from its true source' (*LTH* 680). However, one powerful force at work in his poetry is a resistance to the kind of English that could possibly be attributed to a 'Restoration fop' or even an 'English gentleman', and an honouring of the speech he grew up with in the Calder Valley and the South Yorkshire coalfield. As he said in an oft-quoted interview, 'Whatever other speech you grow into, presumably your dialect stays alive in a sort of inner freedom, a separate little self ... Without it, I doubt if I would ever have written verse.'[6] Again by 'dialect' he means not primarily a variant of language with its own vocabulary and syntax, but a form of speech, with distinctive sounds and rhythms – that is, not Received Pronunciation. This is most obvious in the Anglo-Saxon lexis, short vowels, consonantal diction tending to monosyllable, short syntactical units and unfussy simile in a passage such as the opening of 'View of a Pig': 'The pig lay on a barrow dead. / It weighed, they said, as much as three men ... // It was less than lifeless, further off. / It was like a sack of wheat' (*CP* 76). It is even detectable in the first Laureate poem, published for the christening of Prince Harry, especially in the simile evocative of working-class domesticity: 'Rain didn't so much fall as collapse. / The pavements danced, like cinders in a riddle' (*CP* 803).

This is a well-known feature of Hughes's poetry, but what is particularly interesting is the powerful interanimation of the themes of class and war in his work, as suggested by his Note to the poem for the Queen Mother's birthday. Everyone who is familiar with Hughes will be aware that for him the two decisive moments of English history are the Civil War and the First World War. The Civil War is central to what might be called his ideological construction of English history, the progressive displacement of the sacred and the feminine by the forces of patriarchal monotheism and scientific rationality. The First World War is central to his personal formation. He intriguingly linked the two when, in a review of an anthology of First World War poetry, he described that conflict as a still unfinished civil war (WP 43). In saying that, he had in mind the way in which the enemy in First World War poetry was the establishment at home which sent young men to be slaughtered, rather than the Germans. He didn't, of course, have in mind a simplistic opposition between officers and enlisted men, and this was certainly a civil war in which he imagined Wilfred Owen and his father being on the same side; but he probably did imagine the enemy, like the defeated royalists who triumphed at the Restoration, speaking with the accents of English gentlemen.

Tim Kendall has taken Hughes critics to task, rightly, for underestimating the importance of war in his poetry. However, Kendall represents this importance primarily in terms of a struggle with Hughes's war-poet precursors, specifically Owen and Keith Douglas, of the kind popularized by Harold Bloom's *The Anxiety of Influence*. Kendall illuminatingly points out that by titling his poem about Parnell's campaign against flogging in the army, an event that preceded the First World War, 'Wilfred Owen's Photographs', Hughes erects the war as 'the point of origin to which the meaning of all other episodes should be referred'.[7] Early war poems such as 'Bayonet Charge' are, as Kendall says, heavily influenced by Owen, and Hughes had good reason for wanting to escape from imaginative entrapment in a territory so definitively owned by another poet. Hughes said at a reading in Australia in 1976 that he had 'finally decided that really [the War] had nothing to do with me', and in 1962 had written the poem 'Out' to 'get rid of the entire body of preoccupation'.[8] However, Kendall risks making this seem like a purely literary anxiety, saying that Hughes's 'new approach to war' in the 1960s was 'initiated by his need to establish a less subordinate relationship to his war-poet predecessors'.[9]

'Out' certainly reads as an attempted exorcism of the war's grip on the poet's imagination. It ends:

So goodbye to that bloody-minded flower.
You dead bury your dead.
Goodbye to the cenotaphs on my mother's breasts.
Goodbye to all the remaindered charms of my father's survival.
Let England close. Let the green sea-anemone close.   (*CP* 166)

Paradoxically the poem in which Hughes declares the end of his preoccupation is also the first in which he deals with its real cause, which is not a matter of anxiety of influence, but his father's trauma, and the decisive effect this had on the development of his own identity. While the ticking of the clock dragged William Hughes 'bodily from under / The mortised four-year strata of dead Englishmen / He belonged with', the young Ted, 'small and four, / Lay on the carpet as his luckless double, / His memory's buried, immovable anchor' (*CP* 165). The evocation of the trenches that follows this is more than a transmitted memory: the present tense establishes it as the emotional landscape in which the child's consciousness is formed: 'Under rain that goes on drumming its rods and thickening / Its kingdom, which the sun has abandoned, and where nobody / Can ever move again from shelter'. A year after writing 'Out', Hughes broadcast a memoir of his childhood in which he said of the Calder Valley, 'I can never lose the impression that the whole region is in mourning for the first world war'. By his own account his childhood was lived between the poles of the moor, where he led a paradisal existence hunting animals with his brother, and the valley bottom, which he called 'a descent into the pit'.[10] 'Out' is more surely a confession and recapitulation of imaginative entrapment than a ridding of it. The emotional vehemence, verging on hysteria, of its conclusion enacts a desire not a fulfilment. The extremity of that desire, and the impossibility of its fulfilment, is marked by the need for 'England' itself to 'close'.

Nevertheless it is true that for the next fifteen years the primacy of the First World War was in abeyance in Hughes's poetry. Wars of one kind or another rage in *Crow* and *Gaudete*, but, as Kendall says, Hughes has found 'a prior myth which denies the [First] war its privileged place as prime mover'.[11] However, at the very time when Hughes made his declaration that the war had nothing to do with him, he was beginning to plan the project in which it returned with its full significance. In 1976 he began his collaboration with Fay Godwin on what was to become, first, *Remains of Elmet* (1979), and finally *Elmet* (1994). Hughes has written that the original inspiration for this project was autobiographical, but that a combination of deference to Godwin's photographic art and what he called, at the end of his life, 'diabolical fear of subjectivity' diverted him into composing 'impersonal mood-pieces'.[12] When he brought out the revised version *Elmet* in 1994 he included a number of poems about his family, which had in the meantime appeared in *Wolfwatching* (1989), in a somewhat haphazard attempt to return to the original inspiration. But for the motives that diverted Hughes into impersonality, the *Elmet* project might have been his *Prelude*. As in 'Out', the First World War is crucial to the growth of this poet's mind, but the influence is extended to cover a whole generation, region and class.

Perhaps Hughes's most piercing evocation of the sense that his birthplace was in mourning for the war is the poem 'First, Mills', and above all the two lines, 'the bottomless wound of the railway station / That bled this valley to death'. The flow of conscripted men taken away from the valley by train is imaginatively fused with the flow of blood as they died in the trenches. The idea that the war was a civil war is hinted at in the line 'The towns and the villages were sacked' (CP 462–3). The violence of the war is brought home to the place from which the soldiers set out – just as they are metonymically already bleeding as they get on the train, so the conscription is imagined as an act of violence by an armed force against a civilian population.

Again and again in *Remains of Elmet* the war is closely identified with the region's industrial past. Many of these poems are odd elegies, fiercely resentful of the way of life, the passing of which they record. The identification of war and industry gives some of these poems a powerful ideological thrust, as in 'Hill-Stone Was Content': 'It let itself be conscripted / Into mills. And it stayed in position / Defending this slavery' (CP 463). The discipline of war and the discipline of industry reinforce each other – conscription serves to produce a compliant workforce; the conscripted men (both literal and metaphorical) identify with their oppression, enacting it as a defiant heroism; industry like war reduces the workers to replaceable functions, alienating them from their own humanity. Hughes was no Marxist, but this poem provides memorable images for many aspects of Marx's analysis of economic relationships. The stone, which is the protagonist of a number of the poems, is clearly anthropomorphized, but also represents the wild spirit of the place. As Hughes wrote to Fay Godwin when he was beginning work on the sequence,

> What grips me about the place, I think, is the weird collision of that terrible life of slavery – to work, cash, Methodism – which was an heroic life really, and developed heroic virtues – inside those black buildings, with that wilderness, which is really a desert, more or less uninhabitable. The collision of the pathos of the early industrial revolution . . . with the wildness of the place. The terribleness of it was sealed by the First World War – when the whole lot were carted off and slaughtered, as a sort of ultimate humiliation and helplessness. (*LTH* 379)

'Hardcastle Crags' opens with the pastoral injunction, 'Think often of the silent valley, for the god lives there'. The ensuing poem, however, retorts that a native of Hughes's generation is attuned to sounds beneath the silence of the famous beauty-spot, which rob it of its pastoral innocence and pagan spirit, and these are sounds both of industry and of war: 'But here the leaf-loam silence / Is old siftings of sewing machines and shuttles . . . / And the beech-tree solemnities / Muffle much cordite'. The poem concludes with the speaker haunted by 'The love-murmurs of a generation of slaves / Whose bones melted in Asia Minor' (*CP* 456). (William Hughes was one of only seventeen survivors of a whole regiment of local men who perished at Gallipoli.) One of the most notable attempts in *Elmet* to make the sequence more personal is the transformation of this poem into 'Leaf Mould', in which the speaker's sensitivity to the ghosts of the 'generation of slaves' is attributed to the influence of his mother, who used to walk weeping in the woods when he was still in the womb. If in 'Out' he was his father's 'luckless double', in this poem he is his mother's 'step-up transformer': her personal grief for 'her girlhood and the fallen' is transformed into his mourning for 'Paradise and its fable' (*CP* 768).

'Leaf Mould' is one of a group of poems, first published in *Wolfwatching*, that Hughes wrote as a 'correction', as he put it, of the 'over-determined plan' of *Remains of Elmet*.[13] In these poems the war ('For the Duration', 'Dust as We Are', 'Walt') and working-class deprivation ('Slump Sundays', 'Climbing into Heptonstall') figure strongly. Assuming that Hughes began *Birthday Letters* in the 1970s, these poems can be considered, with the Laureate poems, as one of Hughes's two last new modes of original poetry. In a sense they are the underside of the Laureate poems, the 'offspring' of the First World War in working clothes rather than court dress.

Hughes describes these poems as 'reminiscence or tribute' but, as in a more extreme form in 'Out', the memorializing impulse clashes with a resentful desire to erase the past. In 'Climbing into Heptonstall' a tourist guide is interrupted by a 'madman' who is the voice of the real history of the region. He sings a tuneless song of 'stone-deep deprivation' to obliterate what is presumably the guide's sanitized version of the past. His motive is not to memorialize the victims of deprivation, but to 'Sweep from the soul's attic / Spinners, weavers, tacklers, dyers, and their infants / . . . Burn the record break the monument' (*CP* 750–2). As with the less explicitly crazed speaker of 'Out', however, naming that which must be obliterated serves only to lodge it more securely in the consciousness. Characteristically the war itself leaks into the poems that are primarily about working-class deprivation. 'Slump Sundays', ostensibly about the spiritual 'mouldering' of a mill town in the 1930s, cannot do without references to the Somme and no man's land, while the madman of 'Climbing into Heptonstall' begins his rant with 'Wash the blood', which can only be the blood that leaked away through the railway station in 'First, Mills'.

Surprisingly, Hughes chose not to reprint the two most moving of these poems in *Elmet*. 'Source' and 'Dust As We Are' combine to explore the emotional landscape in which the poet grew up, and the inescapable presence of the war. 'Source' is about his mother's unexplained, chronic weeping. Why did she weep even though her husband returned safe from the war? Why did her weeping continue into Hughes's own childhood? Had she 'got into a habit, / Maybe during the war, of connecting yourself / To something beyond life, a mourning / That repaired you / And was necessary'? The 'Source' of the title is the unexplained (but almost certainly war-related) origin of this weeping, but it is also by implication the origin of something in Hughes himself, her 'step-up transformer', since her weeping 'Could dissolve yourself, me, everything / Into this relief of your strange music' (*CP* 757–8).

This maternal music, sad and ambiguous but comforting, is counterpointed by a different and more certainly war-related paternal influence in 'Dust As We Are'. And both these influences are illuminated by the passage from *The Prelude* to which the title 'Dust As We Are' ironically alludes:

> Dust as we are, the immortal spirit grows
> Like harmony in music; there is a dark
> Inscrutable workmanship that reconciles
> Discordant elements, makes them cling together
> In one society. How strange that all
> The terrors, pains, and early miseries,
> Regrets, vexations, lassitudes interfused
> Within my mind, should e'er have borne a part,
> And that a needful part, in making up
> The calm existence that is mine when I
> Am worthy of myself![14]

'Dust As We Are' echoes 'Out': where in the earlier poem he was his father's 'luckless double', in this one he is his 'supplementary convalescent'. But it differs from 'Out' in the much greater intimacy and tenderness with which Hughes writes about his father, and in the abandonment of the attempt to exorcise the influence of the war. Hughes has written few more delicately tender lines than these:

> I divined,
> With a comb,
> Under his wavy, golden hair, as I combed it,
> The fragility of skull. And I filled
> With his knowledge. (*CP* 753)

The wavy, golden hair corresponds to the outward appearance of youthful, vigorous masculinity in the father who 'took up his pre-war *joie de vivre*', and who allows his young son to comb his hair in a touchingly simple family scene (especially in an age when physical expressions of affection between fathers and sons were unusual). But the scene turns disturbingly into a *memento mori*, anticipating the Webster-like young poet who looked forward to seeing 'every attitude showing its bone' in the grave ('Soliloquy', CP 26). The poem continues:

> After mother's milk
> This was the soul's food. A soap-smell spectre
> Of the massacre of innocents. So the soul grew.
> A strange thing, with rickets – a hyena.
> No singing – that kind of laughter.   (CP 753–4)

His mother's weeping is a 'strange music' that can perhaps be assimilated to Wordworth's untroubled and, some might say, complacent harmonizing of 'early miseries' into an idealized 'calm existence' of adulthood. The title of this poem instructs us to construe it as a sarcastic rejection of the Wordsworthian harmony. Wordsworth lived through, and was to a degree made as a poet by, the terrors and pains of the French Revolution. But Hughes's soul was formed by an even more apocalyptic event that preceded his birth. Like rickets – an image tellingly drawn from the working-class deprivation Hughes witnessed in his youth – the war formed or deformed him before he knew what was happening to him. The downbeat, stoical, accepting note on which the poem ends contrasts with and undercuts the defiant conclusion of 'Out'. It proves that Hughes was deluding himself when he said that the war 'had nothing to do with me'.

I began this chapter by saying that in accepting the Laureateship Hughes nailed his flag to the mast of the establishment. Yet in the course of it we have seen evidence that he strongly and even militantly espoused a cultural resistance to a 'courtly' ruling class. This contradiction is also played out in his writing about war: portraying the First World War as a civil war in which the victims were the common people, 'sacked' and bled to death, but in the Second World War exalting the Queen Mother as the 'incarnation' of 'the ring of the people' (CP 1221). Hughes was a writer of far too great intelligence and integrity not to be aware of this contradiction. He wrote to Keith Sagar, whose only quarrel with Hughes concerned his 'flattery' of the Royal Family, 'You don't have to defend it, Keith. You only have to say you don't like that kind of verse'; but in the same letter he wrote that monarchs 'can only reign if they are created by the unity of a group' (LTH 509–10). He had experienced the national culture as a force both of division and of unity: the division felt by a young poet told by an establishment figure that his verse is 'unsayable'; the unity of the threatened nation huddling round the idealized figures of King and Queen in World War Two. His writing about the division is perhaps more convincing than that about unity. But Hughes was committed to the belief that poetry has a healing function. When writing for children he tried to exercise that function by the simple expedient of making the poetry 'upbeat'. Sean O'Brien sees an interesting similarity between the poetry for children and the Laureate verse, for here too there is a similar simplification.[15] Drawing on the monarchy to cast spells for the unity of the nation, Hughes could not afford to acknowledge the division by which he was so deeply marked.

NOTES

1. Peter Reading, 'Turning on the water works', *Sunday Times* (28 June 1992), Review section, p. 13.
2. Undated (but almost certainly contemporary with accession or coronation of Elizabeth II), Mss 854, Box 1, ff. 38, Emory.
3. TH to Frieda Hughes, 14 February 1975. Mss 1014, Box 1, ff. 53, Emory.
4. Mss 644, Box 83, ff. 90, Emory.
5. Tony Harrison, 'Them & [uz]', ll. 17–18, *Selected Poems*, 2nd edn (Harmondsworth: Penguin, 1987).
6. Ekbert Faas, 'Ted Hughes and *Crow*', *Ted Hughes: The Unaccommodated Universe* (Santa Barbara: Black Sparrow Press, 1980), p. 202.
7. Tim Kendall, *Modern English War Poetry* (Oxford: Oxford University Press, 2006), p. 204.
8. Ted Hughes at Adelaide Festival Writers' Week, March 1976, http://ann.skea.com/Adelaide.htm, accessed 14 January 2010.
9. Kendall, *War Poetry*, p. 213.
10. Ted Hughes, 'The Rock', *The Listener* 70 (19 September 1963), pp. 421–3.
11. Kendall, *War Poetry*, p. 213.
12. Ted Hughes, 'Poetry Book Society Bulletin' 142 (Autumn 1989), p. 3. TH to Keith Sagar, 14 October 1998, Add. 78761, f. 66, BL.
13. Hughes, 'Poetry Society Bulletin' 142, p. 3.
14. William Wordsworth, *The Prelude* (1850), 1, 342–51.
15. Sean O'Brien, *The Deregulated Muse: Essays on Contemporary British and Irish Poetry* (Newcastle upon Tyne: Bloodaxe, 1998), p. 39.

12

ALEX DAVIS

Hughes and his critics

The critical reception of Hughes's work has often generated impassioned pronouncements, on occasion courting hyperbole.[1] Writing in a 1975 post-script to a reprint of *Articulate Energy*, Donald Davie expressed exasperation at what he took to be Hughes's rejection of 'the terms of the contract [between the poet and his readers] accepted by the Movement poets' in the 1950s. In its place, he averred, Hughes 'accepted instead, as he may have learnt afterwards with dismay, the terms of that grosser contract which put him on a par with Mick Jagger'. In other words, Hughes, in line with his North American contemporary Allen Ginsberg, had capitulated to the zeitgeist and its witless revolt, in Davie's jaundiced opinion, '*against civilization*'.[2] By way of con-trast, in the same year in which Davie's postscript appeared, Seamus Heaney gave a lecture at Berkeley, documenting how Hughes 'recalled English poetry in the fifties from a too suburban aversion of the attention from the elemen-tal', in the course of which Hughes is likened by Heaney not to the Stones' front-man, Jagger, but Shakespeare's 'Poor Tom on the heath, a civilized man tasting and testing the primitive facts'.[3] Linking Davie's and Heaney's dis-parate evaluations is the contentious issue of Hughes's 'primitivism', his belief in that which Harold Bloom identifies as a recurrent preoccupation of those he somewhat reductively dubs the 'last romantics' (whose number include, beside Hughes, W. B. Yeats, D. H. Lawrence and Robert Graves): the desir-ability of 'a preternatural catharsis to heal a magical spirit in us'.[4] This is, of course, the theme of many of Hughes's critical writings, culminating in his extraordinary analysis of Shakespeare's 'Tragic Equation' (*SGCB* 1 and *passim*)[5] and his late reflections on the shamanic dimensions to T. S. Eliot's poetry in *A Dancer to God*. Hughes's critical reception is understandably dominated by a comparable concern with the poetry's recurrent exploration of the chthonic spirit which, in *Shakespeare and the Goddess of Complete Being*, Hughes describes as a potentially 'renovating spirit'– that force ani-mating 'poor' or 'Mad Tom' in *King Lear*, and which crucially facilitates the king's 'rebirth' amid the tempestuous elements on the heath (*SGCB* 275).

Keith Sagar's seminal *The Art of Ted Hughes* is governed by a concern with the poet as a shaman-figure, 'whose function,' Sagar avers, 'is to make the dangerous journey, on behalf of his society, into the spirit world' of his personal and the collective unconscious.[6] First published in 1975, an expanded second edition (1978) covers Hughes's work up to and including *Cave Birds* and *Gaudete*.[7] The book builds on Sagar's short but cogent British Council publication of 1972 in reading Hughes's work along what are in effect Leavisite lines, as a diagnostic and potentially curative response to civilization and its discontents. To this end, his study largely eschews any close-reading of the formal features of Hughes's poetry in favour of an at times passionate endorsement of its social relevance.

Sagar's more recent book-length study, *The Laughter of Foxes: A Study of Ted Hughes*, continues his earlier work's preoccupation with the 'healing power' of Hughes's vision, for which, again, he makes the highest claims.[8] But Sagar has his reservations about Hughes's output post-*River* in this regard, arguing that 'the body of work on which Hughes's reputation should stand . . . is almost everything he wrote in the seventies and very early eighties', from *Season Songs* to *River*.[9] Sagar thus not only marginalizes the early poetry on which Hughes's reputation was made, but also, in placing the most value on the creative period preceding Hughes's acceptance of the Laureateship (of the occasional poetry expected of the role Sagar revealingly says nothing),[10] he plays down the importance of two of Hughes's late, most celebrated works: *Tales from Ovid* and *Birthday Letters*. For Sagar these collections are overly dependent on pre-existing material, whether Ovid's original text or the biographical facts of Hughes's relationship with Sylvia Plath. This is surely to do an injustice to both Hughes's extraordinarily vivid, if somewhat disjunctive, versions of passages from the *Metamorphoses* and the Ovidian pathos (if not wit) of the elegiac epistolary poems.[11]

Ekbert Faas's *Ted Hughes: The Unaccommodated Universe* (1980) also takes as its theme the internalized quest-romance Sagar identifies as the core of Hughes's achievement: 'the story of a quester's descent to save his desecrated bride from the underworld through his self-sacrifice'.[12] Faas, however, chooses to interpret this journey as a transmutation of Hughes's personal life and his tragic relationships with Plath and Assia Wevill (the latter of which would be harshly anatomized by Hughes in *Capriccio*). Faas's study concentrates on *Crow* and *Gaudete*, though he makes reference to earlier collections, and his postscript touches on Hughes's subsequent work up to, and including, *Moortown*. For Faas, none of these works from the late 1970s 'marks a radical new departure', though *Cave Birds* he reads as a summation of themes explored in *Crow* and *Gaudete*.[13] While not wholly untrue, such a statement dramatically underplays the remarkable differences between *Cave Birds* and

Gaudete on the level of form and structure, and passes over in silence the sheer range of styles in the poems collected in *Moortown*. Of great interest to Hughes's readers are two interviews with Hughes conducted by Faas, included as an appendix to his study: on *Crow*, from 1970, and *Gaudete*, from 1977.[14] Hughes's comments on *Crow* here, and as quoted in other critical studies, should be read in conjunction with the fascinating 'The Story of Crow', reconstructed with Hughes's permission in Sagar's *The Laughter of Foxes*, which provides a 'framework' of the 'epic folk-tale' of which the published *Crow* is only fragments drawn from the first two-thirds of the projected narrative.[15]

The mythical and anthropological *materia poetica* of Hughes's poetry, especially as deployed in the 1970s sequences Sagar and Faas admire, is explored by Stuart Hirschberg in his *Myth in the Poetry of Ted Hughes* (1981).[16] Hirschberg posits a triadic shape to Hughes's poetic career from the 1950s through the 1970s, from the shaman-persona of the earlier work, via the trickster-figure of *Crow*, to the scapegoats of Prometheus and Lumb in *Prometheus on His Crag* and *Gaudete*. Hirschberg's analysis of the latter work is exemplary in its attentiveness to the wide range of intertexts informing, and giving resonance to, the doppelgänger's shallow sexual escapades and the Epilogue's haunting lyricism. However, while extremely useful as a resource for identifying some of the more obscure allusions in these texts, Hirschberg's over-arching thesis is too cramped a Procrustean bed into which to squeeze Hughes's prolix body of work from this period. The treatment of Hughes's recourse to myth in Joanny Moulin's *Ted Hughes: New Selected Poems* (1999) is perhaps truer to its eclectic and capacious quality than Hirschberg's.[17] For Moulin, Hughes's mature mythic method is a form of Orphism, of psychic descent and return. From *Crow* on, Hughes constructs a cosmos from a range of interrelated sources, in a manner that finds an analogue in Claude Lévi-Strauss's famous comparison of mythmaking to the handiwork of the *bricoleur*.

Likewise, there is something a little too neat about Hirschberg's claim that Hughes's and Plath's poetry comprise, as it were, a pair of Yeatsian gyres, in which each unwinds contrariwise to the other, the self-probing of the Epilogue poems to *Gaudete* matching the purportedly equally tentative mood of Plath's early poems. Tracy Brain's analysis of the relationship between Hughes's and Plath's poetry is less tidy than Hirschberg's argument would allow for, and, arguably, the more suggestive for it. Brain sees each poet's work as cross-pollinating that of the other, or, to use her own metaphor, as engaged in a colloquy or dialogue in which influence is reciprocal rather than one-sided.[18]

In *Re-Making Poetry: Ted Hughes and a New Critical Psychology* (1991), Nick Bishop conjoins the psychological quest or 'inward exploration' of Hughes's poetry to the mythic *bricolage* of *Crow*, *Gaudete* and *Cave Birds*, arguing that with these sequences Hughes finds a mythopoeia adequate to the task of giving a narrative shape to the psychic drama only touched upon by the individual lyrics of *The Hawk in the Rain* and *Lupercal*.[19] Drawing upon Jungian analytical psychology, in which we know Hughes was steeped, Bishop perceives Hughes's work in the 1970s as a sustained record of the need to engage with and realize the transfigurative power of the repressed anima archetype, as embodied in the terrible yet prospectively beneficent feminine presences central to, or, as is largely the case in *Crow*, latent in, these sequences.

Bishop extends his Jungian framework to encompass collections subsequent to *Cave Birds*, perceiving, in a less highly wrought collection such as *River*, the fruits of the internal journey in that volume's meditation on humanity's deepened existential experience of the natural world. Ann Skea's *Ted Hughes: The Poetic Quest* (1994) shares Bishop's interest in the importance of aspects of Jung's thought to the unfolding mythos of Hughes's poetry, primarily that of *Cave Birds*, but also in *Remains of Elmet* and *River*.[20] Skea examines in detail Jung's contention that the medieval and renaissance practice of alchemy, its desire to transform base matter into alchemical gold or lapis, corresponds to his conception of psychic 'individuation': that is, the quest to achieve an enlarged Self through the unification of one's divided being. The relevance of this to a deeper comprehension of *Cave Birds: An Alchemical Cave Drama* is undeniable, and Skea's comprehensive mapping of stages of the alchemical synthesis onto the sequence not only adds to the reader's understanding of the individual poems, but indirectly testifies to their strikingly vivid transmutation of arcane materials. Although not part of her critical remit, the absence of a comparative dimension to Hughes's use of alchemical symbolism is a loss to Skea's analysis. Hughes's poetic engagement with analytical psychology has been related to that of Peter Redgrove and Seamus Heaney;[21] but there is a glaring lacuna in the criticism to date in the lack of sustained readings of *Crow*, *Cave Birds* and *Gaudete* in relation to other important post-war sequences drawing on Jung, such as Charles Olson's *The Maximus Poems*, Thomas Kinsella's *Nightwalker*, *Notes from the Land of the Dead* and *One*, and John Peck's *M*.

The novelty of Craig Robinson's *Ted Hughes as Shepherd of Being* (1989) – which covers Hughes's poetry from *The Hawk in the Rain* to *Flowers and Insects* – is his claim that parallels can be drawn between some key aspects of Hughes's thought and the ideas of Jung's contemporary Martin Heidegger.[22] It must be said that there is no concrete proof that Hughes had read the controversial German philosopher, but Robinson's suggestion that the latter's belief that our technocratic capitalist society and modern rationalism have exiled us from Being (understood as the generalized 'meaning' of entities, not their individual substance) does find a chime in Hughes's concern that we reidentify with the inner core of our common humanity and with the world in which we are existentially 'thrown'. Heidegger's contention that the rot set in as far back as Plato is obliquely echoed in the subtitle to *Cave Birds* that Hughes told Terry Gifford and Neil Roberts he had at one point considered before discarding it: 'The Death Of Socrates and his Resurrection in Egypt' (*LTH* 395). However, the subtitle Hughes eventually settled on, *An Alchemical Cave Drama*, points to the closer affinity between the sequence and Jung's concept of individuation (to which Robinson does pay attention) than with Heidegger's reflections on the dualistic thinking endemic to the Western philosophical tradition.

There is also the faint danger in Robinson's comparison of tarring Hughes, by implication, with the brush of Heidegger's Nazism, which some commentators see as inextricable from his philosophical agenda. After all, as Hughes observes to Ekbert Faas in a 1970 interview, the bird-persona of 'Hawk Roosting' in *Lupercal* has been 'accused of being a fascist' by certain critics, whereas what he actually 'had in mind was that in this hawk Nature is thinking'.[23] Putting to one side the question as to whether the poem celebrates violence or not (and the critics are divided), it is of course fatuous to correlate the Hawk's monologue with the political convictions of its author.[24] That said, Hughes's sceptical response to the deeply reactionary politics of the novelist and British fascist Henry Williamson (author of *Tarka the Otter*, among other works Hughes admired)[25] does not preclude the possibility that the ideological underpinning of his own poetry is deeply conservative, even 'authoritarian', as John Lucas has contended in an otherwise not unsympathetic reading.[26]

Drawing on psychoanalytical theory, Jacqueline Rose proposes a more dialogic reading of the political unconscious of Hughes's poetry. 'Hawk Roosting', she maintains, is characteristic of Hughes's (and Plath's) poetry's propensity to be culpable in that of which it, nevertheless, offers a critique – in the hawk's case that of 'an emblem of pure identity in its fascist mode'.[27] Given its historical horizon, Hughes's hawk's uncompromising mindset equally might be taken as ventriloquizing the technocratic, totalitarian politics of the Cold War, thus sounding an echo of Heidegger's late work. Indeed, in a rare example of a thoroughly materialist interpretation of Hughes's poetry, Stan Smith in the mid 1970s contextualized the early poetry in the climate of post-war deadlock, as 'Russia and America circle each other' (*CP* 62). For Smith the abundant but often constrained energy and power conveyed by Hughes's signature animal poems of this period express both the psychological and social malaise of the Cold War, and a yearning to transcend such an impasse.[28]

If many of the foregoing studies of Hughes tend to concentrate on the themes or sources of his poetry, Terry Gifford and Neil Roberts's *Ted Hughes: A Critical Study* (1981) – while not eschewing such matters – pays closer attention to its formal properties.[29] Leonard M. Scigaj describes their book, in his valuable précis of criticism of Hughes up until 1992, as taking a 'somewhat Leavisite approach' to Hughes.[30] This is, if not wholly inaccurate, a trifle reductive: Sagar's *The Art of Ted Hughes*, as noted above, is a better example of such an approach. Gifford and Roberts's careful attention to the language of Hughes's poems takes its cue from Hughes's description of Keith Douglas's poetry as possessing '[a] utility general-purpose style, as, for instance, Shakespeare's was, that combines a colloquial prose readiness with poetic breadth, a ritual intensity and music of an exceedingly high order with clear direct feeling' (*WP* 215). Thus, while Gifford and Roberts rightly draw attention to, and analyse at length, the boldness and surety of Hughes's use of figurative language, they also emphasize the power with which he can employ a range of registers, from plain or informal to the heightened, often within a single poem. In this study, which covers Hughes's work up to and including *Moortown*, Gifford and Roberts view *Cave Birds* as Hughes's crowning achievement to date, their evaluation informed less by the (admittedly ambiguous)[31] transfiguration of the protagonist, than by their belief that in this sequence Hughes's language is disciplined yet sensuous, the sequence unified despite its occasional unevenness.

The title of Leonard M. Scigaj's *Ted Hughes: Form and Imagination* (1986) points to a comparable concern to that of Gifford and Roberts with the formal properties of the poetry. For Scigaj, Hughes's work evolves through three distinct phases: an early formalist period, in which the poetry is deeply coloured by Hughes's reading in the poetry and poetics of John Crowe Ransom, is succeeded by the 'mythic surrealism' of *Wodwo* and *Crow*,[32] itself strongly marked by Hughes's interest in the *Bardo Thödol*,[33] which, in turn, gives way from the mid 1970s to *River* to a quasi-mystical, pantheistic vision. Scigaj's division of Hughes's career into three chapters is less schematic than Hirschberg's, and his close readings more supple. His interpretation of the middle phase (as of 1983) of Hughes's career is particularly careful in its treatment of the biographical trauma behind certain poems: such experience, he insists, must be seen as an 'analogue ... that influences and parallels, but does not determine, the thought and content of the poems'.[34] In his injunction against committing what is tantamount to the New Critical heresy of the 'biographical fallacy', Scigaj echoes the very formalism to which he argues Hughes at the outset of his career was deeply indebted. Scigaj's book is written in the long shadow of such North American formalism, and one of its avowed aims is to rejuvenate interest in Hughes's poetry in an American readership precisely through attentiveness to its compellingly varied style.

In 1992, Scigaj would lament the continuing 'decline in reader and scholarly interest' in Hughes, not confined to, but especially acute in, the United States: both the failure of North American publishers to reprint recent collections and the 'fallout' from Ted and Olwyn Hughes's restrictions on copyright permissions for Plath's unpublished works, damaging Hughes's American reputation at that date.[35] To this one might add Hughes's diminished critical fortunes in the 1970s and 1980s, prior to his lionization (in Britain, at any rate) in the last years of his life. Much of the derogation of Hughes in this period centres on the purported lack of formal intricacy to his work, evidence, for a number of critics, of his failure to absorb the lessons of literary modernism. Veronica Forrest-Thomson, in 1978, accuses *Crow* of exhibiting 'bad Naturalisation': in the case of 'Song for a Phallus', for example, she writes, 'The most we could say would be that the nursery jingle echoes the theme of infantile helplessness', the poem otherwise possessing little in the way of self-reflexive 'Artifice'.[36] Reviewing *Gaudete* in the same year as Forrest-Thomson's study was published, Terry Eagleton complains that the volume's narrative, despite its fantastic or 'non-realistic' subject-matter, is written in a mode still indebted to the mimetic conventions of 'traditional realism', which it only 'superficially' appears to transgress.[37]

Along related lines, Anthony Easthope has more recently contended that 'Key aspects' of Hughes's language 'remain indelibly pre-Modernist', specifically the manner in which his diction strives for 'transparency' in the face of the 'natural object'.[38] To this it might be objected that mimesis was a cornerstone of early Anglophone modernism – witness the exacting aesthetic demands of T. E. Hulme and the ambitions of Imagism. Be this as it may, Easthope chooses to contrast Hughes with contemporary poets in whose work he detects the enabling legacy of modernism as he rather narrowly conceives it, J. H. Prynne and Tom Raworth, whose poems challenge transparency of meaning through innovatively destabilizing the predominantly referential function of language.

For A. D. Moody, conversely, the metaphorical richness of Hughes's poetry constitutes an irresponsible evasion of reality, comparable to the startling, but misleading, defamiliarization of lived experience in Craig Raine's 'Martian' poems. Moody maintains that the language of the poems is very far from transparent, being overly dependent on 'association and simile'; and the result, particularly in *Crow*, is a crude 'sensationalizing of both experience and language'.[39] Moody's denunciation is marred by its bombast, but it has at least the virtue of emphasizing the rhetorical, as opposed to the referential, dimension to Hughes's work. Paul Bentley's *The Poetry of Ted Hughes: Language, Illusion and Beyond* (1998) begins by observing that the vividly mimetic quality of Hughes's poems should not blind us to their preoccupation with their own medium – namely, words. Yet where Moody hears verbal obfuscation, Bentley finds 'a marked uneasiness … with language as a medium of representation' in Hughes's rendering of the extra-linguistic world.[40] By means of a theoretically nuanced reading – informed by Mikhail Bakhtin, Jacques Lacan and Julia Kristeva, among others – Bentley convincingly links Hughes's figurative exuberance to an awareness of the 'limitations and failings of language' in its asymptotic approach to the unrepresentable Lacanian Real ('Hughes seems to imply that all languages are in a sense "mythical" constructs, provisional attempts to represent the universe within the terms available'.[41])

Bentley's poststructuralist reading is to be welcomed. Hughes studies remained largely untroubled by the 'theory wars' of the 1970s and 1980s, and, while the 1990s saw a gradual cessation of hostilities, it remains the case that theory-driven readings of Hughes have been relatively scarce. An obvious exception to this state of affairs is ecocriticism's growing engagement with his work. There is no little irony in the fact that Keith's Sagar's fulminations against the depredations of 'post-modern critical theorists' on literary studies should appear in the foreword to the work in which he stands revealed as an ardent ecocritic, *Literature and the Crime Against Nature: From Homer to Hughes* (2005).[42] Sagar's book makes a plea for the crucial importance to ecology of the imagination and hence the vital significance of the poetry of a writer like Hughes. Leonard M. Scigaj can be credited with beginning this trend in criticism of Hughes,[43] but, beginning with an essay, 'Gods of Mud: Hughes and the Post-pastoral', and a chapter in his *Green Voices* (1995), Terry Gifford's work has largely defined the field. Gifford holds that Hughes's poetry has come to exhibit a 'post-pastoral' stance, which is that of a 'literature … which avoids the closed circle of both "pastoral" idealized celebration and the "anti-pastoral" simple correction of it'.[44] Of course, since Virgil's *Eclogues*, pastoral poetry's 'idealization' of rural life is shadowed by the harshness of historical reality: witness the dispossession of the shepherds Meliboeus and Moeris in *Eclogue* 1 and *Eclogue* 9, respectively, whose evictions reflect events in the Italian countryside in the context of the civil wars. But 'post-pastoralism', according to Gifford, is a process in which the acknowledgement of our bodily and psychic affinity with nature produces an awareness of humanity's exploitation of the earth, and a consequent need humbly to atone for this crime.

If Hughes's version of pastoral is not Virgil's, nevertheless, both poets share a deep concern with national identity and history. Tom Paulin has argued for Hughes's entrenched nationalism, and the latter's acceptance of the Poet Laureateship in 1984 might be seen as confirming this claim.[45] More subtly, Neil Roberts's searching chapter on the 'Laureate project' in his *Ted Hughes: A Literary Life* (2006) contrasts the eccentric 'personal myth' of nation and crown underpinning Hughes's occasional Laureate verse with the public voice Tennyson was able to achieve in the role in an ideologically distinct era.[46] Roberts's study, as its title implies, grounds its explications of the poetry in the circumstances of the life, but without losing sight of the fact that Hughes's importance lies, first and foremost, in his work. To that end, Roberts provides one of the soberest and most illuminating accounts of Plath's centrality to Hughes's writing, especially in her stylistic influence on his work but also her posthumous presence in the 'apostrophic elegies' collected as *Birthday Letters*.[47] Drawing extensively on archival manuscript materials held at Emory University and the British Library, Roberts's succinct discussion of *Crow* comprises the best starting point for a reader intrigued by the sequence's composition and ultimate collapse amidst the debris of its idiosyncratic mythic framework. Of equal value is the discussion of the narrative structures of *Gaudete* and *Cave Birds*, and those volumes' riven exploration of the 'masculine guilt' in which they understandably had their origin.[48] Roberts's study is usefully supplemented by Terry Gifford's 2009 contribution to the Routledge Guides to Literature Series, *Ted Hughes*,[49] which provides a concise biography, evaluations of all the major works and a judicious history of their critical reception.

By the end of the first decade of the twenty-first century, the reception Gifford charts has reached global proportions. In China, the ecocritic Chen Hong has written on Hughes's depiction of the 'animality' common to human and animal alike.[50] The Indian scholar Usha V. T. also stresses the ecological imperative of Hughes's work, while attending to the related – in Usha's reading – issue of the representation of femininity in the poetry, and the function of women in Hughes as avatars of a fertility goddess.[51]

Hughes's well-known anecdote of the dream in which a burnt fox disturbingly convinced him not to continue to read English at Cambridge (see *WP* 8–9) is clearly indicative of a mentality largely unreceptive to the kind of writing this chapter has surveyed. Yet admirers of Hughes have much to be grateful for in that such a charred intercessor has not disturbed the academic study of his work.

NOTES

1. Given the large body of secondary literature on Hughes, this chapter is necessarily selective; for further information on Hughes and his critics, the following surveys of the field are highly recommended: Leonard M. Scigaj, 'Introduction', in Leonard M. Scigaj (ed.), *Critical Essays on Ted Hughes* (New York: G. K. Hall, 1992), pp. 1–38; Sandie Byrne, *The Poetry of Ted Hughes: A Reader's Guide to Essential Criticism* (Cambridge: Icon Books, 2000); and Terry Gifford, *Ted Hughes* (London: Routledge, 2009), pp. 99–148.

2. Donald Davie, *Articulate Energy: An Inquiry into the Syntax of English Poetry*, new edn (London: Routledge and Kegan Paul, 1976), pp. xiii–xiv. Davie's response to Hughes, it is fair to add, generally took the form of qualified praise: see his searching 1967 review of *Wodwo* reprinted in Donald Davie, *With the Grain: Essays on Thomas Hardy and Modern British Poetry*, ed. Clive Wilmer (Manchester: Carcanet, 1998), pp. 239–41; and Donald Davie, *Under Briggflatts: A History of Poetry in Great Britain 1960–1988* (Manchester: Carcanet, 1989), *passim*. On Hughes and another iconic rock star, cf. Ian McMillan, 'Ted Hughes is Elvis Presley', in his *Dad, the Donkey's on Fire* (Manchester: Carcanet, 1994), pp. 19–21.

3. Seamus Heaney, *Preoccupations: Selected Prose 1968–1978* (London: Faber, 1980), p. 153.

4. Harold Bloom, *The Ringers in the Tower: Studies in Romantic Tradition* (Chicago: University of Chicago Press, 1971), p. 9.

5. In addition to Chapter 10 above, for an account of 'Ted Hughes's Shakespeare', see Neil Corcoran, *Shakespeare and the Modern Poet* (Cambridge: Cambridge University Press, 2010), pp. 181–240.

6. Keith Sagar, *The Art of Ted Hughes*, 2nd edn (Cambridge: Cambridge University Press, 1978), p. 3.

7. The text of *Cave Birds* discussed by Sagar in *The Art of Ted Hughes* differs considerably from that published in the same year as his expanded study. Ten poems from the sequence of thirty-one read at the Ilkley Festival in 1975 were first published in a sumptuous limited edition by Scolar Press in 1975; the heavily revised trade edition of 1978 is described on its dust-jacket as the 'first full general edition'. For details, see the relevant entry in Keith Sagar and Stephen Tabor, *Ted Hughes: A Bibliography 1946–1995*, 2nd edn (London: Mansell, 1998).

8. Keith Sagar, *The Laughter of Foxes: A Study of Ted Hughes*, 2nd edn (Liverpool: Liverpool University Press, 2006), p. ix.

9. *Ibid.*, p. xi.

10. With the exception of a brief reference to a note by Hughes appended to 'Rain-Charm for the Duchy', a poem, incidentally, originally intended for *River* and composed with no intended allusion to Prince Harry's christening; see Neil Roberts, *Ted Hughes: A Literary Life* (Basingstoke: Palgrave Macmillan, 2006), pp. 155 and Chapter 8 above.

11. On the 'Ovidian logic' to Hughes's two final collections, see Philip Hardie, 'Introduction', in *The Cambridge Companion to Ovid*, ed. Philip Hardie (Cambridge: Cambridge University Press, 2002), p. 2. See also Anne-Marie Tatham, 'Passion *in extremis* in Ted Hughes's *Tales from Ovid*', in Roger Rees (ed.), *Ted Hughes and the Classics* (Oxford: Oxford University Press, 2009), pp. 177–98.

12. Ekbert Faas, *Ted Hughes: The Unaccommodated Universe* (Santa Barbara: Black Sparrow, 1980), p. 11.

13. *Ibid.*, p. 141.

14. The first is a reprinting of 'Ted Hughes and Crow: An Interview with Egbert Faas', *London Magazine* 10:10 (1971), pp. 5–20. Faas also includes as a further appendix a generous selection of Hughes's critical writing, not all of which found its way into *WP*.

15. See Sagar, *The Laughter of Foxes*, pp. 170–80.

16. Stuart Hirschberg, *Myth in the Poetry of Ted Hughes* (Dublin: Wolfhound Press, 1981).

17. Joanny Moulin, *Ted Hughes: New Selected Poems 1957–1994* (Paris: Didier-Érudition, 1999).

18. See Tracy Brain, *The Other Sylvia Plath* (Harlow: Longman, 2001), pp. 177–216; see also Neil Roberts, 'The Common Text of Sylvia Plath and Ted Hughes', *Symbiosis* 7:1 (2003), pp. 157–73; and Diane Middlebrook, 'The Poetry of Sylvia Plath and Ted Hughes: Call and Response', in Jo Gill (ed.), *The Cambridge Companion to Sylvia Plath*, (Cambridge: Cambridge University Press, 2006), pp. 156–171. Still valuable in its treatment of Hughes and Plath's relationship is Margaret Dickie Uroff, *Sylvia Plath and Ted Hughes* (Urbana and Chicago: University of Illinois Press, 1979).

19. Nick Bishop, *Re-making Poetry: Ted Hughes and a New Critical Psychology* (London: Harvester Wheatsheaf, 1991), p. 109.

20. Ann Skea, *Ted Hughes: The Poetic Quest* (Armidale: University of New England Press, 1994). For studies by Skea on Hughes, magic and the occult, see her website: *The Ted Hughes Homepage*, <http://ann.skea.com/ THHome.htm>.

21. See Terry Gifford and Neil Roberts, 'Hughes and Two Contemporaries: Peter Redgrove and Seamus Heaney', in Keith Sagar (ed.), *The Achievement of Ted Hughes* (Manchester: Manchester University Press, 1983), pp. 91–106.

22. Craig Robinson, *Ted Hughes as Shepherd of Being* (Basingstoke: Macmillan, 1989).

23. Faas, *The Unaccommodated Universe*, p. 199.

24. For reservations about the purported violence of *Lupercal*, see John Press, 'Violence in Verse', review of *Lupercal*, by Ted Hughes, *Sunday Times* (3 April 1960); and Calvin Bedient, *Eight Contemporary Poets* (Oxford: Oxford University Press, 1974), pp. 95–118. The most intemperate critiques of Hughes on this topic are those of David Holbrook. See David Holbrook, 'The Cult of Hughes and Gunn', *Poetry Review* 54 (1963), pp. 167–83; and David Holbrook, 'Ted Hughes's *Crow* and the Longing for Non-Being', in Peter Abbs (ed.), *The Black Rainbow: Essays on the Present Breakdown of Culture* (London: Heinemann, 1975), pp. 32–54.

25. See *LTH* 234: 'He [Williamson] was a great Fascist, dreamed he had been called to do for England what Hitler did for Germany, etc., and made a great mess of his life with Hitlerism.' Hughes's memorial address for Williamson tactfully excludes mention of his fascism: Ted Hughes, 'A Memorial Address', in Brocard Sewell (ed.), *Henry Williamson: The Man, The Writings: A Symposium* (Padstow: Tabb House, 1980), pp. 159–65.

26. See John Lucas, *Modern English Poetry from Hardy to Hughes: A Critical Survey* (London: Batsford, 1986), p. 194.

27. Jacqueline Rose, *The Haunting of Sylvia Plath* (London: Virago, 1991), p. 156.

28. See Stan Smith, *Inviolable Voice: History and Twentieth-Century Poetry* (Dublin: Gill and Macmillan, 1982), pp. 150–69. On the mythic in Hughes's poetry (and others') as a hankering for a 'transcendence' of the vicissitudes of post-war society, see Terry Eagleton, 'Myth and History in Recent Poetry', in Michael Schmidt and Grevel Lindop (eds.), *British Poetry since 1960: A Critical Survey* (Oxford: Carcanet, 1972), p. 239.

29. Terry Gifford and Neil Roberts, *Ted Hughes: A Critical Study* (London: Faber and Faber, 1981).

30. Scigaj, 'Introduction', p. 5.

31. After all, 'At the end of the ritual / up comes a goblin' (*CP* 440).

32. Leonard M. Scigaj, *The Poetry of Ted Hughes: Form and Imagination* (Iowa City: University of Iowa Press, 1986), p. xiv.

33. Commonly referred to in English as *The Tibetan Book of the Dead*; see the excerpts from Hughes's rendering of the work in *ST* 1–13.

34. Scigaj, *The Poetry of Ted Hughes*, p. 87.

35. Scigaj, 'Introduction', pp. 2, 3. The situation Scigaj describes no longer entirely holds: Hughes's *Collected Selected Poems* was published in 2003 by Farrar, Straus and Giroux in the US; while, to take a single instance of her previously unavailable or bowdlerized work, Plath's journals are available in North America as *The Unabridged Journals of Sylvia Plath*, ed. Karen V. Kukil (New York: Random House, 2000).

36. Veronica Forrest-Thomson, *Poetic Artifice: A Theory of Twentieth-Century Poetry* (Manchester: Manchester University Press, 1978), p. 149.

37. Terry Eagleton, 'New Poetry', review of *Gaudete*, by Ted Hughes, *Stand* 19:2 (1978), p. 78.

38. Anthony Easthope, 'The Poetry of Ted Hughes: Some Reservations', in Joanny Moulin, *Lire Ted Hughes: New Selected Poems 1957–1994* (Paris: Editions du Temps, 1999), p. 21.

39. A. D. Moody, 'Telling It Like It's Not: Ted Hughes and Craig Raine', *Yearbook of English Studies* 17 (1987), p. 178.

40. Paul Bentley, *The Poetry of Ted Hughes: Language, Illusion and Beyond* (London: Longman, 1998), p. 1.

41. *Ibid.*, pp. 36, 37.

42. Keith Sagar, *Literature and the Crime Against Nature: From Homer to Hughes* (London: Chaucer Press, 2005), p. xvi. The concluding chapter of this book reprints Chapter 4 of Sagar's *The Laughter of Foxes*.

43. See Leonard M. Scigaj, *Ted Hughes* (Boston, MA: Twayne, 1991).

44. Terry Gifford, *Reconnecting with John Muir: Essays in Post-Pastoral Practice* (Athens: University of Georgia Press, 2006), p. 12. See also Terry Gifford, *Green Voices: Understanding Contemporary Nature Poetry* (Manchester: Manchester University Press, 1995; 2nd edn CCC Press, 2011); and Terry Gifford, 'Gods of Mud: Hughes and the Post-pastoral', in Keith Sagar (ed.), *The Challenge of Ted Hughes* (Basingstoke: Macmillan, 1994), pp. 129–41.

45. See Tom Paulin, *Minotaur: Poetry and the Nation State* (London: Faber and Faber, 1992), pp. 252–75.

46. Roberts, *Ted Hughes*, p. 166.

47. *Ibid.*, p. 202.

48. *Ibid.*, p. 99.

49. See note 1 above.
50. See Chen Hong, *Bestiality, Animality, and Humanity* (Wuhan: Central China Normal University Press, 2005).
51. See Usha V. T., *Modern English Literature: The Real and the Imagined: The Poetic World of Ted Hughes* (Jaipur: Mangal Deep Publications, 1998).

Primary Works

Books

The Hawk in the Rain (London: Faber and Faber, 1957).
Lupercal (London: Faber and Faber, 1960).
Meet My Folks (London: Faber and Faber, 1961).
The Earth-Owl and Other Moon People (London: Faber and Faber, 1963).
How the Whale Became (London: Faber and Faber, 1963).
Nessie the Mannerless Monster (London: Faber and Faber, 1964).
Recklings (London: Turret Books, 1966).
Poetry in the Making (London: Faber and Faber, 1967).
Wodwo (London: Faber and Faber, 1967).
The Iron Man (London: Faber and Faber, 1968).
Seneca's Oedipus (London: Faber and Faber, 1969).
Crow (London: Faber and Faber, 1970).
The Coming of the Kings (London: Faber and Faber, 1970).
A Choice of Shakespeare's Verse (London: Faber and Faber, 1971; 2nd edn 1991).
Earth-Moon (London: Rainbow Press, 1976).
Season Songs (London: Faber and Faber, 1976).
Gaudete (London: Faber and Faber, 1977).
Cave Birds (London: Faber and Faber, 1978).
Moon-Bells and Other Poems (London: Chatto and Windus, 1978).
Orts (London: Rainbow Press, 1978).
Moortown (London: Faber and Faber, 1979).
Remains of Elmet (London: Faber and Faber, 1979).
A Primer of Birds (Devon: Gehenna Press, 1981).
Under the North Star (London: Faber and Faber, 1981).
Selected Poems 1957–1981 (London: Faber and Faber, 1982).
River (London: Faber and Faber, 1983).
What Is the Truth? (London: Faber and Faber, 1984).
Flowers and Insects (London: Faber and Faber, 1986).
Ffangs the Vampire Bat and the Kiss of Truth (London: Faber and Faber, 1986).
The Cat and the Cuckoo (Devon: Sunstone Press,1987).
Moon-Whales and Other Moon Poems (New York: Viking, 1988).
Tales of the Early World (London: Faber and Faber, 1988).
Moortown Diary (London: Faber and Faber, 1989).

Wolfwatching (London: Faber and Faber, 1989).
Capriccio (Devon: Gehenna Press, 1990).
A Dancer to God (London: Faber and Faber, 1992).
Rain-Charm for the Duchy (London: Faber and Faber, 1992).
Shakespeare and the Goddess of Complete Being (London: Faber and Faber, 1992).
The Iron Woman (London: Faber and Faber, 1993).
The Mermaid's Purse (Devon: Sunstone Press, 1993).
Three Books (Cave Birds, Remains of Elmet, River) (London: Faber and Faber, 1993).
Difficulties of a Bridegroom (London: Faber and Faber, 1995).
Elmet (London: Faber and Faber, 1994).
Winter Pollen (London: Faber and Faber, 1994).
New Selected Poems 1957–1994 (London: Faber and Faber, 1995).
The Dreamfighter and Other Creation Tales (London: Faber and Faber, 1995).
Collected Animal Poems, 4 vols. (London: Faber and Faber, 1995).
Spring Awakening (London: Faber and Faber, 1995).
Blood Wedding (London: Faber and Faber, 1996).
Tales from Ovid (London: Faber and Faber, 1997).
By Heart (London: Faber and Faber, 1997).
Birthday Letters (London: Faber and Faber, 1998).
Howls & Whispers (Devon: Gehenna Press, 1998).
Phèdre (London: Faber and Faber, 1998).
Alcestis (London: Faber and Faber, 1999).
The Oresteia (London: Faber and Faber, 1999).
Collected Plays for Children (London: Faber and Faber, 2001).
Collected Poems (London: Faber and Faber, 2003).
Collected Poems for Children (London: Faber and Faber, 2005).
Selected Translations (London: Faber and Faber, 2006).
Letters of Ted Hughes (London: Faber and Faber, 2007).
Timmy the Tug (London: Thames and Hudson, 2009).

Uncollected essays

'Myth and Education', 1970, *Children's Literature in Education*, 1, pp. 55–70. (Importantly different from the revised version included in *Winter Pollen*.)

Recordings

The Thought-Fox and Other Poems, read by Ted Hughes, Faber and Faber, 1994.
Ted Hughes Reading his Poetry, HarperCollins Audio Books, 1996.
Nessie The Mannerless Monster and *The Iron Wolf*, read by Ted Hughes, Faber/ Penguin, 1996.
Tales of the Early World, read by Ted Hughes, Faber/Penguin, 1996.
The Dreamfighter and Other Creation Tales, read by Ted Hughes, Faber/Penguin, 1996.
Ffangs the Vampire Bat and the Kiss of Truth, read by Ted Hughes, Faber/Penguin, 1996.
The Iron Woman, read by Ted Hughes, Faber/Penguin, 1996.
The Iron Man, read by Ted Hughes, Faber/Penguin, 1997.
How the Whale Became and Other Stories, read by Ted Hughes, Faber/Penguin, 1997.
By Heart: 101 Poems to Remember, read by Ted Hughes, Faber/Penguin, 1997.

Crow, read by Ted Hughes, Faber/Penguin, 1997.

Tales from Ovid, read by Ted Hughes, Faber/Penguin, 1998.

Poetry in the Making, British Library Sound Archive, 2008.

The Spoken Word – Ted Hughes. Poems and short stories (a 2CD set drawn from BBC Radio broadcasts), British Library Sound Archive, 2008.

The Spoken Word – Ted Hughes. Poetry in the Making *and* Season Songs (a 2CD set of five BBC Radio broadcasts for schools, plus two programmes reading *Season Songs*), British Library Sound Archive, 2008.

The Artist and the Poet: Leonard Baskin and Ted Hughes in conversation 1983. A documentary DVD by Noel Chanan, 2009.

The Spoken Word – Sylvia Plath. ('Two of a Kind' interview), British Library Sound Archive, 2010.

Secondary Works

Biographical

Boyanowsky, Ehor, *Savage Gods: In the Wild with Ted Hughes* (Vancouver: Douglas and McIntyre, 2009).

Feinstein, Elaine, *Ted Hughes: The Life of a Poet* (London: Weidenfeld and Nicolson, 2001).

Gammage, Nick (ed.), *The Epic Poise: A Celebration of Ted Hughes* (London : Faber and Faber, 1999).

Hughes, Ted, *Letters of Ted Hughes* (London: Faber and Faber, 2007).

Huws, Daniel, *Memories of Ted Hughes 1952–1963* (Nottingham: Five Leaves Publications, 2010).

Koren, Yehuda and Eilat Negev, *A Lover of Unreason: The Life and Tragic Death of Assia Wevill* (London: Robson Books, 2006).

Middlebrook, Diane, *Her Husband* (London: Little, Brown, 2004).

Moulin, Joanny, *Ted Hughes: la terre hantée. Biographie.* (Paris: Aden, 2007).

Myers, Lucas, *Crow Steered, Bergs Appeared* (Sewanee: Proctor Press, 2001).

Stevenson, Anne, *Bitter Fame: A Life of Sylvia Plath* (London: Viking, 1989).

Tennant, Emma, *Burnt Diaries* (Edinburgh: Canongate, 1999).

Weissbort, Daniel, *Letters to Ted* (London: Anvil, 2002).

Bibliographical

Sagar, Keith and Stephen Tabor, *Ted Hughes: A Bibliography 1946–1995* (London: Mansell, 1998).

Websites

http://ann.skea.com/THHome.htm (managed by Ann Skea).

www.earth-moon.org (managed by Claas Kazzer).

www.keithsagar.co.uk/tedhughes.html (managed by Keith Sagar).

www3.sympatico.ca/sylviapaul/hughes_archives.htm (Centre for Ted Hughes Studies, managed by Sylvia Paul).

www.theelmettrust (The Elmet Trust).

www.thetedhughessociety.org

Reviews of criticism

Byrne, Sandie, *The Poetry of Ted Hughes: A Reader's Guide to Essential Criticism* (Cambridge: Icon Books, 2000).

Gifford, Terry, *Ted Hughes* (London: Routledge, 2009).

Scigaj, Leonard M., *Critical Essays on Ted Hughes* (New York: G. K. Hall, 1992).

Critical studies

Bassnett, Susan, *Ted Hughes* (Tavistock: Northcote House, 2008).

Bentley, Paul, *The Poetry of Ted Hughes: Language, Illusion and Beyond* (London: Longman, 1998).

Bishop, Nick, *Re-Making Poetry* (London: Harvester Wheatsheaf, 1991).

Clark, Heather, *The Grief of Influence: Sylia Plath and Ted Hughes* (Oxford: Oxford University Press, 2011).

Gifford, Terry and Neil Roberts, *Ted Hughes: A Critical Study* (London: Faber and Faber, 1981).

Hadley, Edward, *The Elegies of Ted Hughes* (London: Palgrave Macmillan, 2010).

Hirshberg, Stuart, *Myth in the Poetry of Ted Hughes* (Dublin: Wolfhound Press, 1981).

Moulin, Joanny, *Ted Hughes: La langue rémunérée* (Paris: L'Harmattan, 1999).

Roberts, Neil, *Ted Hughes: A Literary Life* (Basingstoke: Palgrave Macmillan, 2006).

Ted Hughes: New Selected Poems (Penrith: Humanities-Ebooks.co.uk, 2007)

Robinson, Craig, *Ted Hughes as Shepherd of Being* (Basingstoke: Macmillan, 1989).

Sagar, Keith, *The Art of Ted Hughes* (Cambridge: Cambridge University Press, 1975; 2nd edn 1978).

The Laughter of Foxes (Liverpool: Liverpool University Press, 2000; 2nd edn 2006).

Nature and Ted Hughes: 'Terror and Exultation' (www.keithsagar.co.uk, 2009).

Scigaj, Leonard M., *The Poetry of Ted Hughes: Form and Imagination* (Iowa: University of Iowa Press, 1986).

Ted Hughes (Boston: Twayne, 1991).

Skea, Ann, *The Poetic Quest* (Armidale: University of New England Press, 1994).

Collections of critical essays

Dyson, A. E. (ed.), *Three Contemporary Poets: Thom Gunn, Ted Hughes & R. S. Thomas* (Basingstoke: Macmillan, 1990).

Moulin, Joanny (ed.), *Lire Ted Hughes: New Selected Poems 1957–1994* (Paris: Editions du Temps, 1999).

(ed.), *Ted Hughes: Alternative Horizons* (London: Routledge, 2004).

Rees, R. D. (ed.), *Ted Hughes and the Classics* (Oxford: Oxford University Press, 2009).

Sagar, Keith (ed.), *The Achievement of Ted Hughes* (Manchester: Manchester University Press, 1983).

(ed.), *The Challenge of Ted Hughes* (London: Macmillan, 1994).

Schuchard, Ronald (ed.), *Fixed Stars Govern a Life* (Atlanta: Academic Exchange, Emory University, 2006).

Scigaj, Leonard M. (ed.), *Critical Essays on Ted Hughes* (New York: G. K. Hall, 1992).

Articles, essays and chapters in books

Bedient, Calvin, *Eight Contemporary Poets* (Oxford: Oxford University Press, 1974).

'Ted Hughes's Fearful Greening', *Parnassus*, 14:1 (1987), pp. 150–63.

Corcoran, Neil, *English Poetry since 1940* (London: Longman, 1993).

Shakespeare and the Modern Poet (Cambridge: Cambridge University Press, 2010).

Cox, Brian, 'Ted Hughes (1930–1998): A Personal Retrospect', *The Hudson Review* 52:1 (1999), pp. 29–43.

Csokits, János, 'János Pilinszky's "Desert of Love": A Note', in Daniel Weissbort (ed.), *Translating Poetry: The Double Labyrinth* (Basingstoke: Palgrave Macmillan, 1989).

Eagleton, Terry, 'Myth and History in Recent Poetry', in Michael Schmidt and Grevel Lindop (eds.), *British Poetry Since 1960* (Oxford: Carcanet, 1972).

Faas, Egbert, 'Ted Hughes and Crow', an interview, *London Magazine* 10 (10 January 1971), pp. 5–20.

The Unaccommodated Universe (Santa Barbara: Black Sparrow Press, 1980).

Gifford, Terry, *Green Voices: Understanding Contemporary Nature Poetry* (Manchester: Manchester University Press, 1995; 2nd edn CCC Press, 2011).

'Interview with Fay Godwin', *Thumbscrew* 18 (2001), pp. 114–17.

Greening, John, *Focus on Ted Hughes* (London: Greenwich Exchange, 2007).

Heinz, Drue, 'Ted Hughes: The Art of Poetry LXXI', *Paris Review* 134 (1995), pp. 55–94.

Holbrook, David, 'The Cult of Hughes and Gunn', *Poetry Review* 54 (1963), 167–83.

'Ted Hughes's *Crow* and the Longing for Non-Being', in Peter Abbs (ed.), *The Black Rainbow: Essays on the Present Breakdown of Culture* (London: Heinemann, 1975).

Hong, Chen, *Bestiality, Animality, and Humanity* (Wuhan: Central China Normal University Press, 2005).

Hughes, Frieda, *Forty-Five* (New York: HarperCollins, 2008).

Kazzer, Claas, 'Difficulties of a Bridegroom', *Q/W/E/R/T/Y* 9 (1999), pp. 187–201.

Kendall, Tim, *Modern English War Poetry* (Oxford: Oxford University Press, 2006).

Larrissy, Edward, *Reading Twentieth Century Poetry* (Oxford: Blackwell, 1990).

Lucas, John, *Modern English Poetry from Hardy to Hughes* (London: Batsford, 1986).

Malcolm, Janet, *The Silent Woman: Sylvia Plath and Ted Hughes* (London: Macmillan, 1994).

Maslen, Elizabeth, 'Counterpoint: Collaborations between Ted Hughes and Three Visual Artists', *Word and Image*, 2:1 (January–March 1986), pp. 33–44.

Middlebrook, Diane, 'The Poetry of Sylvia Plath and Ted Hughes: Call, and Response', in Jo Gill (ed.), *The Cambridge Companion to Sylvia Plath* (Cambridge: Cambridge University Press, 2006).

Moat, John, *The Founding of Arvon* (London: Frances Lincoln, 2005).

Moody, David, 'Telling It Like It's Not', *The Yearbook of English Studies* 17 (1987), pp. 166–78.

Moulin, Joanny, *Ted Hughes: New Selected Poems* (Paris: Didier Erudition, 1999).

Muldoon, Paul, *The End of the Poem* (London: Faber and Faber, 2006).

O'Brien, Sean, *The Deregulated Muse* (Newcastle upon Tyne: Bloodaxe, 1998).

Owen, Jane, *The Poetry of Ted Hughes: Author Study Activities for Key Stage 2/3* (London: David Fulton, 2003).

Paulin, Tom, *Minotaur: Poetry and the Nation State* (London: Faber and Faber, 1992).

Roberts, Neil, 'Ted Hughes and the Laureateship', *Critical Quarterly* 27:2 (1985), pp. 3–5.

Narrative and Voice in Postwar Poetry (Harlow: Longman, 1999).

'The Common Text of Sylvia Plath and Ted Hughes', *Symbiosis* 7:1 (2003), pp. 157–73.

Sagar, Keith, *Ted Hughes* (Harlow: Longman for the British Council, 1972).

'Ted Hughes', *Dictionary of National Biography*, vol. XXVIII (Oxford: Oxford University Press, 2004).

Literature and the Crime Against Nature (London: Chaucer Press, 2004).

Ted Hughes and Nature: 'Terror and Exultation' (www.keithsagar.co.uk, 2009).

Schmidt, Michael and Grevel Lindop (eds.), *British Poetry Since 1960* (Oxford: Carcanet, 1972).

Smith, A. C. H., *Orghast at Persepolis* (London: Methuen, 1972).

Thurley, Geoffrey, *The Ironic Harvest* (London: Arnold, 1974).

Uroff, Margaret Dickie, *Sylvia Plath and Ted Hughes* (Chicago: University of Illinois Press, 1979).

Usha, V. T., *Modern English Literature. The Real and the Imagined: The Poetic World of Ted Hughes* (Jaipur: Mangal Deep Publications, 1998).

'Remembering Ted Hughes', *Journal of Literature and Aesthetics*, 7:2 (1999), pp. 81–4.

Wagner, Erica, *Ariel's Gift: Ted Hughes, Sylvia Plath and the Story of* Birthday Letters (London: Faber and Faber, 2000).

Winterson, Jeanette, 'Foreword', *Great Poets of the 20th Century: Ted Hughes* (London: Guardian, 2008).

Wright, Carolyn, 'What Happens in the Heart', *Poetry Review* 89:3 (1999), pp. 3–9.

INDEX

Cambridge Companions to ...

AUTHORS

Edward Albee edited by Stephen J. Bottoms

Margaret Atwood edited by Coral Ann Howells

W. H. Auden edited by Stan Smith

Jane Austen edited by Edward Copeland and Juliet McMaster (second edition)

Beckett edited by John Pilling

Bede edited by Scott DeGregorio

Aphra Behn edited by Derek Hughes and Janet Todd

Walter Benjamin edited by David S. Ferris

William Blake edited by Morris Eaves

Brecht edited by Peter Thomson and Glendyr Sacks (second edition)

The Brontës edited by Heather Glen

Bunyan edited by Anne Dunan-Page

Frances Burney edited by Peter Sabor

Byron edited by Drummond Bone

Albert Camus edited by Edward J. Hughes

Willa Cather edited by Marilee Lindemann

Cervantes edited by Anthony J. Cascardi

Chaucer edited by Piero Boitani and Jill Mann (second edition)

Chekhov edited by Vera Gottlieb and Paul Allain

Kate Chopin edited by Janet Beer

Caryl Churchill edited by Elaine Aston and Elin Diamond

Coleridge edited by Lucy Newlyn

Wilkie Collins edited by Jenny Bourne Taylor

Joseph Conrad edited by J. H. Stape

Dante edited by Rachel Jacoff (second edition)

Daniel Defoe edited by John Richetti

Don DeLillo edited by John N. Duvall

Charles Dickens edited by John O. Jordan

Emily Dickinson edited by Wendy Martin

John Donne edited by Achsah Guibbory

Dostoevskii edited by W. J. Leatherbarrow

Theodore Dreiser edited by Leonard Cassuto and Claire Virginia Eby

John Dryden edited by Steven N. Zwicker

W. E. B. Du Bois edited by Shamoon Zamir

George Eliot edited by George Levine

T. S. Eliot edited by A. David Moody

Ralph Ellison edited by Ross Posnock

Ralph Waldo Emerson edited by Joel Porte and Saundra Morris

William Faulkner edited by Philip M. Weinstein

Henry Fielding edited by Claude Rawson

F. Scott Fitzgerald edited by Ruth Prigozy

Flaubert edited by Timothy Unwin

E. M. Forster edited by David Bradshaw

Benjamin Franklin edited by Carla Mulford

Brian Friel edited by Anthony Roche

Robert Frost edited by Robert Faggen

Gabriel García Márquez edited by Philip Swanson

Elizabeth Gaskell edited by Jill L. Matus

Goethe edited by Lesley Sharpe

Günter Grass edited by Stuart Taberner

Thomas Hardy edited by Dale Kramer

David Hare edited by Richard Boon

Nathaniel Hawthorne edited by Richard Millington

Seamus Heaney edited by Bernard O'Donoghue

Ernest Hemingway edited by Scott Donaldson

Homer edited by Robert Fowler

Horace edited by Stephen Harrison

Ted Hughes edited by Terry Gifford

Ibsen edited by James McFarlane

Henry James edited by Jonathan Freedman

Samuel Johnson edited by Greg Clingham

Ben Jonson edited by Richard Harp and Stanley Stewart

James Joyce edited by Derek Attridge (second edition)

Kafka edited by Julian Preece

Keats edited by Susan J. Wolfson

Lacan edited by Jean-Michel Rabaté

D. H. Lawrence edited by Anne Fernihough

Primo Levi edited by Robert Gordon

Lucretius edited by Stuart Gillespie and Philip Hardie

Machiavelli edited by John M. Najemy

David Mamet edited by Christopher Bigsby

Thomas Mann edited by Ritchie Robertson

Christopher Marlowe edited by Patrick Cheney

Andrew Marvell edited by Derek Hirst and Steven N. Zwicker

TOPICS